DISTANZ

Franz Wanner

FOES AT THE EDGE OF THE FRAME

Herausgegeben von / Edited by Stephanie Weber

DUAL-USE

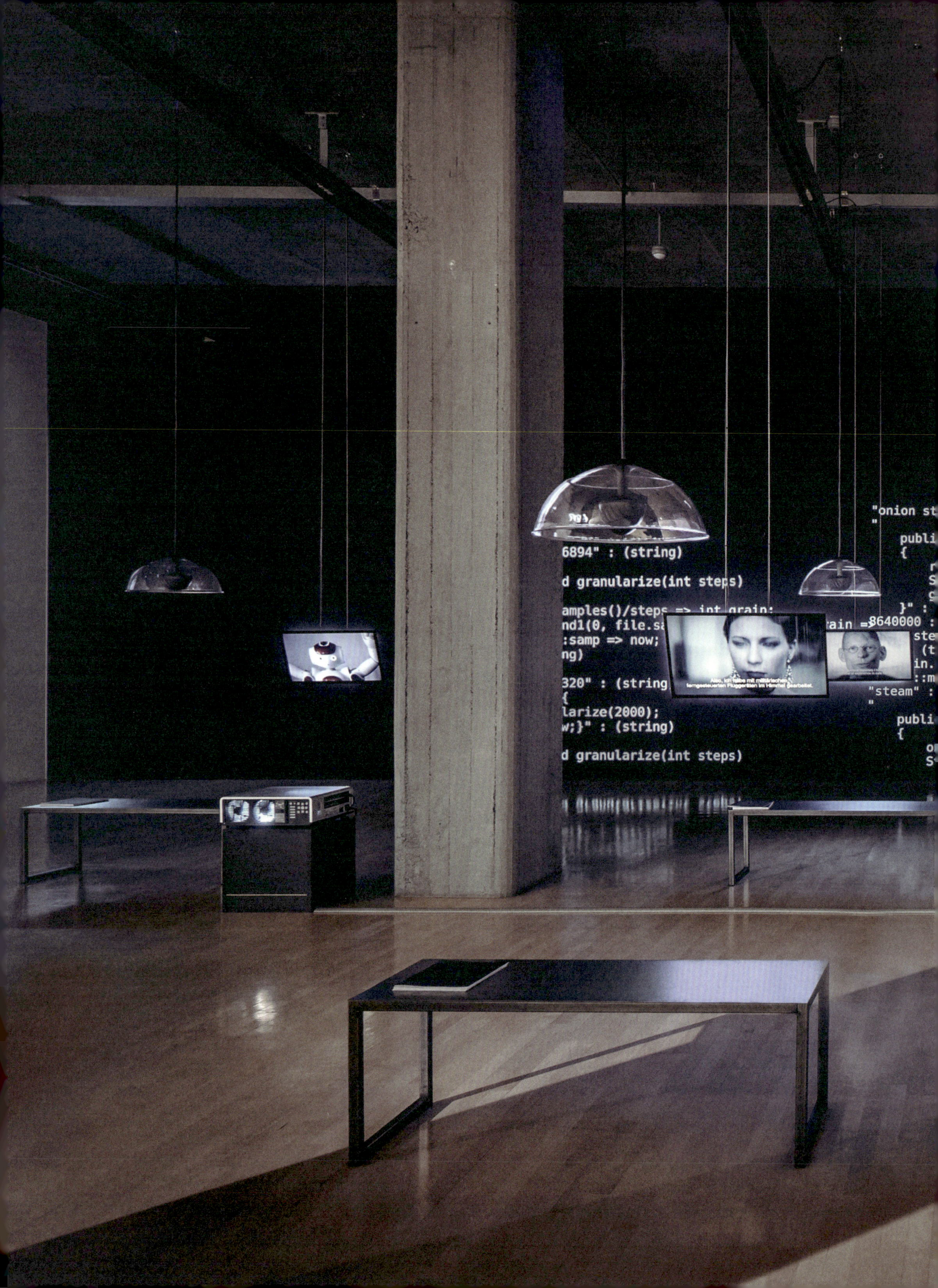
"onion st
publi
6894" : (string)
d granularize(int steps)
amples()/steps => int grain;
nd1(0, file.sa
:samp => now;
ng)
8640000 :
320" : (string
larize(2000);
w;}" : (string)
"steam" :
publi
d granularize(int steps)

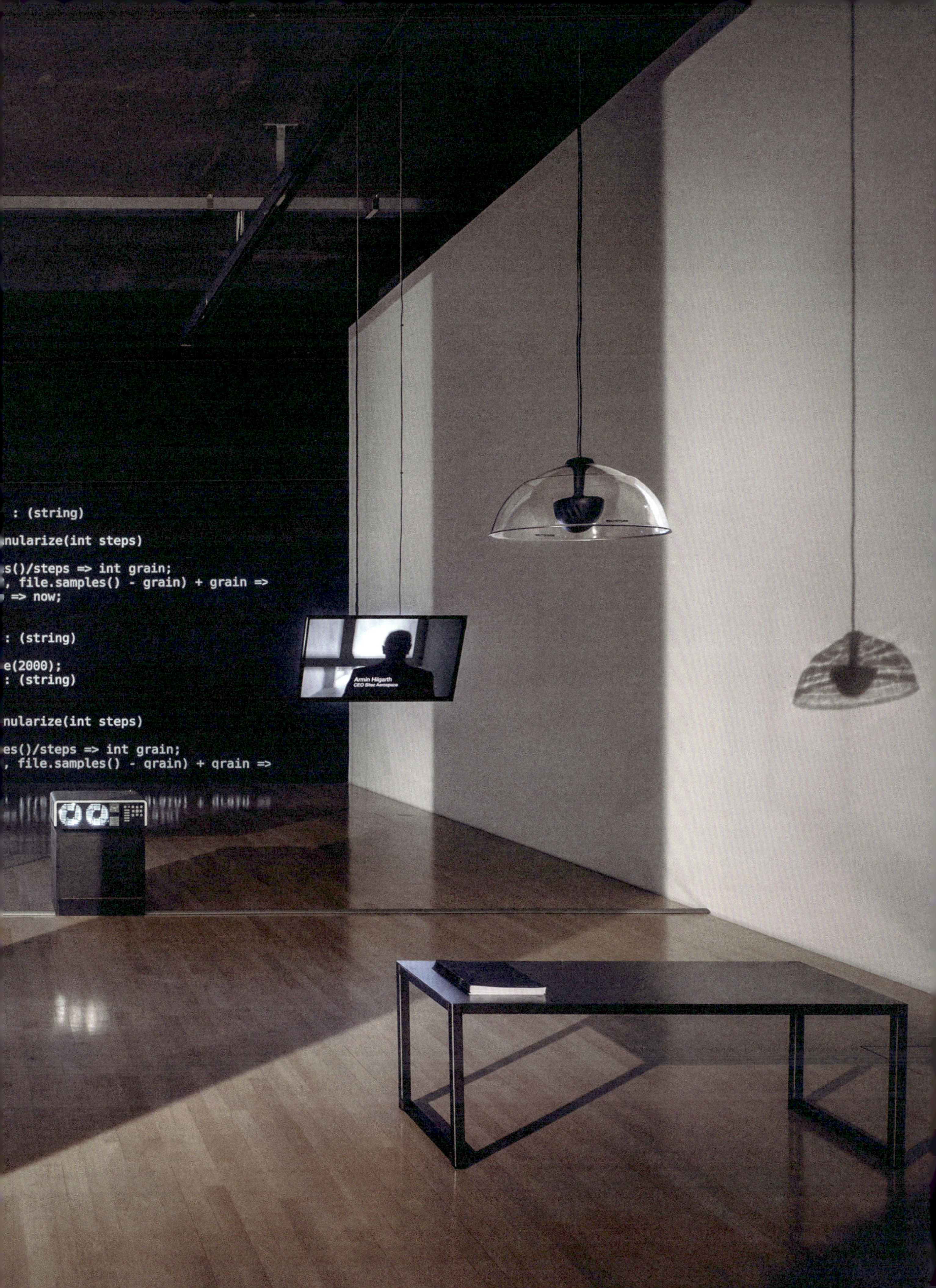
: (string)
nularize(int steps)
s()/steps => int grain;
, file.samples() - grain) + grain =>
=> now;
: (string)
e(2000);
: (string)
nularize(int steps)
es()/steps => int grain;
, file.samples() - grain) + grain =>
Armin Hilgarth
CEO Sitec Aerospace

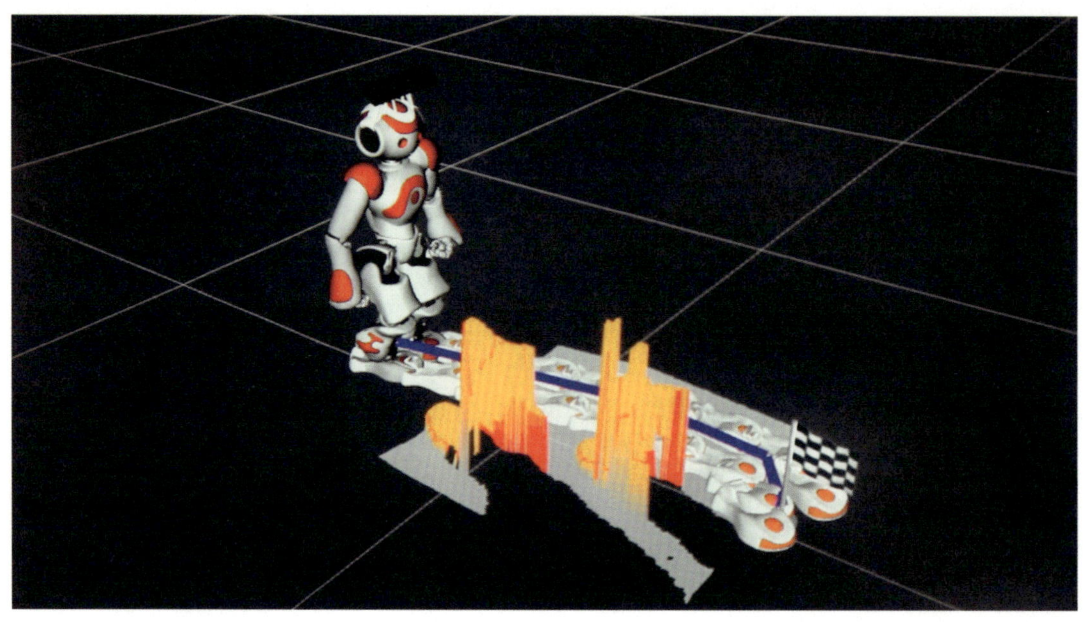

Seite / Pages 6–9
Installation *DUAL-USE*, Ausstellung *Favoriten III*, Städtische Galerie im Lenbachhaus und Kunstbau München, 2016
Installation *DUAL-USE*, exhibition *Favoriten III*, Städtische Galerie im Lenbachhaus und Kunstbau München, Munich, 2016

DUAL-USE
5-Kanal-Installation, 2016

DUAL-USE I: Global Cocktail, 4 Min.
DUAL-USE II: Biosprengstoff, 1 Min.
DUAL-USE III: Kampfmodel, 3 Min.
DUAL-USE IV: Or do we have the same?, 11 Min.
DUAL-USE V: Weltverzweiflungsmaschine, Programmcode, – ∞

Die Fünf-Kanal-Installation *DUAL-USE* zieht den titelgebenden Begriff in Zweifel. Vier von der Decke hängende Bildschirme zeigen Protagonist*innen einer globalisierten Waren- und Wissensproduktion. Die Tätigkeit einer Drohnenpilotin der US-Armee, die auch als Model arbeitet, wird von Dauerregen unterlaufen – weder der Strike noch das Shooting lassen sich bei Niederschlag erfolgreich durchführen. Ein Chemieprofessor sitzt im Explosionswind, während er seinen Rüstungsauftrag im deutschen Bildungssystem verteidigt. Der Geschäftsführer eines Rüstungszulieferers ist von Knallgeräuschen seiner eigenen Produkte irritiert. Eine Entwicklerin humanoider Roboter begegnet deren Potenzialen zwischen Krieg und Kinderzimmer.

Den Videos werden spezifische Störgeräusche entnommen und in eine Programmierung eingespeist, die sie auf Wahrscheinlichkeiten basierend zu einem Dual-Use-Ambientsound kombiniert und in Echtzeit im Raum wiedergibt. Die ökonomisierten Ambitionen der Akteur*innen steigern die Performance der Weltverzweiflungsmaschine. Sie verbreitet das algorithmische Grundrauschen einer militarisierten Massenkultur, die ihr eigenes Störgeräusch permanent produziert und nicht mehr wahrnimmt. Der Programmcode, der dem Schallgebilde zugrunde liegt, läuft als großflächig projizierter Zeichenstrom unablässig über die Rückwand des Ausstellungsraums.

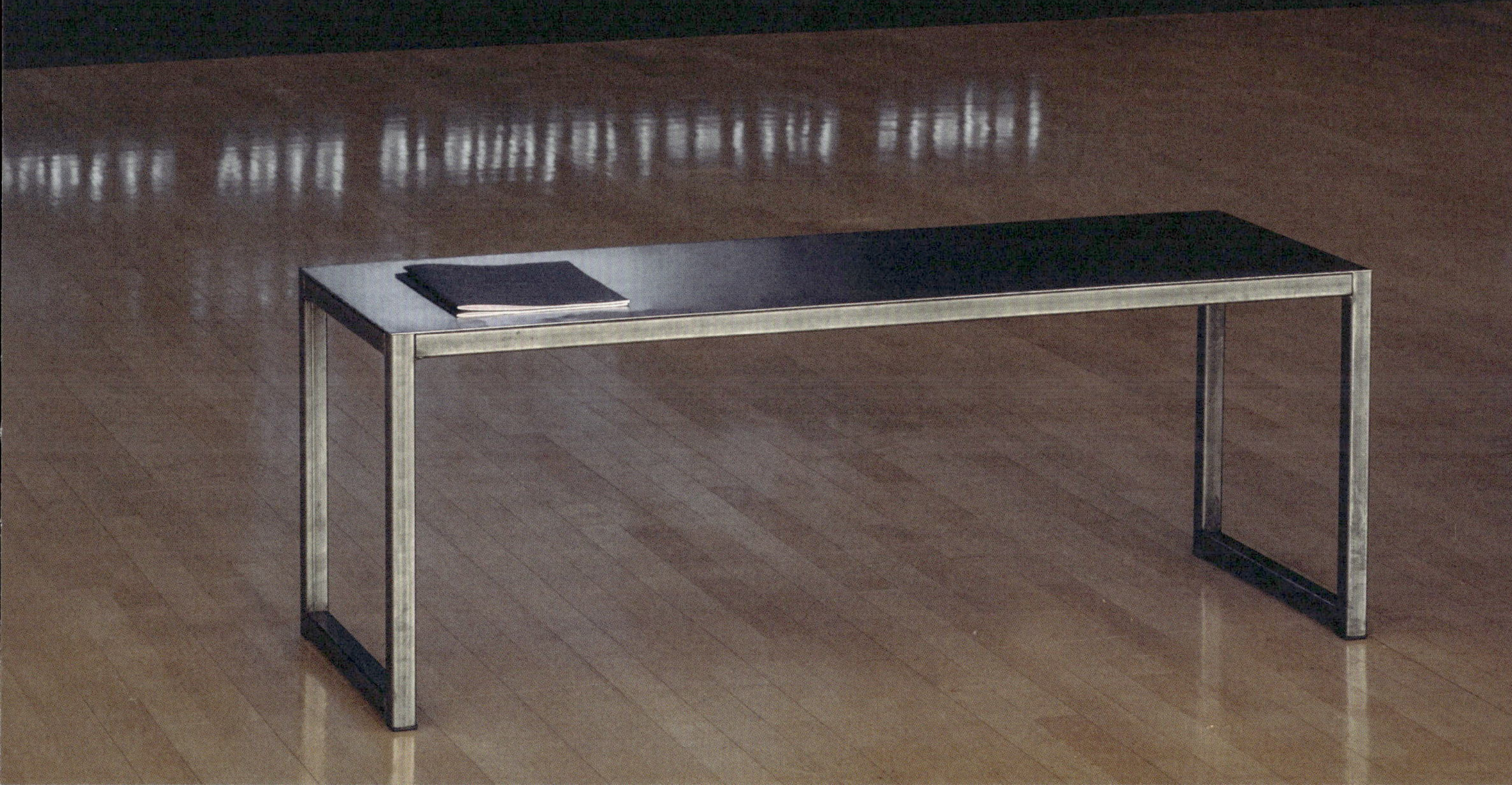
100::ms=>now;
" : (string)
i => float 0.8827
incval => file.
100::ms=>now;
" : (string)
i => float 0.8834 ;
incval => file.gain;
100::ms=>now;
" : (string)
(string)
ublic void granularize(int steps)

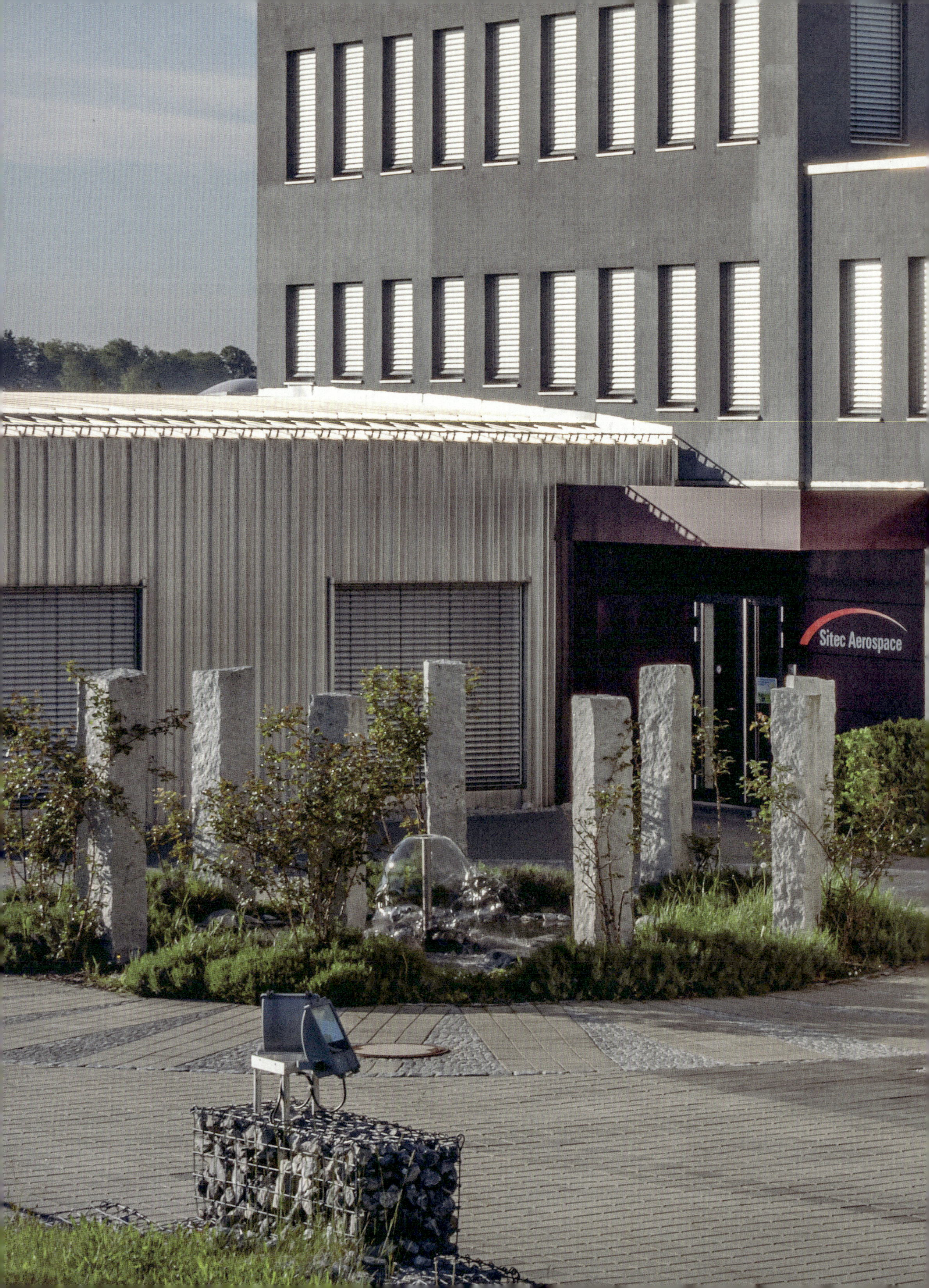
Sitec Aerospace

DUAL-USE I: Global Cocktail, 4 Min., Stills
DUAL-USE I: Global Cocktail, 4 min., stills

Links / Left
Kunst am Bau, *Stonehenge*
Percent for art, *Stonehenge*

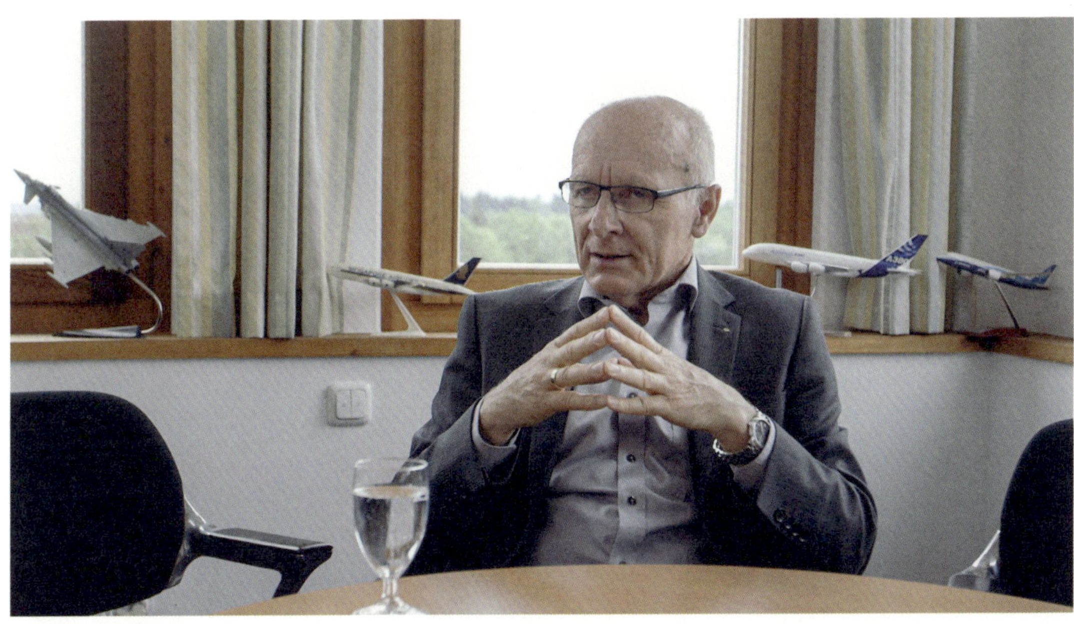

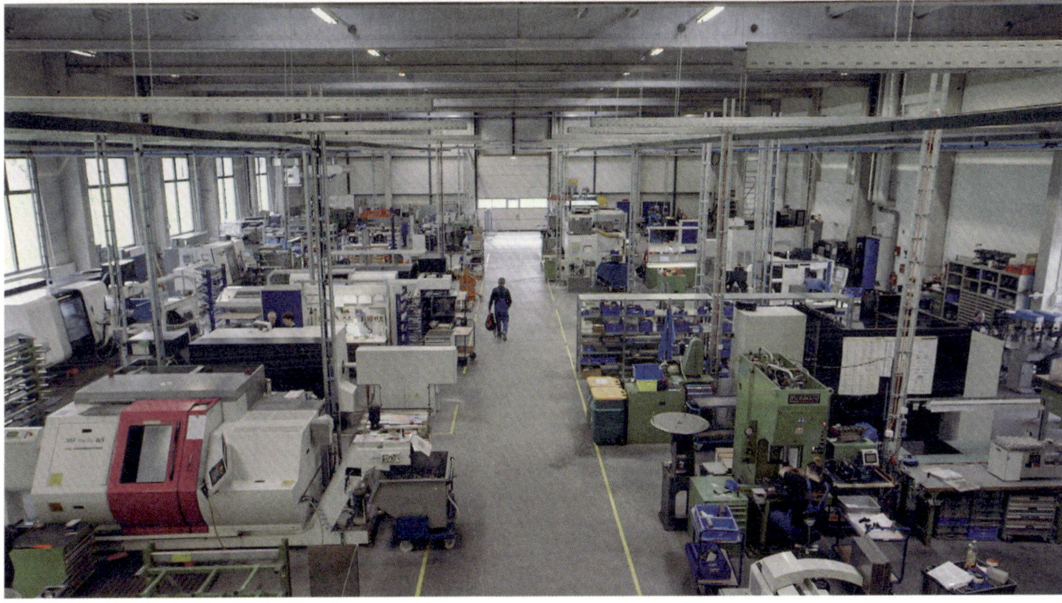

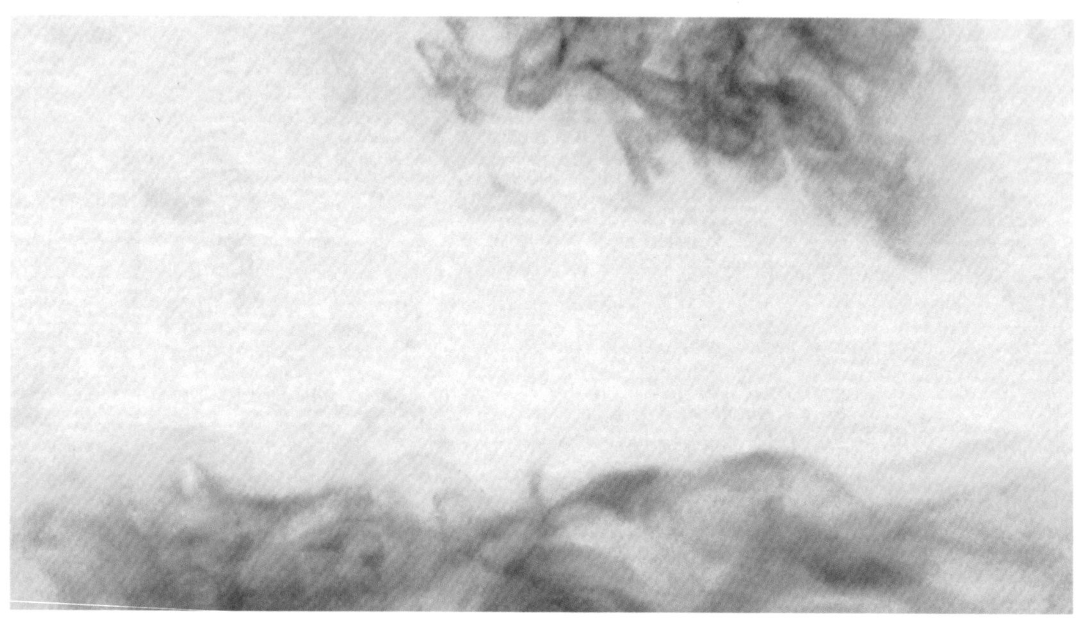

DUAL-USE II: Biosprengstoff, 1 Min., Stills
DUAL-USE II: Environmentally Friendly Explosives, 1 min., stills

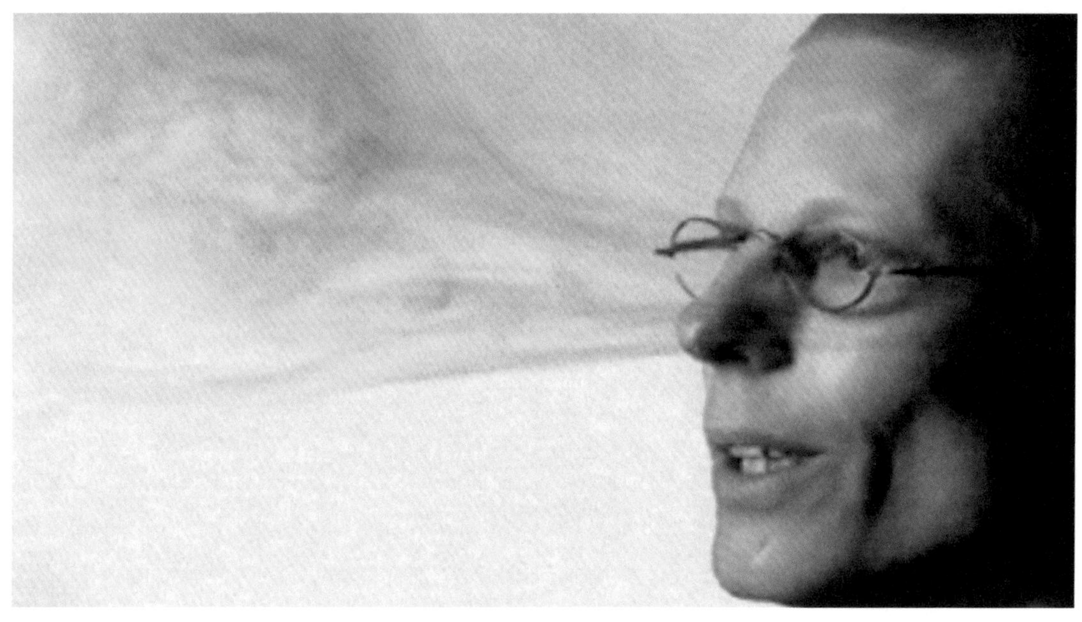

DUAL-USE
5-channel installation, 2016

DUAL-USE I: Global Cocktail, 4 min.
DUAL-USE II: Environmentally Friendly Explosives, 1 min.
DUAL-USE III: Combat Model, 3 min.
DUAL-USE IV: Or do we have the same?, 11 min.
DUAL-USE V: World Desperation Machine, program code, – ∞

The 5-channel video installation *DUAL-USE* raises questions about the term used for the title. Four screens hanging from the ceiling display protagonists of a globalized production of commodities and knowledge. The actions of a female US Army drone pilot, who works concurrently as a model, are undermined by incessant rain—neither the strike nor the shooting can be executed successfully during the rainfall. A chemistry professor sits in the wind of an explosion while he defends his armaments commission within the German educational system. The executive of an armaments supplier is disturbed by the banging sounds of his own product. A female developer of humanoid robots encounters their potential somewhere between warfare and nursery.

Disturbing noises were taken from the videos and fed into a program that combines them into a dual-use ambient sound based on probabilities and reproduces them in real time in the art space. The economized ambitions of the protagonists intensify the performance of the world desperation machine. It disseminates the algorithmic ambient noise of a militarized mass culture, which permanently produces its own disturbing noise, albeit one that it is no longer aware of. The program code on which the sonic form is based runs continually in the form of an extensive, projected stream of characters across the back wall of the exhibition space.

Air and Space Operations Center AOC
US-Militärbasis Ramstein, Deutschland, koordiniert seit 2011 Exekutionen per Drohne
US military base Ramstein, Germany, has coordinated executions by drone since 2011

DUAL-USE III: Kampfmodel, 3 Min., Stills
DUAL-USE III: Combat Model, 3 min., stills

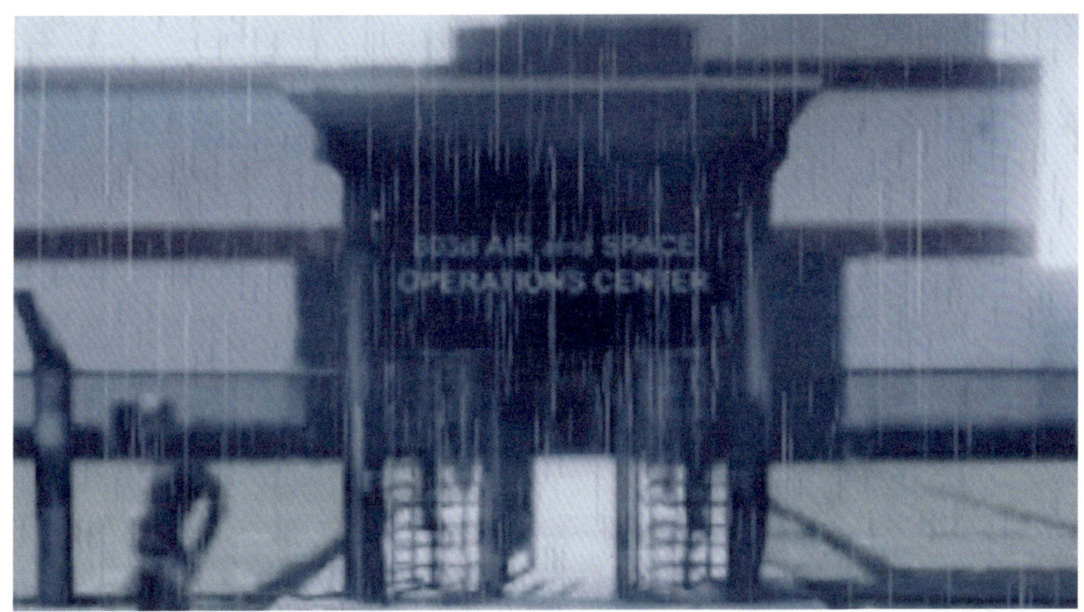
OPERATIONS CENTER

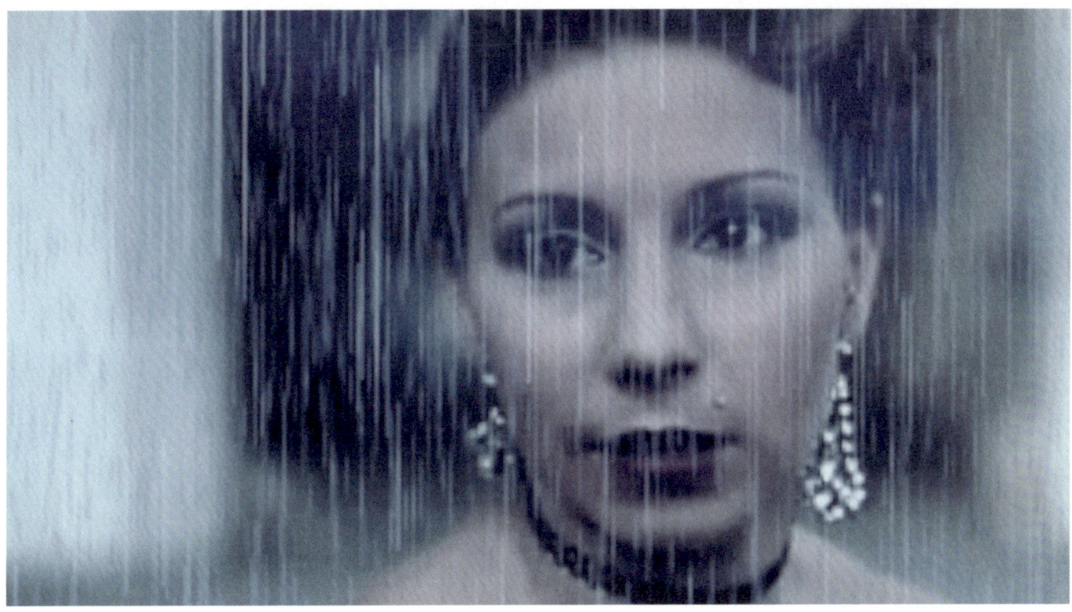

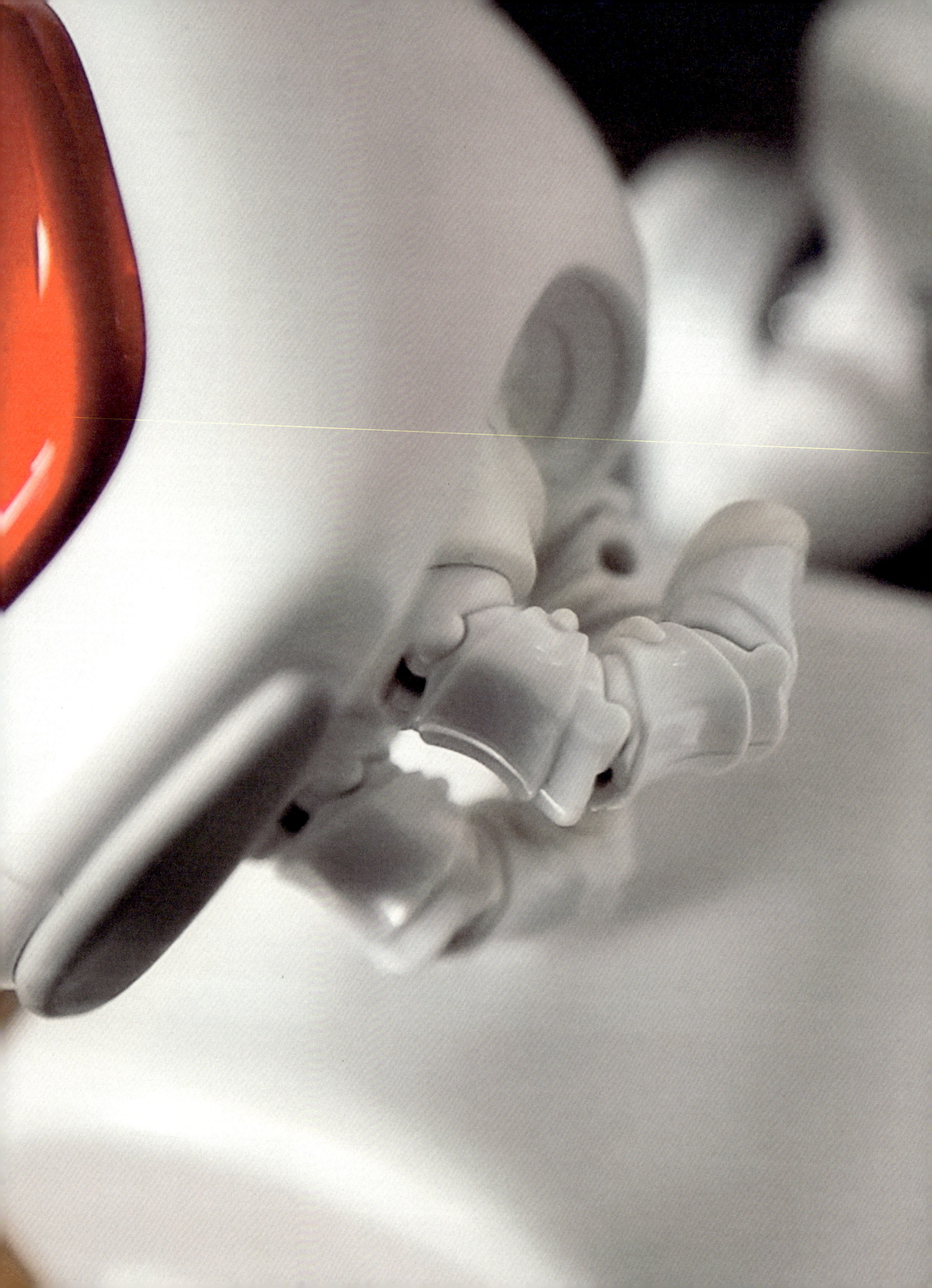

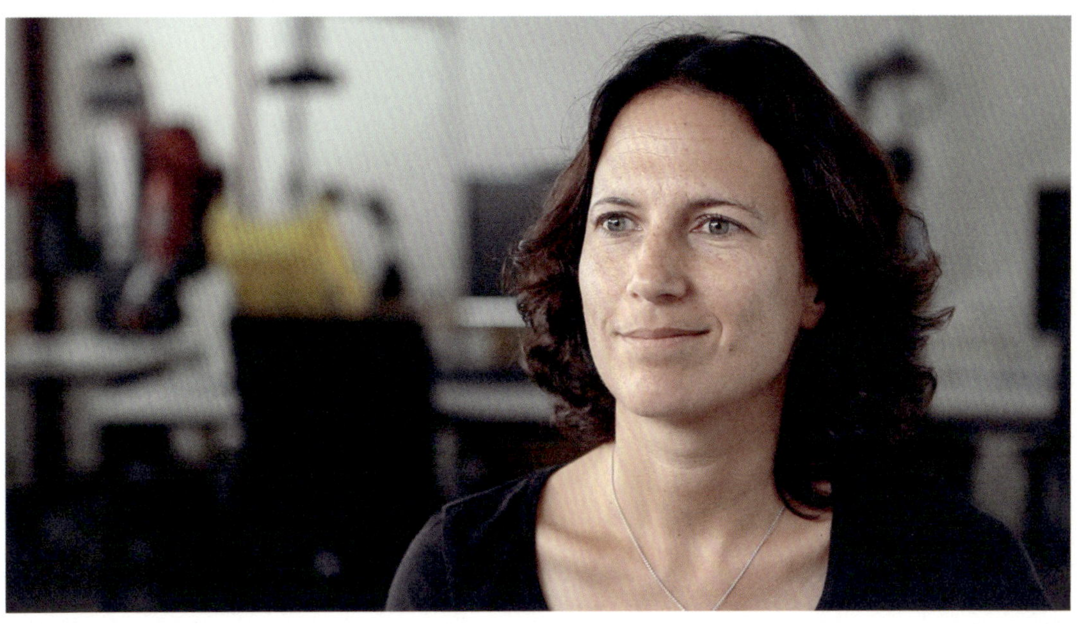

DUAL-USE IV: Or do we have the same?, 11 Min., Stills
DUAL-USE IV: Or do we have the same?, 11 min., stills

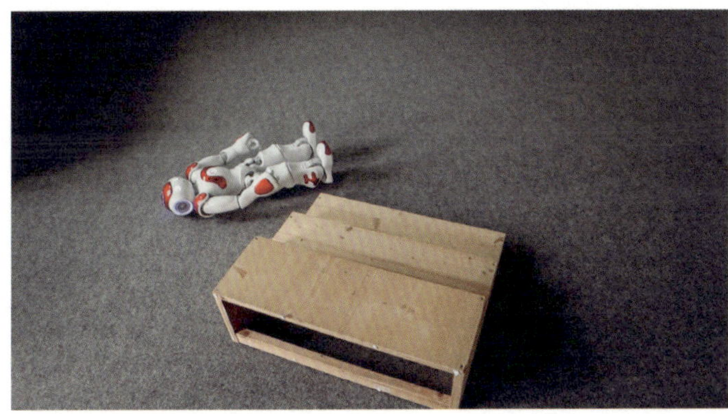

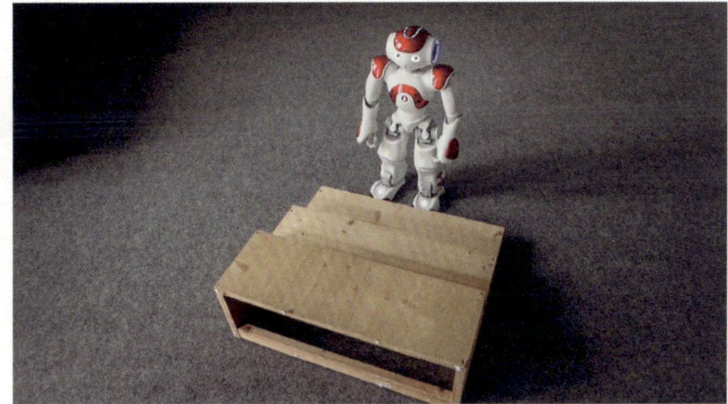

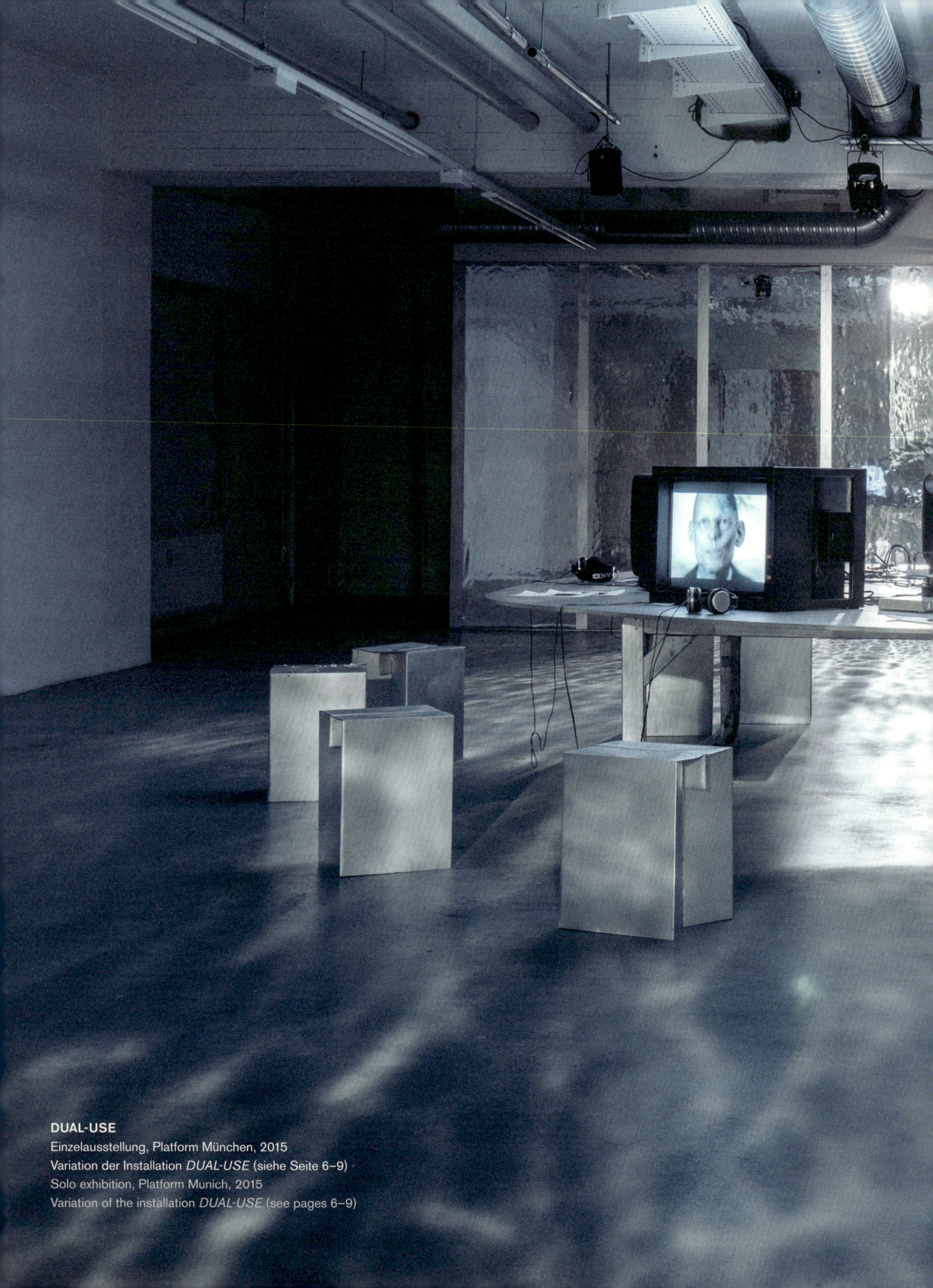

DUAL-USE
Einzelausstellung, Platform München, 2015
Variation der Installation *DUAL-USE* (siehe Seite 6–9)
Solo exhibition, Platform Munich, 2015
Variation of the installation *DUAL-USE* (see pages 6–9)

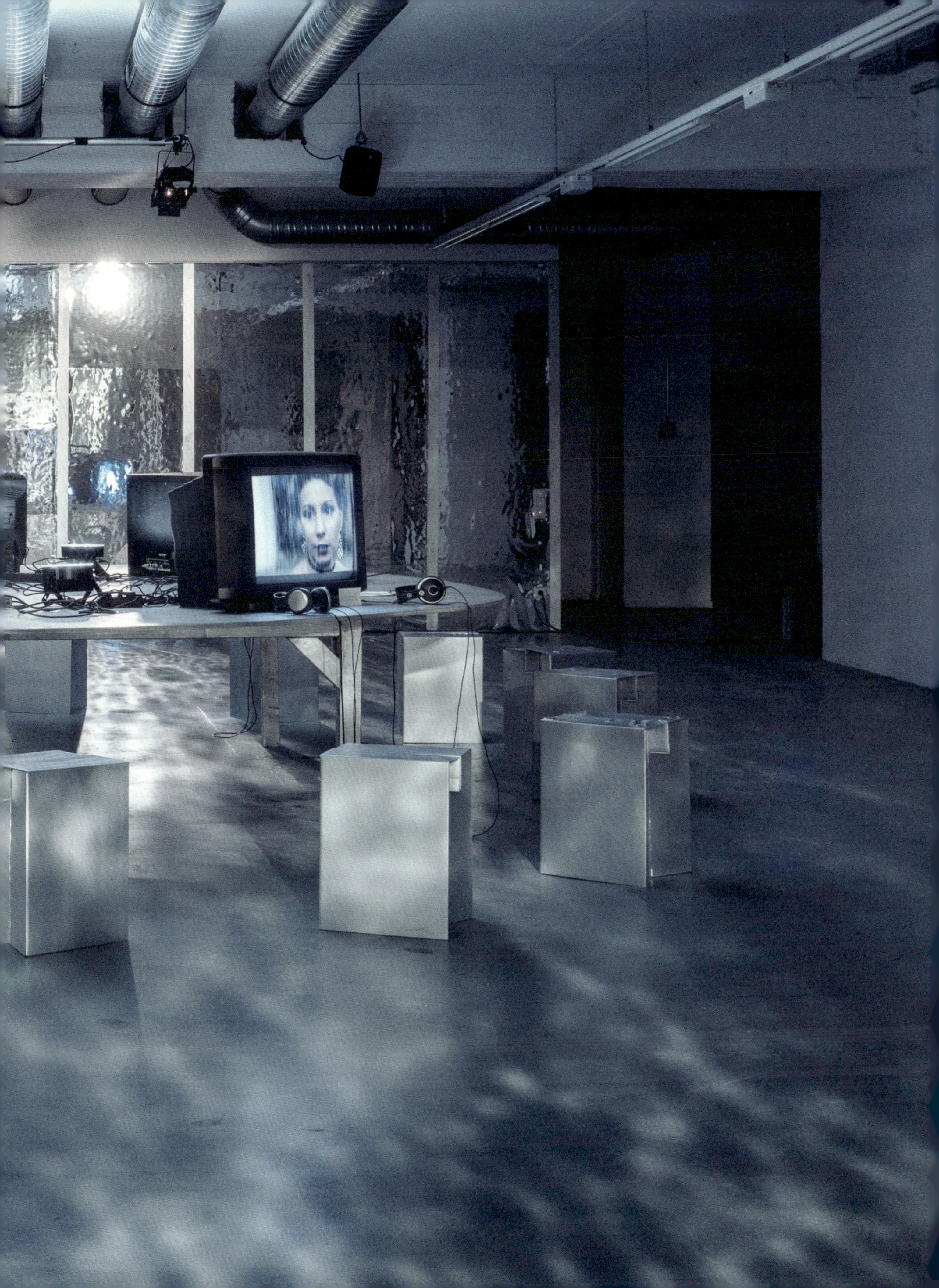

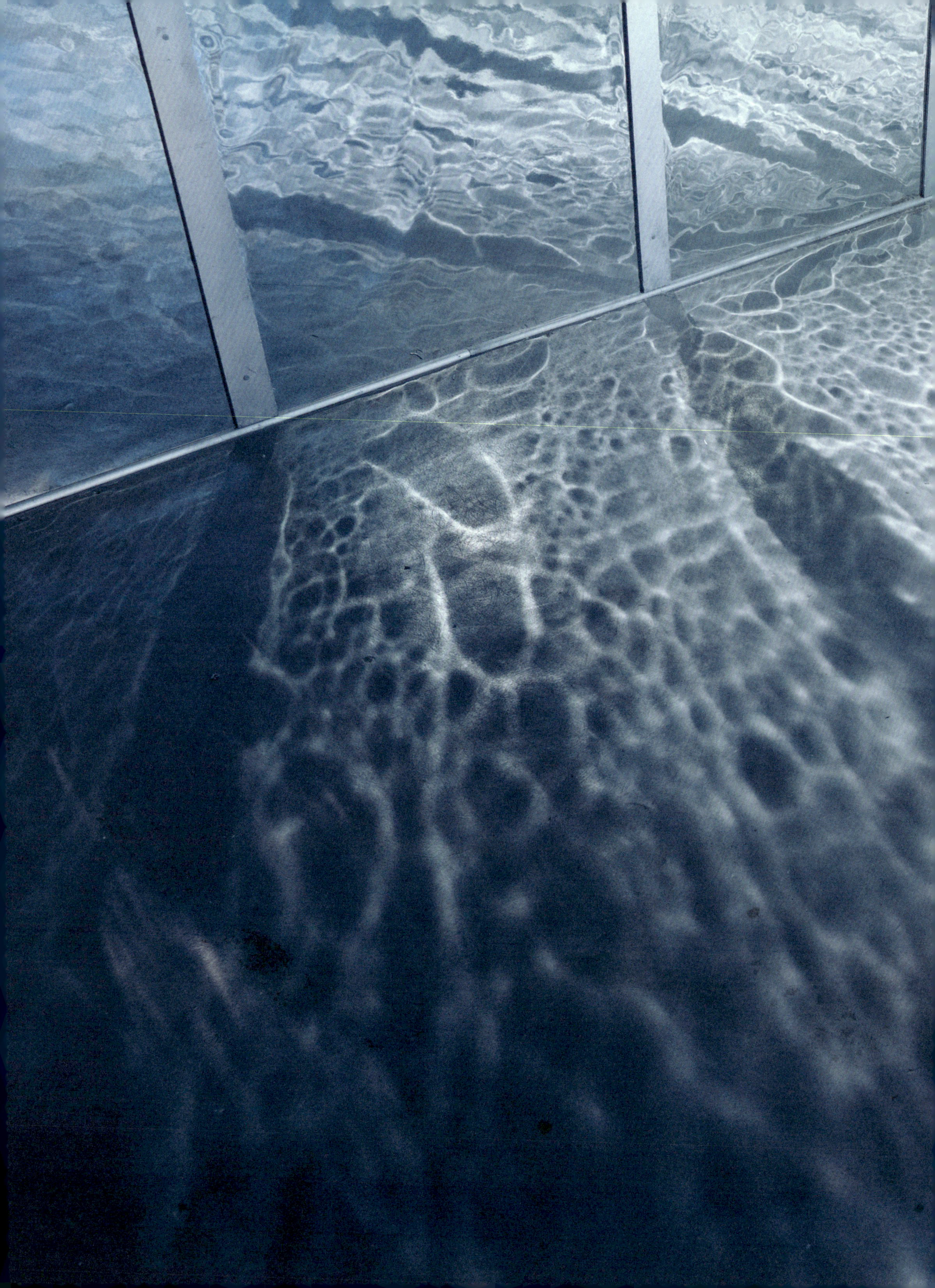

Stephanie Weber

Sprachrauschen: Gedanken zu zwei Arbeiten Franz Wanners

„We only see what we look at. Looking is an act of choice." John Berger, *Ways of Seeing*, 1972

Ein JPEG, das vor Kurzem online kursierte, enthielt eine Liste „amerikanischer" Namen, die sich ein japanischer Spieldesigner in den 1990er-Jahren für ein Baseball-Computerspiel ausgedacht hatte.[1] Die Namen der Teammitglieder klangen nordamerikanisch, waren es aber bei genauerem Hinsehen nicht. Dabei waren es meist nicht mehr als ein paar Buchstaben, die Sleve McDichael, Karl Dandleton oder Raul Chamgerlain als Fiktion entlarvten. Die lexischen Ausreißer fußten auf einer Reihe realistischer und vertrauter kultureller Annahmen über Nordamerika: ein Hauch schottischer und irischer Ahnen (Bobson Dugnutt), ein Anteil US-Präsident (Glenallen Mixon), durchwoben von einem nordamerikanischen Kosmopolitismus, der einen Onson Sweemey oder Anatoli Smorin hätte hervorbringen können. Es war genau dieses *beinahe* Richtige, die geringfügige Verfremdung, die die Wirklichkeit klarer hervortreten ließen.

Sich nun dem eigenen gesellschaftlichen Umfeld so zu nähern, als wäre es fremd, ist ungleich schwieriger, wenn nicht unmöglich. Franz Wanner versucht es nichtsdestotrotz. In seinen Arbeiten lassen sich Strategien der Aneignung, Imitation und Verfremdung beobachten, die sich – und auf diesen Aspekt konzentriert sich der folgende Text – in besonderer Weise auch auf sprachlicher Ebene bewegen. Für die beiden hier besprochenen Arbeiten hat der Künstler einen engen Fokus auf seine unmittelbare geografische und soziale Umgebung, auf München und das Münchner Umland, gelegt. Wobei der Ort an sich, sei es Moskau und Bad Tölz oder Duisburg und New York, für Wanner eine lediglich exemplarische Rolle spielt, also keine essenzielle oder gar existenzielle Funktion erfüllt. Seine Beobachtungen der vergangenen sieben Jahre galten der bundesdeutschen Rüstungsindustrie und ihren Exporten, der Migration und der Asylpolitik der Europäischen Union sowie dem Verhältnis des deutschen Nationalsozialismus mit dem ihm nachfolgenden nihilistischen Wohlstandsimperativ. Sprache, in Form von selbstverfassten, zitierten, zweckentfremdeten Texten, sowie die Montage von existierendem Bildmaterial dienen Wanner dabei als zentrales Arbeits- und Analysewerkzeug.

Wanner lehnt die Beschreibung seiner Arbeit als investigativ ab. Obgleich sein Prozess häufig erstaunliche Informationen hervorbringt, deckt der Künstler weniger auf, als dass er genau hinsieht und nachfragt. Eine Vorliebe für allgemein zugängliche Quellen – Websites von privaten und staatlichen Einrichtungen wie etwa der ortsansässigen Universität und ihrer Forschungsinstitute, des deutschen Verteidigungsministeriums oder der Firma für „Luftfahrttechnik" im Münchner Umland, Zeitungsartikel, Stadtpläne und Besichtigungen vor Ort – ist Ausdruck einer Arbeitsmethode, die privilegierter Informationen nicht bedarf und bedürfen möchte.

Es geht Wanner weder darum, düstere Geheimnisse aus den Tiefen eines Archivs an das Tageslicht zu befördern, noch darum, Tatsachen durch dokumentarische Akribie richtigzustellen. Vielmehr beschäftigt ihn die Frage, wie viel offensichtlich Düsteres wir uns heute kollektiv bemühen zu übersehen. In einem Interview bezeichnete er die gesellschaftlich verbreitete Fähigkeit, selbst die augenscheinlichsten politischen Widersprüche aus der bewussten Wahrnehmung zu katapultieren, als „kollektive kognitive Dissonanz",[2] die zum Symptom der Wohlstandsgesellschaften (hier der deutschen) geworden sei. Für diese Verdrängung setzt der Künstler kein kollektives nationales Trauma voraus, sondern einen erlernten Bürger*innenpragmatismus in einem Staat, der sich aus den Trümmern eines selbst verursachten Kriegs als aller Ideologien entledigtes Wunderkind des Wirtschaftsliberalismus neu erfand. Mit trockenem bis schwarzem Humor sowie einer systematischen Vermischung von belegbaren Quellen, fiktiven Geschichten und Zitaten aus Filmen, Fernseh- oder Onlinereportagen und anderem führt er seine Analysen der Pathologie des Übersehenwollens innerhalb des aktuellen bundesdeutschen Moments und dessen Idiomen vor.

Die konsequente Fortschreibung dieser Form von kognitiver Dissonanz ist Thema von Wanners Fünf-Kanal-Videoinstallation *DUAL-USE* (2016). „Dual Use" ist ein Begriff, der vor allem in der Exportkontrolle verwendet wird und der Güter „mit doppeltem Verwendungszweck" bezeichnet, die sowohl für zivile als auch für militärische Zwecke dienen können.[3] Die erklärte Absicht der Dual-Use-Bestimmung ist es, die Ausfuhr von Waren zu erschweren, die für militärische Zwecke genutzt werden könnten. Die Doppelbödigkeit des Begriffs ist nicht zu übersehen oder vielmehr: Sie ist ihm explizit namentlich eingeschrieben, während die implizite Kontrollfunktion der Verordnung langer Erklärungen und noch längerer Güterlisten bedarf. Genau diese Doppelbödigkeit ist es dann auch, die den Bezug auf Dual Use zu einem beliebten militärischen Schachzug macht: Unter dem Deckmantel zivilen Gebrauchs können zivile Forschung (etwa an der Universität) und Fördermittel für militärische Zwecke abgegriffen und das Ganze zugleich geleugnet werden (denn die Forschung *könnte* auch einem zivilen Zweck zugutekommen). Es ist genau diese unverhohlen schizophrene Beschaffenheit des Dual-Use-Konzepts, die Wanners Interesse weckte.

Die Installation besteht aus vier im Raum verteilten Monitoren, die von einer Projektion eines vertikal fortlaufenden Computercodes hinterfangen werden. Die vier Videos zeigen vom Künstler selbst geführte und gefilmte sowie gefundene und collagierte Interviews mit jeweils einem*r Gesprächspartner*in: Thomas Klapötke, Chemieprofessor an der Ludwig-Maximilians-Universität München (LMU), der umweltfreundliche Sprengstoffe für die US-amerikanische Armee entwickelt; die ehemalige US-Drohnenpilotin Danielle Balderston, heute Gothic Model; Armin Hilgarth, CEO der Firma Sitec Aerospace in Bad Tölz; und die Professorin für humanoide Roboter Maren Bennewitz von der Universität Bonn. Alle Interviewten versuchen mehr oder minder geschickt, das eigene (berufliche) Handeln zu naturalisieren und somit der eigenen Verantwortung zu entkoppeln, oder es, wie im Fall Balderstons, theatralisch zu überhöhen. Verschiedene hörbare Irritationsmomente stören die jeweilige Erzählung der Sprechenden: Der CEO von Sitec Aerospace, der Wanner gegenüber die Harmlosigkeit der hier produzierten Technik betont, schreckt bei einem Knall, der aus der Fabrik hallt, zusammen; Danielle Balderston, die im Abendkleid von ihren tödlichen Treffern als Pilotin berichtet,[4] ist durch den strömenden Regen kaum zu hören. Selbstverständlich „passieren" diese Irritationsmomente nicht einfach, sondern sind Wanners sorgfältiger und subjektiver Schnitt- und Tonarbeit geschuldet. Er bezeichnet diese Unterbrechungen selbst als „Störgeräusche". Diese Störgeräusche speisen den Computercode, der hinter den Monitoren endlos die Wand hinunterscrollt. Roland Barthes verwandte Mitte der 1950er-Jahre erstmals den Begriff des „Codes", um das Produktionsverhältnis von Macht und Sprache zu bezeichnen. Er bezog sich dabei konkret auf die kolonialfranzösische Sprache oder „Schreibweise"[5] zur Zeit des Algerienkriegs, deren Vokabular wie ein Code funktioniere, da es keinerlei Verhältnis zur Realität habe, oder aber ein diametral entgegengesetztes. In dieser Sprache wurden die Kolonisierung Nordafrikas zur „französischen Präsenz" und die einheimischen Bewohner*innen zu „muslimischen Populationen". Die Absicht dieser Schreibweise, so Barthes, sei die Herstellung einer Übereinstimmung zwischen (kolonialfranzösischen) Normen und Fakten. Als „kosmetische" Sprache ziele sie darauf ab, die eigentlichen Tatsachen mit einem „Sprachrauschen" („bruit de langage") zu bedecken. In Wanners Installation verdecken die als Code visualisierten Störgeräusche nicht die von den Interviewten vorgetragenen Tatsachen, sondern spielen vielmehr die Rolle eines Exzesses, der wie ein irreparables Leck im Wassertank die kosmetischen Diskurse der Interviewten perforiert. Diese Störungen oder Verfremdungen werden auf verschiedene Art und Weise verstärkt und betreffen auch die Rolle der Betrachterin, der – obwohl sich die ideologische Haltung des Künstlers abzeichnet – kein eindeutiger Standpunkt ermöglicht wird. So ist beispielsweise die Wissenschaftlerin aus Bonn durch ihre offene, ungekünstelte Art Sympathieträgerin und will sich in die Reihe der anderen Protagonist*innen nicht ganz einfügen. Die zwei vom Künstler selbst geführten und gefilmten Gespräche unterscheiden sich zudem in Dramatik, Bild- und Tonqualität derart von den zwei Fernsehproduktionen, dass man nicht umhinkann, sich zu fragen, wie viel Inszenierung und Affekt in jedem einzelnen der Gespräche steckt, gerade in jenen, die besonders „natürlich" wirken. Durch diese mal mehr, mal weniger erkennbaren schnitttechnischen und somit semantischen Eingriffe zeichnet sich sowohl in *DUAL-USE* sowie in den noch zu besprechenden *Battle Management Drawings* (2017) ein bestimmtes gesellschaftliches Idiom ab. Dieses zeigt sich – im Sinne von Susanne Leebs Interpretation des derridaschen Idiom-Begriffs in *Die Wahrheit in der Malerei* (1992) – nie selbst, sondern kristallisiert sich an den „Bruchstellen" historischer, sozialer, politischer oder ökonomischer Art. Der Zug (Derridas „trait") werde erst dort sichtbar, wo eine Bildsprache an- oder umgeeignet, zitiert wird.[6]

Für das Video *Biosprengstoff* (2016) verwendet Wanner Ausschnitte verschiedener von 3sat und ARD produzierten Dokumentationen über den LMU-Chemiker Thomas Klapötke. Anders als in den TV-Beiträgen ziehen sich in Wanners Version Rauchschwaden durch das Video, das außerdem mit Szenen aus Friedrich Dürrenmatts 1964 entstandener Verfilmung der *Physiker* gespickt ist. Der erzielte Effekt ist hier geradezu komödiantisch mit dem Resultat, dass „das böse Gewissen und die schlechte Absicht der Apologetik",[7] die aus den keinesfalls komödiantisch intendierten Worten des Wissenschaftlers sprechen, umso unüberhörbarer werden. Er empfinde es „als Auszeichnung", für die „sicherlich größte Armee der Welt" zu arbeiten, sagt Klapötke. Zudem habe er „natürlich" das Recht auf „Selbstverteidigung und Landesverteidigung" – ein bezeichnender Widersinn, spricht der deutsche Wissenschaftler doch von der US-Armee.[8] Auch die von Barthes analysierte Kolonialsprache diente dazu, kalkulierte und ökonomisch motivierte Taten in ein Wortgewand des Natürlichen zu kleiden. Dank ihr wurde die französische Gewalt zur objektiven Notwendigkeit, zum Resultat eines höheren Willens, der „eine zynische Realität mit einer vornehmen Moral"[9] absicherte.

„I'd like to write a poetry that could speed up a dialectical continuity in discontinuity & thus make visible whatever is forced into invisibility by police realism [...]" (Sean Bonney, „Letter on Poetics (after Rimbaud)", 2011).[10]

Die Battle Management Language (BML), auf die Wanners *Battle Management Drawings* Bezug nehmen, ist eine seit 2001 militärisch entwickelte Sprache, die keinerlei Mehrdeutigkeit kennen soll. Man muss keine Linguistin sein, um der Behauptung einer unmissverständlichen Kommunikation mit Zweifeln zu begegnen, weshalb Wanner die vom Wachtberger Fraunhofer-Institut mitentwickelte Sprache auch als „linguistisches Wunder"[11] bezeichnet. Konzeptuell ist die BML gewissermaßen der Straight-Edge-Gegenpol des promiskuitiven Dual-Use-Begriffs. Auf fünf vertikal installierten Flachbildschirmen schieben sich abwechselnd zwei kurze Texte und Fotografien ins Sichtfeld. Extrem kondensiert im Inhalt und affektlos im Ton, scheinen die substantivträchtigen Texte – man könnte sie auch als analytische Poesien beschreiben – selber in dieser Funktionssprache verfasst zu sein; zumindest spielt Wanner darauf an. Diese Vermutung wird durch ihren Inhalt ad absurdum geführt, da den Texten auf minimalem Raum ein Maximum an Widerspruch eingeschrieben ist. Dieser Eindruck verstärkt sich durch die Fotografien: Eine Drohne schwebt vor dem Tölzer Kalvarienberg mit malerischer Barockkirche; dem Kurztext zur Entwicklung von Technologien, die Menschen anhand von Haut- und Haarfarbe erkennen sollen, stellt Wanner ein Foto beiseite, in dem das mächtige Radom des Fraunhofer-Instituts hinter einem ordentlich eingezäunten Einfamilienhaus aufragt. In den Texten prallen die Widersprüche zum Teil in ein und demselben Satz aufeinander: „gesicherte Heimat" und „feindliches Gebiet" (S. 36 / *Battle Management Drawing II*), „massenkulturelle ‚Gedenkaktion'" (S. 48 / *Battle Management Drawing IV*); an anderer Stelle ergibt sich das Grauen aus dem Kontrast zwischen realpolitischer Sprachform und Gegenstand wie in *Battle Management Drawing I* (S. 35): „*Ein mobiler Roboter registriert in einem gemeinsamen Projekt des Fraunhofer-Instituts und der Universität Bonn die Haut- und Haarfarbe von Menschen, um Individuen selbstständig zu erkennen und zu verfolgen. Die Bewaffnung autonomer Systeme in Deutschland sei unumgänglich, besagt eine Studie des* Büros für Technikfolgen-Abschätzung beim Deutschen Bundestag. *Maschinen erweisen sich als fähig, eigenständig Waffen zu betätigen.*"

Die Battle Management Language soll unter anderem verwendet werden, um unbemannten Drohnen Befehle zu erteilen; eine Situation, die *Battle Management Drawing II* zugrunde liegt (S. 36–37). Wanner flicht (nicht nur) hier Militärjargon in den Kurztext ein – „Fernlenkvideos", „flexible Kampfzone", „feindzentriert" – und macht sich so ein paranoides Idiom zu eigen, das mit gutem Grund die größtmögliche Abstraktion von gelebter Realität und ihrem Ausdruck anstrebt. Diese sprachliche Abstraktion ist kein bloßes Resultat kafkaesker bürokratischer Strukturen, sondern verfolgt bestimmte Ziele, worauf Wanner konkret in *Battle Management Drawing IV* (S. 48–49) verweist. Er thematisiert hier die Weigerung der deutschen Bundeswehr, Kriegstraumata als solche anzuerkennen und psychotherapeutisch behandeln zu lassen: „*Die Absicht des Bundes ist [...] nicht die Lebendigkeit, sondern die Tauglichkeit.*" Die Tauglichkeit eines Menschen, anders als die Lebendigkeit, betrifft ausschließlich seine oder ihre Funktion, seine oder ihre Zweckmäßigkeit. Wanner lenkt mit dieser markanten Gegenüberstellung unsere Aufmerksamkeit auf den Kern einer militärisch-neoliberalen und gesellschaftlich über diesen Komplex hinaus verbreiteten „Schreibweise". Anders als die Objekte und „blinden Kräfte" von „Sprache und Stil" ist die Schreibweise, laut Barthes, eine „Funktion"; „[...] sie ist die durch ihre soziale Bestimmung umgewandelte literarische Ausdrucksweise, sie ist die in ihrer menschlichen Intention ergriffene Form, die somit an die großen Krisen der Geschichte gebunden ist".[12] Diese ideologisch verankerte und verankernde Sprache und ihre sozioökonomische Funktion sind eine konkrete Schreibweise der Bundesrepublik, die durch Wanners behutsame semantische Eingriffe zeitweise in aller Schärfe hervortritt. Man fühlt sich an den britischen Poeten Sean Bonney erinnert, der „die aride Realität der Gefängnisstrafe und der Polizeipatrone" als die „reale Poetik des Kapitals"[13] bezeichnet. Keine Sprache, keine Schreibweise ist folgenreicher, folgenschwerer als die staatlich verordnete und betriebene, deren Konsequenzen nicht ästhetischer, sondern konkreter, materieller und sozialer Natur sind.

1 Vgl. https://twitter.com/lrgmnn/status/813635533658144768/photo/1 [abgerufen am 20.11.2019].

2 Franz Wanner im Interview mit Philippine Régniez: „La frontière entre civil et militaire est brouillée", in: *Usbek & Rica*, Paris, 3. Juli 2018, https://usbeketrica.com/article/la-frontiere-entre-civil-et-militaire-est-brouillee [abgerufen am 20.11.2019]. Die Übersetzung des Zitats aus dem Französischen übernahm die Verfasserin.

3 Zu diesen Gütern zählen laut EU-Verordnung Waren, die „sowohl für nichtexplosive Zwecke als auch für jedwede Form der Unterstützung bei der Herstellung von Kernwaffen oder sonstigen Kernsprengkörpern verwendet werden können" (Art. 2, Abs. 1, EG Dual-Use-Verordnung).

4 Eine der TV-Dokumentationen, aus denen sich Wanner die Aufnahmen für sein Video aneignete, heißt wahrhaftig *Der Todesengel* (NDR).

5 Im Sinne von Barthes' Begriff der „écriture".

6 Susanne Leeb, „Die kleinen ‚k's der Kunst", in: *Texte zur Kunst*, Heft 108 (2017), S. 32–56, hier S. 33.

7 Karl Marx, *Das Kapital*, Bd. 1, Vorwort zur zweiten Auflage, Anaconda Verlag, Köln 2009, S. 39–46, hier S. 41. In seinem kurzen Exkurs über die Geschichte der politischen Ökonomie schreibt Marx über den Moment, als die französische und deutsche Bourgeoisie an Macht gewann, dass dieser das Ende der wissenschaftlichen bürgerlichen Ökonomie einleite. Das ganze Zitat passt wunderbar auf die Situation des LMU-Wissenschaftlers: „Es handelte sich jetzt nicht mehr darum, ob dies oder jenes Theorem wahr sei, sondern ob es dem Kapital nützlich oder schädlich, bequem oder unbequem, ob polizeiwidrig oder nicht. An die Stelle uneigennütziger Forschung trat bezahlte Klopffechterei, an die Stelle unbefangner wissenschaftlicher Untersuchung das böse Gewissen und die schlechte Absicht der Apologetik."

8 Es sei denn, wir unterstellen Klapötke, dass er entlang der seit 2001 überhöhten Konfliktlinien zwischen „Abendland" und „Morgenland" denkt.

9 Roland Barthes, „Afrikanische Grammatik", in: ders., *Mythen des Alltags*, aus dem Französischen von Horst Brühmann, Suhrkamp Verlag, Berlin 2010, S. 178–186, hier S. 178.

10 http://abandonedbuildings.blogspot.com/2011/06/letter-on-poetics.html [abgerufen am 20.11.2019].

11 Franz Wanner, „Battle Management Language – Sprachlose Mythen militärischer Strukturen", Vortrag im Haus der Wissenschaft Bremen, 16. März 2019, vorab abgedruckt in: Informationsstelle Militarisierung e. V. (Hg.), *Krieg im Informationsraum. Zum 21. Kongress der Informationsstelle Militarisierung*, Tübingen 2018, http://www.imi-online.de/download/Informationsraum2018-Web.pdf, S. 32–39 [abgerufen am 20.11.2019].

12 Roland Barthes, *Am Nullpunkt der Literatur*, aus dem Französischen von Helmut Scheffel, Suhrkamp Verlag, Frankfurt am Main 1985, S. 20f.

13 Sean Bonney, „Notes on Militant Poetics" 1/3, http://abandonedbuildings.blogspot.com/2012/03/notes-on-militant-poetics-1-3.html [abgerufen am 20.11.2019]. Die Übersetzung der Zitate aus dem Englischen übernahm die Verfasserin.

Stephanie Weber

The Rustle of Speech: Thoughts on Two Works by Franz Wanner

"We only see what we look at. Looking is an act of choice." John Berger, *Ways of Seeing*, 1972

A JPEG that recently did the rounds online contained a list of "American" names a Japanese games designer had thought up during the 1990s for use in a baseball computer game.[1] The names of the team members *sounded* North American, but upon closer inspection were not. In fact, what gave away Sleve McDichael, Karl Dandleton, and Raul Chamgerlain as fictive characters was a matter of just a few letters. The lexical deviations were based on a series of realistic and familiar cultural assumptions about North America: a hint of Scottish and Irish ancestry (Bobson Dugnutt), a helping of US President (Glenallen Mixon), interwoven with a North American cosmopolitanism that could have produced an Onson Sweemey or an Anatoli Smorin. It was precisely this *almost* correctness, this slight slip, that enabled the reality to be seen more clearly.

To approach one's own social environment in a similar manner, as if it were foreign, is infinitely more difficult, impossible even. Franz Wanner takes a stab at it nonetheless. In his works, we can observe strategies of appropriation, imitation, and alienation which, consistently, if not exclusively, operate on a linguistic level. It is on this aspect that the following text will concentrate. For the two works under discussion here, the artist has focused closely on his immediate geographical and social surroundings, namely Munich and its environs. For Wanner, the place itself, be it Moscow and Bad Tölz or Duisburg and New York, is used merely as an example and thus fulfills no essential function, let alone an existential one. His observations over the past seven years have been directed toward the German armaments industry and its exports, the European Union's policies on migration and asylum, and the relationship of German National Socialism to the ahistorical imperative of prosperity that succeeded it. Language, in the form of texts he has written himself, or which he quotes or alters, and the montage of existing pictorial material serve Wanner as a fundamental tool for his work and analyses.

Wanner rejects any description of his work as investigative. Although his process frequently yields little-known information, the artist is more a careful observer inquiring into things that we all know exist rather than one who unmasks or exposes them. A characteristic feature of his work method is a predilection for sources that are publicly accessible: websites of private and state institutions such as the local university and its research institutes, the German Ministry of Defense, or the aeronautical engineering company in the environs of Munich—as well as newspaper articles, town plans, and site visits. He neither needs nor wishes to make use of privileged information.
Wanner is not seeking to unearth dark secrets from the depths of an archive and bring them to light, nor does he aim to set the records straight by means of meticulous documentary work. His greater concern is to question how many glaringly disturbing facts we collectively agree to disregard. In an interview, he described the socially widespread ability to catapult even the most obvious political contradictions out of our conscious awareness as "collective cognitive dissonance"[2] – a commonly shared symptom of capitalist societies (in this case, in Germany). The artist does not see collective national trauma as a necessary prerequisite for this suppression. Instead, he attributes it to a learned civic pragmatism in a state—the wunderkind of economic liberalism—that claimed to have shed all ideology when reinventing itself from the rubble of a self-induced war. With dry humor and a systematic combination of verifiable sources, fictitious stories, and quotes from movies, television, and online reportages, etc., Wanner presents his analysis of the pathology of overlooking what is in plain view within the present-day German moment.

The systematic continuation of this form of cognitive dissonance provides the subject for Wanner's five-channel video installation *DUAL-USE* (2016). The term "dual use" is used above all in export control. It refers to goods "with a dual purpose," which can be used for both military and civilian ends.[3] The declared intention of classifying goods as dual-use is to make it harder to export those that could be used for military purposes. It is impossible to ignore the ambiguity of the term, or rather: this ambiguity is explicitly recorded in the designation itself, while the implicit control function of the regulation demands long explanations and even longer goods lists. It is this very ambiguity that makes the reference to dual use into a popular military gambit: under the guise of civilian use, civilian research (for example at a university) and funding can be tapped for military purposes. It was precisely this schizophrenic nature of the dual-use concept that aroused Wanner's interest.

The installation *DUAL-USE* consists of four monitors distributed throughout the room, framed by a projection of a vertically scrolling computer code. The four videos show interviews conducted and filmed by the artist himself, along with found interviews with a total of four conversation partners: Thomas Klapötke, Professor of Chemistry at Ludwig-Maximilian University in Munich (LMU), who is developing environmentally friendly explosives for the US Army; the former US drone pilot Danielle Balderston, today a gothic model; Armin Hilgarth, CEO of Sitec Aerospace in Bad Tölz; and Maren Bennewitz, Professor for Humanoid Robots at Bonn University. What runs through all interviews is the speakers' positing of their (professional) activities as natural and hence divorced of responsibility. Various audible moments of irritation disrupt or interrupt the narrative of the speakers in each case: the CEO of Sitec Aerospace, who assures Wanner of the harmlessness of the technology being produced by his company, is visibly startled by a bang from the factory; Danielle Balderston, dressed in an evening gown as she tells of her lethal strikes as a pilot,[4] can hardly be heard through the driving rain. The aforementioned moments of irritation do not simply "happen," but are the result of Wanner's careful and subjective editing and sound work. The artist casually describes these interruptions as "interferences." Roland Barthes first used the term "code" in the mid-1950s to describe the relationship between the production of power and language. In doing so, he was referring specifically to the French-colonial language or "writing"[5] at the time of the Algerian War. He likened the colonial vocabulary to a code, one that bore no relationship to reality, but rather represented its very opposite. In this language, the colonization of North Africa was toned down to a "French presence" there; the local inhabitants became "Muslim populations." For Barthes, the intention of this language was to create conformity between (colonial French) norms and facts. In a "cosmetic" procedure, its purpose was to cover the truth of colonial oppression with "the rustle of language" ("bruit de langage"). In Wanner's installation, the interference, visualized in the form of the scrolling code, does not mask the facts described by the interviewees, but rather acts as an excess, which perforates their cosmetic discourses. This subtle alienation is underlined through various means. The observer is not afforded a distinct point of view despite the fact that the artist's own ideological standpoint within the presented scenario is tangible. Maren Bennewitz, the scientist from Bonn, for example, is presented as a likeable figure and does not quite fit in with the other protagonists. Furthermore, the dramaturgy and picture and sound quality of the two conversations conducted and filmed by the artist himself differ from the two television productions to such an extent that we cannot help but ask ourselves how much staging and affect is contained in each of the conversations, especially in those which seem particularly "authentic." Through more or less recognizable interventions in the form of editing, a particular social "idiom" becomes apparent both in *DUAL-USE* and in the *Battle Management Drawings* (2017), which will be discussed next. In the sense of Susanne Leeb's interpretation of Jacques Derrida's idiomatic meaning in *The Truth in Painting* (1992), this social "idiom" itself is never shown but is crystallized at the historical, social, political, or economic "breaking point." Derrida's "trait" becomes visible only where a visual language is quoted in an appropriated or modified form.[6]

For the video *Environmentally Friendly Explosives* (2016), Wanner uses excerpts from various documentaries about the LMU chemist Thomas Klapötke produced by the 3sat and ARD TV networks. Unlike the original television productions, the video in Wanner's version is permeated by billows of smoke and laced with scenes from the 1964 adaptation of Friedrich Dürrenmatt's *The Physicists.* The effect achieved here verges on the comedic, with the result that "the bad conscience and the evil intent of apologetics"[7] become all the more unmistakable. Klapötke considers it an "honor" to work for "what is certainly the world's largest army," Moreover, he "naturally" has the right "to defend himself and to defend the country"—a telling absurdity, since the German scientist is talking here about the US Army.[8] We are reminded here of the colonial language as analyzed by Barthes, which served to cover up calculated economically motivated decisions in the disguise of a natural state of affairs. Thanks to this language, the French violence was presented as an objective necessity, as the result of a higher will that secured "a cynical reality with polite morality."[9]

"I'd like to write a poetry that could speed up a dialectical continuity in discontinuity & thus make visible whatever is forced into invisibility by police realism [...]."[10]

Battle Management Language (BML), to which Wanner's *Battle Management Drawings* refer, has been developed for military use since 2001 and aims to rule out any ambiguity within communication. One does not have to be a linguist to be doubtful of claims of an unequivocal communication, which is why Wanner refers to the language that the Fraunhofer Institute in Wachtberg helped to develop as a "linguistic marvel."[11] Conceptually, the BML is to some degree the straight-edge counterpart to the promiscuous concept of dual use. Wanner's *Battle Management Drawings* consist of five vertically mounted flat screens, each of which shows two short texts and photographs sliding intermittently into view. Extremely condensed in terms of content and factual in tone, these texts, with their preponderance of nouns—they could also be described as analytical poems—seem to have been composed in this functional language; at least this is what Wanner seems to be implying. This conjecture is carried ad absurdum through their content in that the texts record a maximum of contradiction within a minimum of space. This impression is emphasized by the photographs, in which a drone is seen hovering above the Kalvarienberg (Calvary Hill) in Tölz with its picturesque baroque church. Wanner juxtaposes the short text about the development of technologies that claim to recognize people by the color of their skin and hair with a photo in which the massive radome of the Fraunhofer Institute rises up behind a neatly fenced-off, detached, single-family home. Within the texts, the contradictions clash with each other, sometimes within one and the same sentence: "secured homeland" and "hostile territory" (*Battle Management Drawing II*, pp. 36–37), "mass-cultural 'commemoration event'" (*Battle Management Drawing IV*, pp. 48–49). Elsewhere, the horror arises from the contrast between the politically pragmatic linguistic form and the object, as in *Battle Management Drawing I* (pp. 34–35): "In a joint project between the Fraunhofer Institute and the University of Bonn, a mobile robot registers the color of people's skin and hair in order to independently recognize and pursue individuals. According to a study by the Office of Technology Assessment at the German Bundestag (TAB), the arming of autonomous systems in Germany is inevitable. Machines prove capable of operating weapons on their own."

Battle Management Language is intended, among other things, to issue commands to unmanned drones—a situation on which *Battle Management Drawing II* is based (pp. 36–37). Here (but not only here), Wanner weaves military jargon into the short text—"remote-control videos," "flexible combat zone," "enemy-centered"—thereby embracing a specific paranoid idiom that has good reason to strive to achieve the greatest possible abstraction of lived reality and its expression. This linguistic abstraction is no mere absurd result of Kafkaesque bureaucratic structures; it has a psychological objective, as Wanner specifically points out in *Battle Management Drawing IV* (pp. 48–49). Here, he takes as his subject the refusal of the German Armed Forces to recognize war trauma as such and to provide psychotherapeutic treatment: The aim of the Federal Ministry of Defense "is not vitality but fitness." A person's fitness, unlike his or her vitality, applies exclusively to his or her function, his or her suitability. Wanner uses this striking juxtaposition to direct our attention toward the core of a military-neoliberal "form of expression" that is widely used socially beyond this complex. According to Barthes, a mode of writing is—unlike the objects and "blind forces" of "language and style"— a "function"; it is "the literary language transformed by its social finality, form considered as human intention, and thus linked to the great crises of History."[12] This ideologically anchored and anchoring language and its socio-economic function are a concrete form of expression by the Federal Republic, one that occasionally emerges in all its clarity through Wanner's careful semantic intervention. We find ourselves reminded of the British poet Sean Bonney, who describes "the arid realities of the prison sentence and the police bullet" as the "real poetry of capital."[13] No language, no formal style is more momentous, more far-reaching than that ordered and operated by the state and whose consequences are not aesthetic, but of a concrete, material, and social nature.

1 See https://twitter.com/lrgmnn/status/813635533658144768/photo/1 (accessed November 20, 2019).

2 Franz Wanner in an interview with Philippine Régniez, "La frontière entre civil et militaire est brouillée," in *Usbek & Rica*, Paris, July 3, 2018; https://usbeketrica.com/article/la-frontiere-entre-civil-et-militaire-est-brouillee (accessed November 20, 2019) [translated].

3 According to EU regulations, these goods include those which "can be used both for nonexplosive purposes and also for any form of support in the manufacture of nuclear weapons or other explosive nuclear devices" (Art. 2, para. 1, EC Dual-Use Regulation).

4 One of the television documentaries from which Wanner used pictures for his video was indeed called *Der Todesengel* (The Angel of Death) (NDR).

5 In the sense of Barthes's term "écriture."

6 Susanne Leeb, "Die kleinen 'k's der Kunst," in *Texte zur Kunst*, no. 108 (2017), pp. 32–56, here p. 33.

7 Karl Marx, *Das Kapital*, vol. 1, preface to the second edition, Hamburg 2009, pp. 39–46, here p. 41. In his short essay on the history of the political economy, Writing about the moment when the French and German bourgeoisies gained power, Marx says that it marked the end of the scientific bourgeois economy. The full quotation perfectly suits the situation of the scientist at Ludwig-Maximilian University, Munich: "Es handelte sich jetzt nicht mehr

darum, ob dies oder jenes Theorem wahr sei, sondern ob es dem Kapital nützlich oder schädlich, bequem oder unbequem, ob polizeiwidrig oder nicht. An die Stelle uneigennütziger Forschung trat bezahlte Klopffechterei, an die Stelle unbefangener wissenschaftlicher Untersuchung das böse Gewissen und die schlechte Absicht der Apologetik." ["It was thenceforth no longer a question, whether this theorem or that was true, but whether it was useful to capital or harmful, expedient or inexpedient, politically dangerous or not. In place of disinterested enquirers, there were hired prize-fighters; in place of genuine scientific research, the bad conscience and the evil intent of apologetic."] English translation available online at: https://www.econlib.org/book-chapters/chapter-authors-prefaces-to-the-first-and-second-editions-by-karl-marx/ (accessed November 25, 2019).

8 Unless we insinuate that Klapötke is thinking along the lines of conflict between "Occident" and "Orient," which have been exaggerated since 2001.

9 Roland Barthes, "Afrikanische Grammatik," in Barthes, *Mythen des Alltags*, translated from the French by Horst Brühmann, Berlin 2010, pp. 178–86, here p. 178 [translated]. English edition: "African Grammar," in *Mythologies*, transl. Richard Howard and Annette Lavers, New York 2012.

10 Sean Bonney, "Letter on Poetics (after Rimbaud)," 2011, http://abandonedbuildings.blogspot.com/2011/06/letter-on-poetics.html (accessed November 20, 2019).

11 Franz Wanner, "Battle Management Language – Sprachlose Mythen militärischer Strukturen," lecture at the Haus der Wissenschaft Bremen, March 16, 2019, advance printing in Informationsstelle Militarisierung e.V. (ed.), *Krieg im Informationsraum. Zum 21. Kongress der Informationsstelle Militarisierung*, Tübingen 2018; http://www.imi-online.de/download/Informationsraum2018-Web.pdf, pp. 32–39 (accessed November 20, 2019).

12 Roland Barthes, *Am Nullpunkt der Literatur*; English edition: *Writing Degree Zero*, transl. Annette Lavers and Colin Smith with a preface by Sunsan Sontag, 5th edn, New York 1989, p. 14. Available online at https://archive.org/details/writingdegreezer00rola_0/page/14 (accessed November 20, 2019).

13 Sean Bonney, "Notes on Militant Poetics" 1/3, http://abandonedbuildings.blogspot.com/2012/03/notes-on-militant-poetics-1-3.html (accessed November 20, 2019).

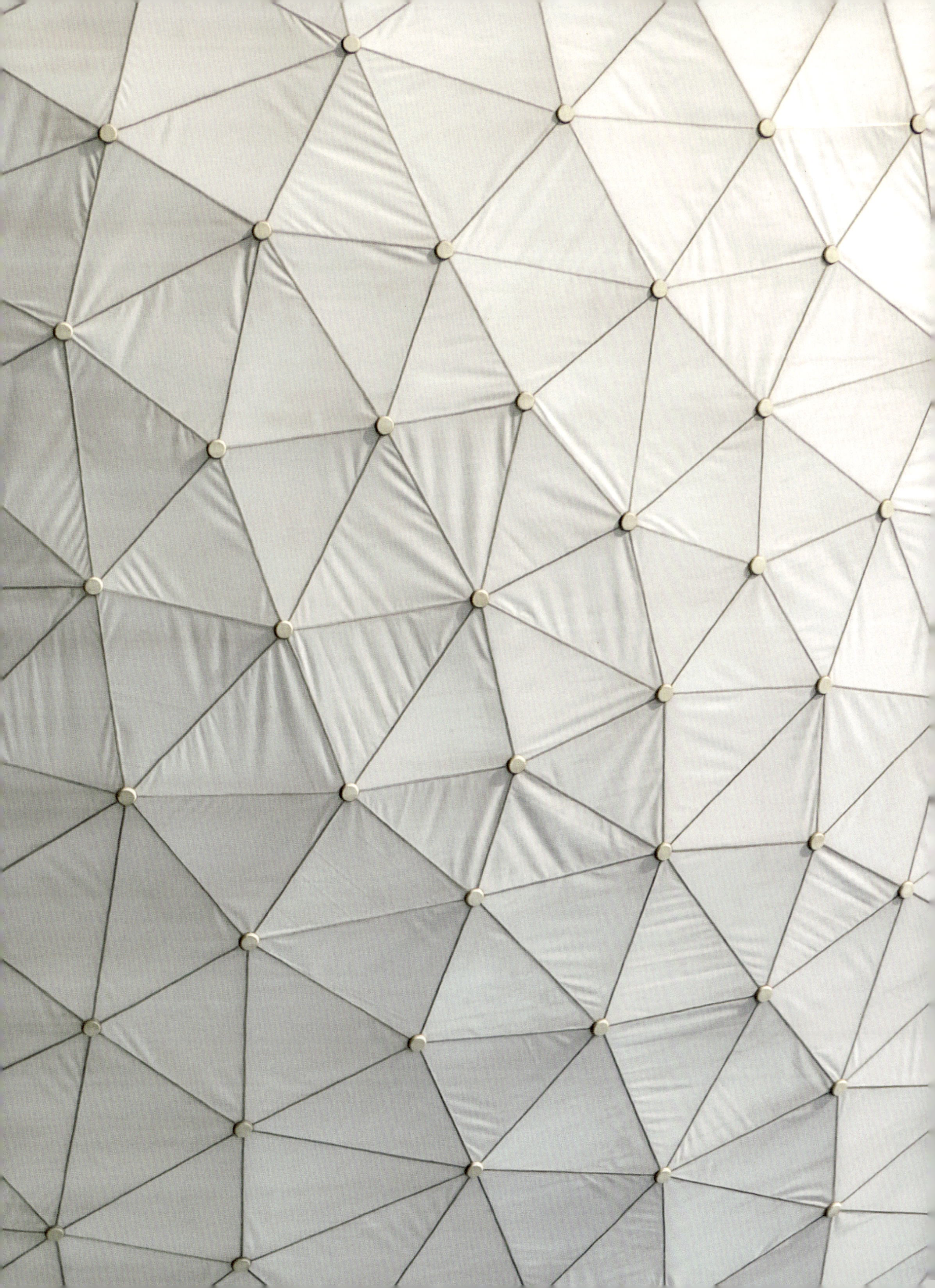

BATTLE MANAGEMENT DRAWINGS

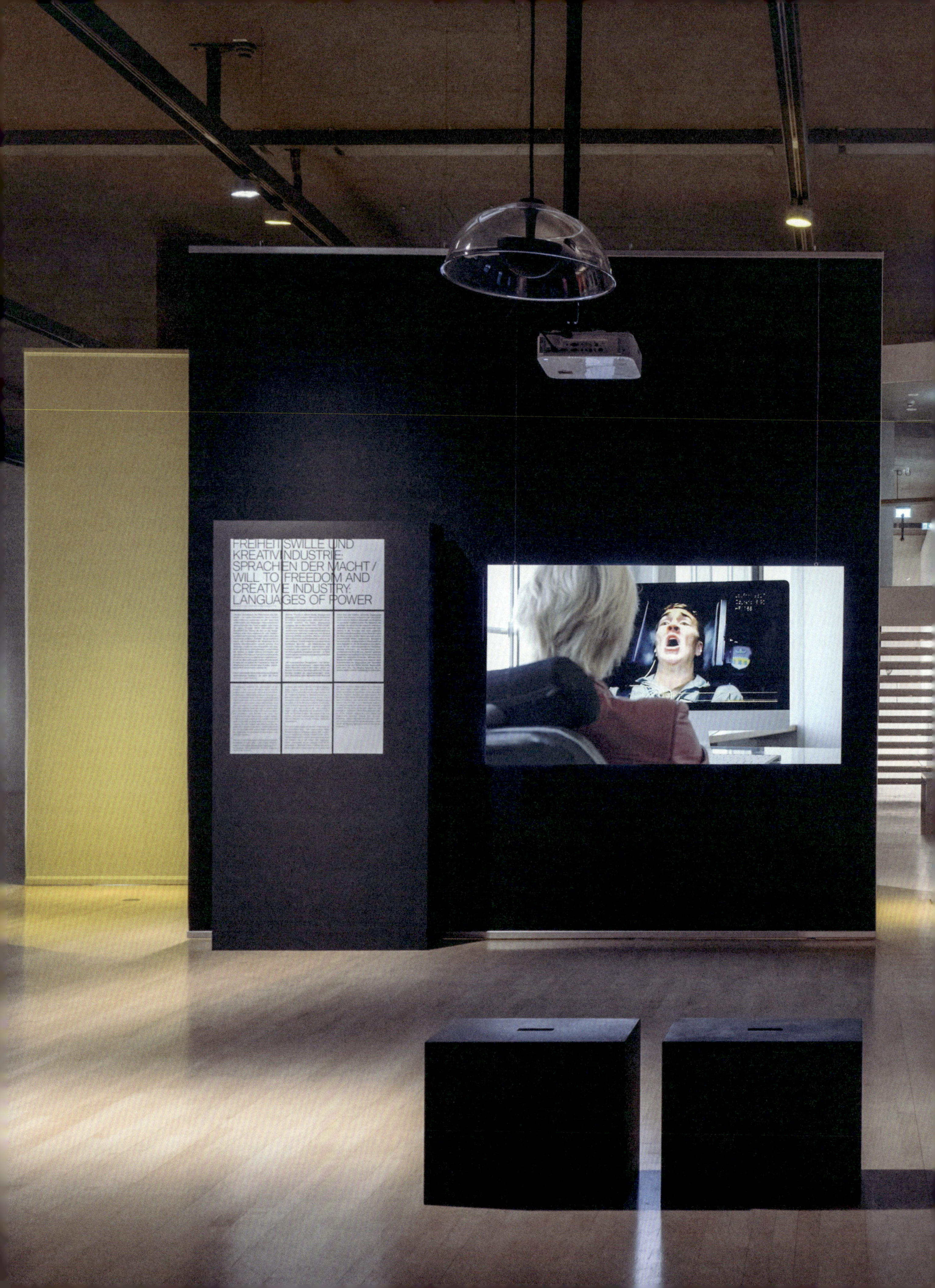
FREIHEITSWILLE UND
KREATIVINDUSTRIE:
SPRACHEN DER MACHT /
WILL TO FREEDOM AND
CREATIVE INDUSTRY:
LANGUAGES OF POWER

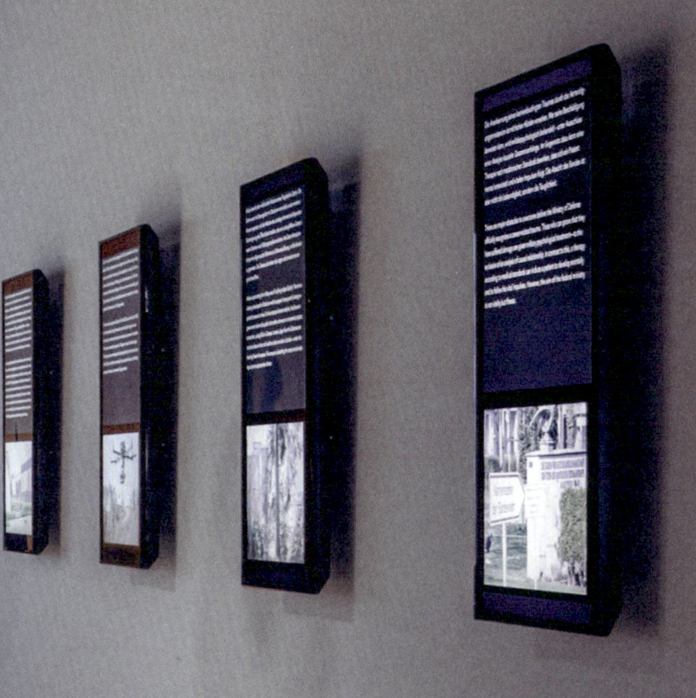

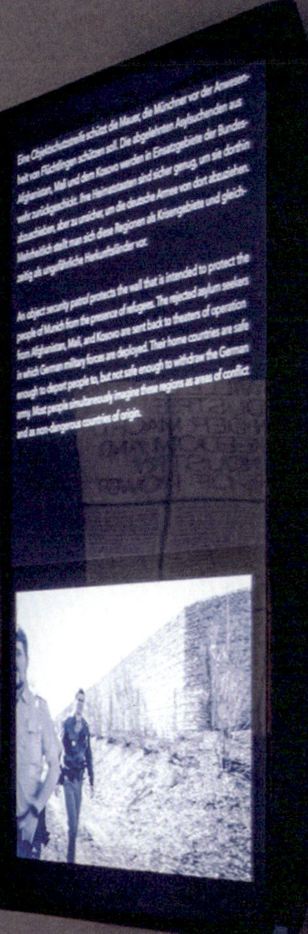

Installationen *Battle Management Drawings I–V*, 2017 und *From Camp to Campus*, 2017/19
Ausstellung *After the Fact. Propaganda im 21. Jahrhundert*,
Städtische Galerie im Lenbachhaus und Kunstbau München, 2017

Installations *Battle Management Drawings I–V*, 2017 and *From Camp to Campus*, 2017/19
Exhibition *After the Fact. Propaganda in the 21st Century*,
Städtische Galerie im Lenbachhaus und Kunstbau München, Munich, 2017

Battle Management Drawing I

Über die Vorgänge im Inneren des Radoms dringt wenig nach außen. In der Nachbarschaft in Wachtberg kursieren Gerüchte, die Militärforscher*innen auf dem umzäunten Gelände unterhielten sich in *Battle Management Language*. Das Fraunhofer-Institut, das die Riesenkugel betreibt, entwickelt die „kontrollierte Sprache ohne Mehrdeutigkeiten", um unbemannten Systemen Befehle zu erteilen.

Little about the proceedings inside the radome reaches the outside. Rumors are circulating in the neighborhood in Wachtberg that military researchers within the fenced-in compound converse in Battle Management Language. The Fraunhofer Institute, which operates the giant sphere, is developing a "controlled language without ambiguities" for issuing orders to unmanned systems.

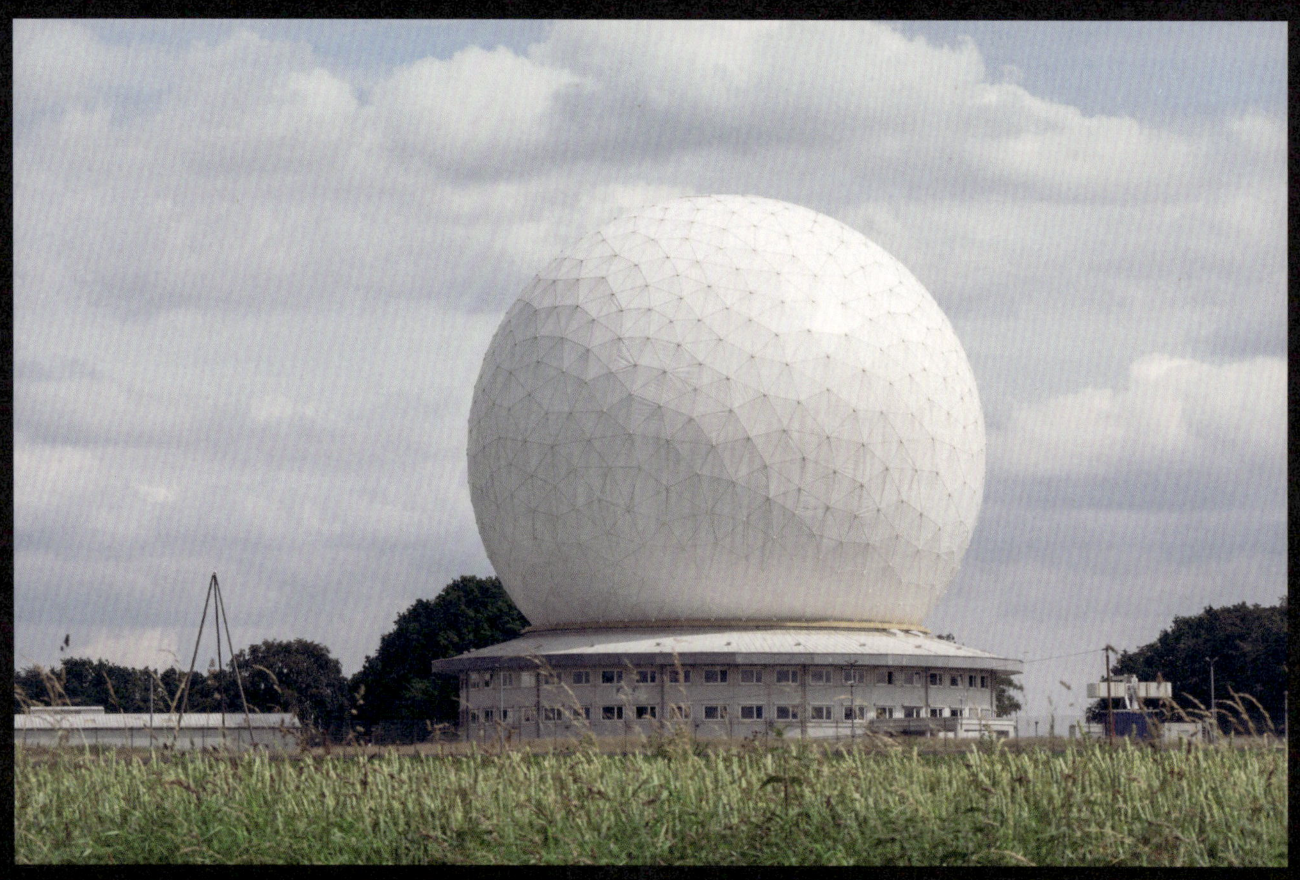

Ein mobiler Roboter registriert in einem gemeinsamen Projekt des Fraunhofer-Instituts und der Universität Bonn die Haut- und Haarfarbe von Menschen, um Individuen selbstständig zu erkennen und zu verfolgen. Die Bewaffnung autonomer Systeme in Deutschland sei unumgänglich, besagt eine Studie des *Büros für Technikfolgen-Abschätzung beim Deutschen Bundestag*. Maschinen erweisen sich als fähig, eigenständig Waffen zu betätigen. Die Frage, ob sich Menschen als fähig erweisen, sich nicht wie Maschinen betätigen zu lassen, beantwortet Lars, der als unbewaffneter Rasenmäher in Wachtberg arbeitet, mit autonomen „Battle Management Drawings".

In a joint project between the Fraunhofer Institute and the University of Bonn, a mobile robot registers the color of people's skin and hair in order to independently recognize and pursue individuals. According to a study by the Office of Technology Assessment at the German Bundestag (TAB), the arming of autonomous systems in Germany is inevitable. Machines prove capable of operating weapons on their own. The question of whether people prove capable of not allowing themselves to be operated like machines is answered by Lars, who works as an unarmed mowing machine in Wachtberg with autonomous "Battle Management Drawings."

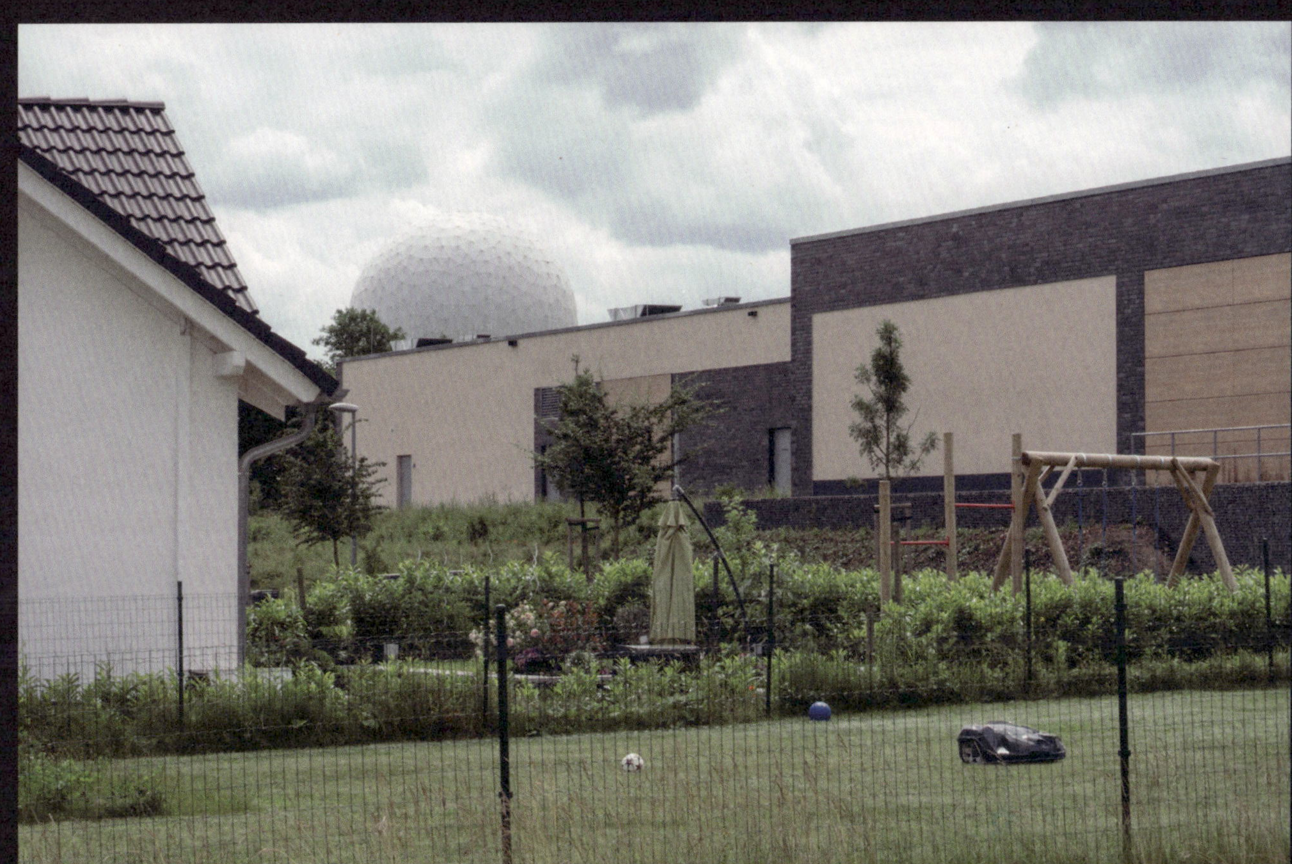

Battle Management Drawing II

Das Dispositiv der Drohne teilt den globalen Raum in zwei Bereiche: die gesicherte Heimat und das feindliche Gebiet, das unter ständiger Beobachtung steht und als flexible Kampfzone nonlinear und feindzentriert verschoben wird.* Die Ausführenden des staatlichen Vorsorgeterrorismus verüben vom Büro aus über bewaffnete Fernlenkvideos Hinrichtungen aus der Luft. Die Tätigkeit lässt sie körperlich unverletzt, kann aber existenzielle Zweifel an ihrer Berufswahl auslösen. Im Gegensatz dazu sind autonome Systeme frei von Identität und funktionieren zweifellos.

The dispositif of the drone divides global space into two domains: secured homeland and hostile territory, the latter of which is under constant observation and shifted around as a flexible combat zone in a nonlinear and enemy-centered way.** Those who carry out preventive state terrorism commit aerial executions from their offices via armed remote-control videos. The work leaves them physically unharmed but can trigger existential doubts about their choice of careers. In contrast, autonomous systems are identity-free and function without doubt.

* Grégoire Chamayou, *Ferngesteuerte Gewalt. Eine Theorie der Drohne*, aus dem Französischen von Christian Leitner, Passagen Verlag, Wien 2014, Teil I. Techniken und Taktiken, Kapitel 1. Methodologien der feindlichen Umgebung, S. 33–36, Kapitel 6. Kill Box, S. 63–70.

** Grégoire Chamayou, *A Theory of the Drone*, translated from the French by Janet Lloyd (New York: The New Press, 2015), part I: Techniques and Tactics, chapter 1: Methodologies for a Hostile Environment, pp. 21–25, chapter 6: Kill Box, pp. 52–59.

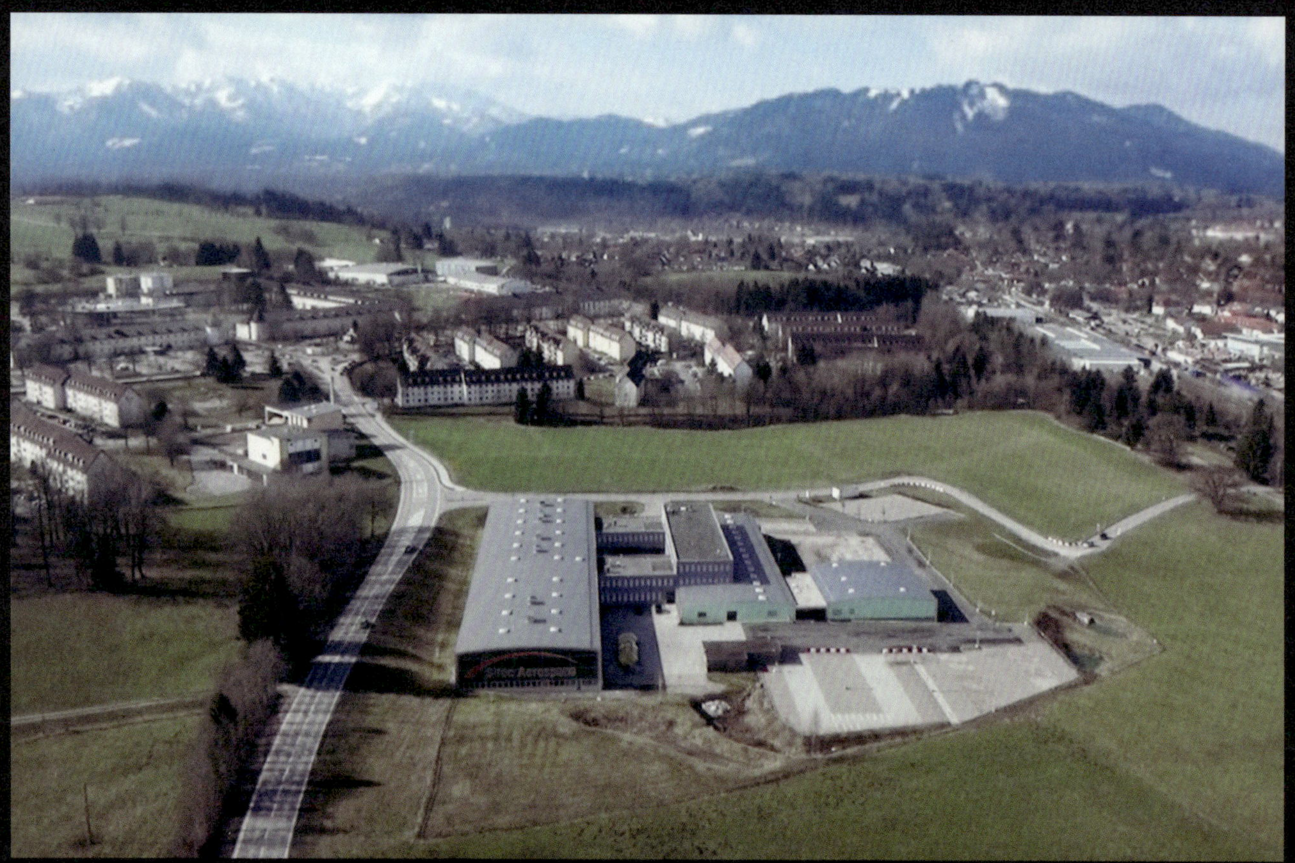

Die Drohne über dem Kalvarienberg in Bad Tölz ist unbewaffnet. Der Berg bot bis 1800 den Exekutionen des Landgerichts eine Bühne. Gegenwärtig ist dort eine ikonisierte Hinrichtung als Dauerinstallation zu sehen. Die Drohne zeichnet Bilder für einen TV-Beitrag über Sitec Aerospace auf. Die Firma sichert den Wohlstand der Region, indem sie sich an der Herstellung des *Tigers* beteiligt. Außer in den Kampfhubschrauber investiert ihre Holdinggesellschaft Temasek auch in Singapurs Zoo.

The drone hovering above the Kalvarienberg (Calvary Hill) in Bad Tölz is unarmed. Until 1800, the hill provided a stage for executions ordered by the regional court. At present, an iconized execution is on display there as a permanent installation. The drone is recording images for a TV segment about Sitec Aerospace. The company secures the region's prosperity through its involvement in the manufacture of the *Tiger*. In addition to investing in the combat helicopter, its holding company, Temasek, also invests in Singapore's zoo.

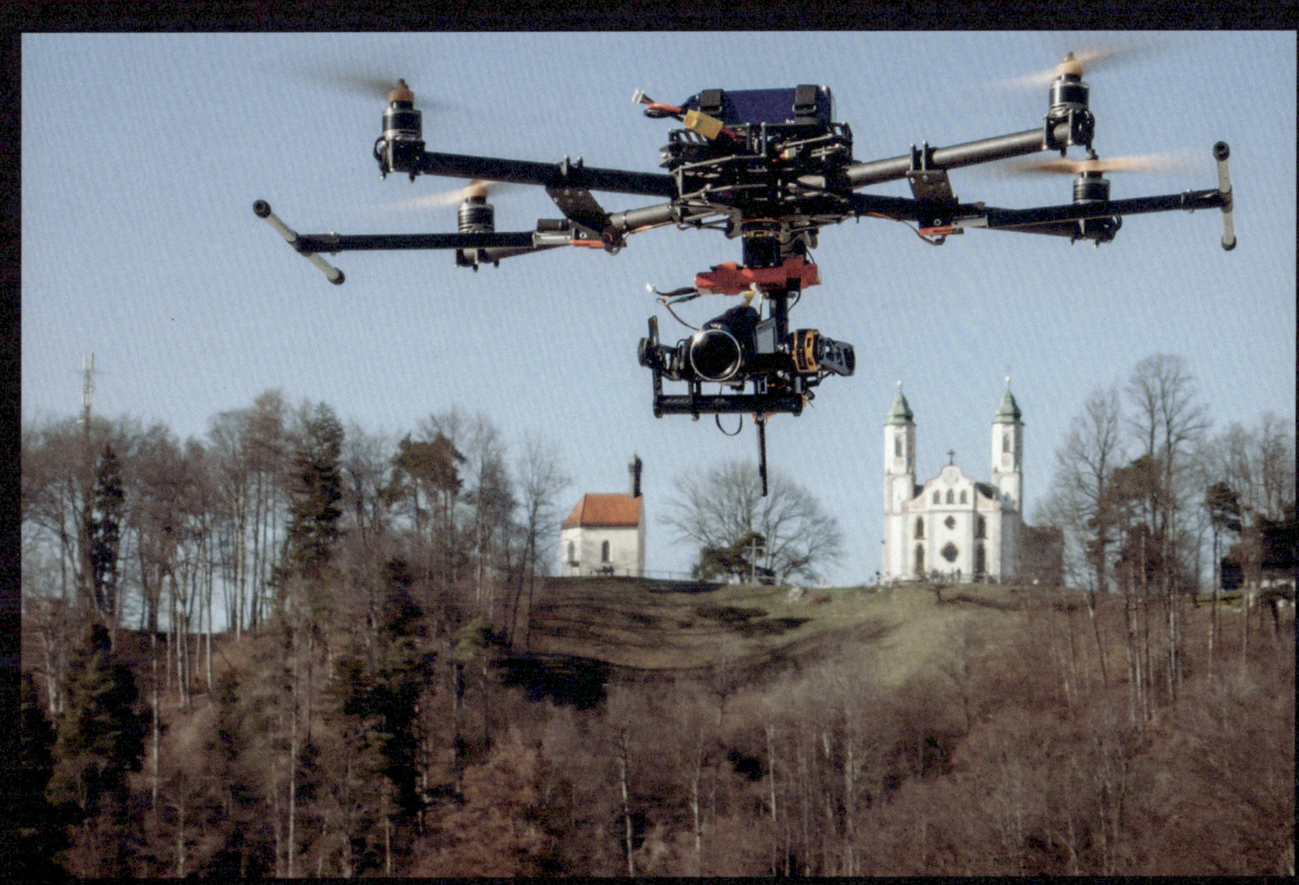

Battle Management Drawing III

Der Ludwig Bölkow Campus in Ottobrunn bei München wird 2013 nach einem NS-Ingenieur benannt. Der Campus basiert auf der ehemaligen Luftfahrtforschungsanstalt, für deren Bau zwei Zwangsarbeitslager für KZ-Häftlinge und Kriegsgefangene eingerichtet wurden. Die Fundamente des Kriegsgefangenenlagers liegen in Sichtweite des heutigen Campus. Ein Bachelorprogramm formt die Studierenden dort zu Kampfpilot*innen. 2016 schreibt die Bayerische Staatsregierung, die Geschichte des Orts sei nicht Inhalt der Forschungs- und Lehrtätigkeit.

In 2013, this campus in Ottobrunn, near Munich, was named after Ludwig Bölkow, the engineer who developed armaments for the Nazi regime. The campus is based on the former aeronautical research institute. For its construction, two forced labor camps were set up nearby for the concentration camp inmates and prisoners of war. The foundations of the former prisoner-of-war camp are within sight of the present-day Ludwig Bölkow Campus, where a bachelor's program now molds the students into combat pilots. In 2016, the government of the State of Bavaria wrote that the site's history was not the subject of research and teaching activities at the campus.

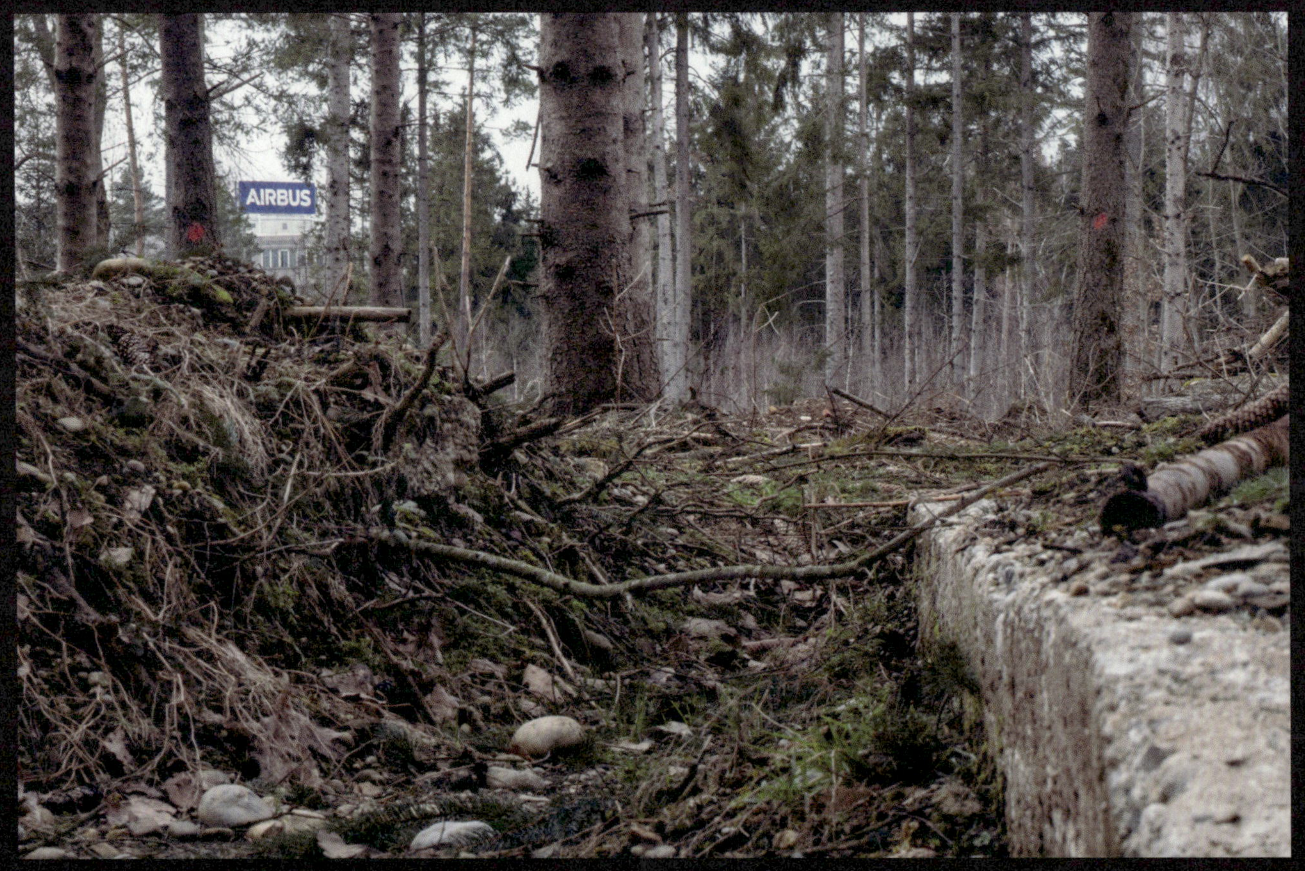

Airbus bewirbt den militärischen Nutzen seines Flugobjekts *Zephyr*. Die Drohne wird in Ottobrunn mit öffentlichen Mitteln entwickelt und an mehrere Armeen exportiert. Auf der Website des Landtags informiert die Bayerische Staatsregierung die Öffentlichkeit darüber, dass am Ludwig Bölkow Campus weder Drohnen- noch Rüstungsprojekte existieren. Als *Green Aerospace* bringe man Algen aus den Bahamas zur Zellwandauflösung, um Biokerosin zu gewinnen. Der Campus absorbiert das Lager und simuliert ein artgerechtes Klima.

Airbus is promoting the military use of its flying object *Zephyr*. The drone is being developed in Ottobrunn with public funding and is exported to several armies. On the state parliament website, the Bavarian government tells the public that neither drones nor armaments projects exist at the Ludwig Bölkow Campus. Instead, algae from the Bahamas are used to dissolve their cell walls in order to obtain aviation biofuels—under the heading Green Aerospace. The campus is absorbing the camp and simulating a species-appropriate climate.

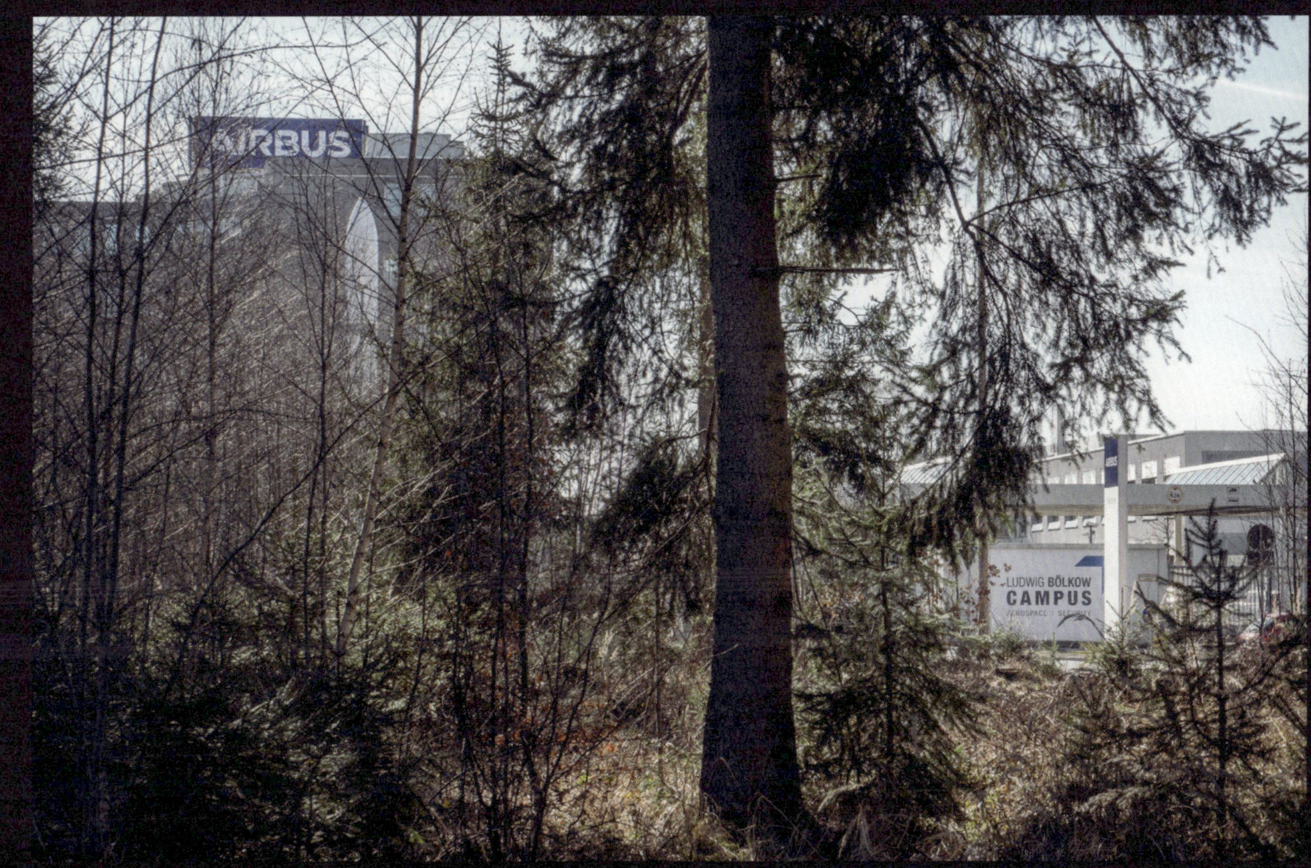

Ortsanalyse I
Öffentliche Raumuntersuchung, früheres Kriegsgefangenenlager, Ludwig-Bölkow-Komplex, Ottobrunn bei München, 4. Juni 2017

Franz Wanner wird mit Interessierten die Orte und Zusammenhänge seiner zur Ausstellung *After the Fact. Propaganda im 21. Jahrhundert* (2017) im Kunstbau des Lenbachhauses entstandenen Arbeiten *Battle Management Drawings* und *From Camp to Campus* aufsuchen, aufzeichnen und verhandeln.

Martina Oberprantacher, Kunstvermittlerin an der Städtischen Galerie im Lenbachhaus und Kunstbau München

Site Analysis I
Public space exploration, former prisoner-of-war camp, Ludwig Bölkow Complex, Ottobrunn, near Munich, June 4, 2017

Franz Wanner will make recordings and negotiate with interested parties during visits to the locations and contexts of his works *Battle Management Drawings* and *From Camp to Campus*; both installations are on display at the Lenbachhaus in the exhibition *After the Fact. Propaganda in the 21st Century* (2017).

Martina Oberprantacher, art educator at the Städtische Galerie im Lenbachhaus und Kunstbau München, Munich

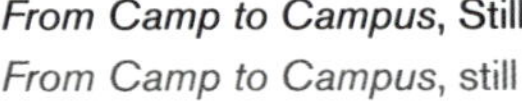

From Camp to Campus, Still
From Camp to Campus, still

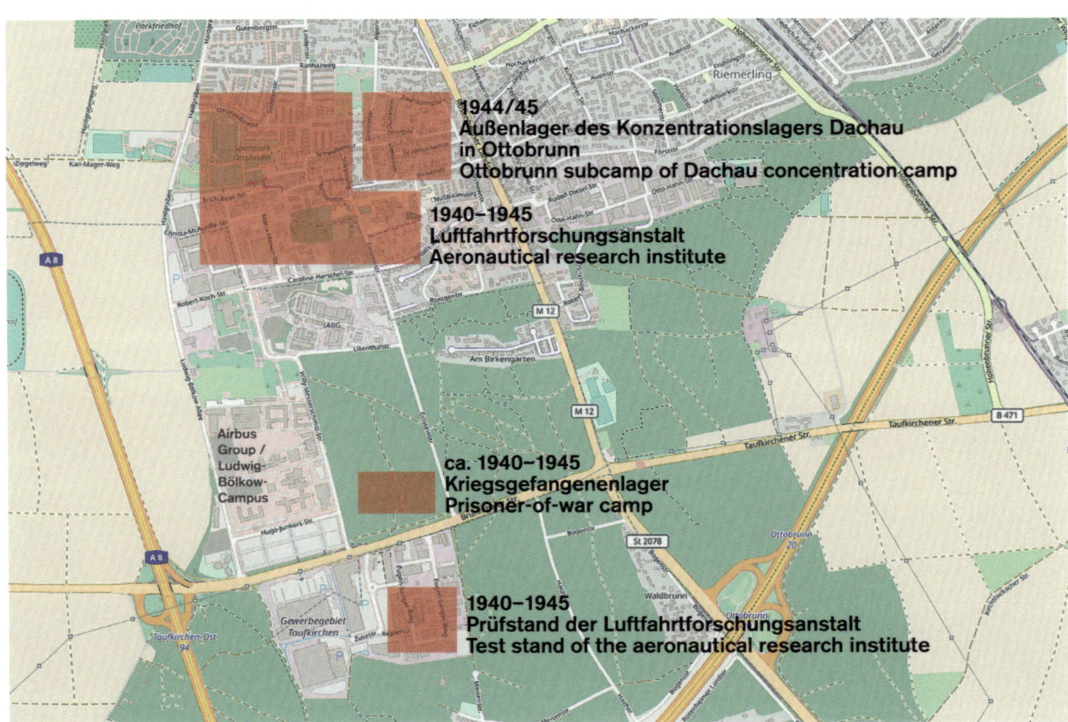

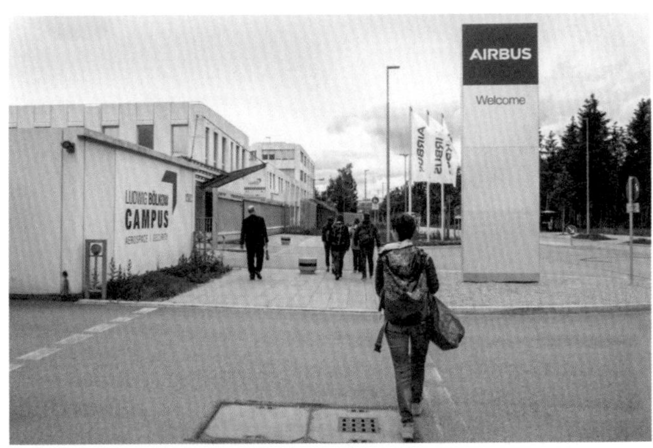

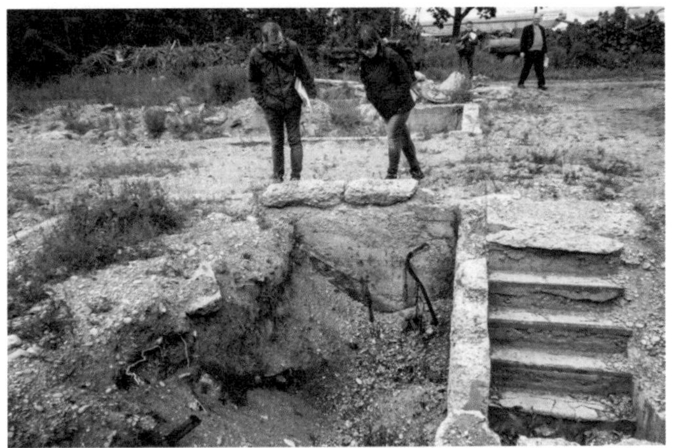

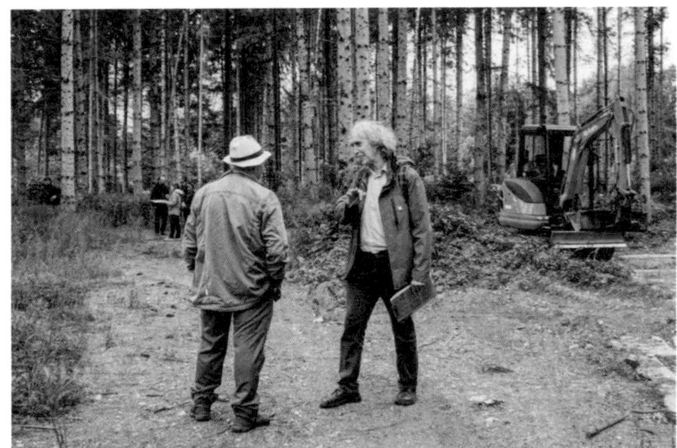

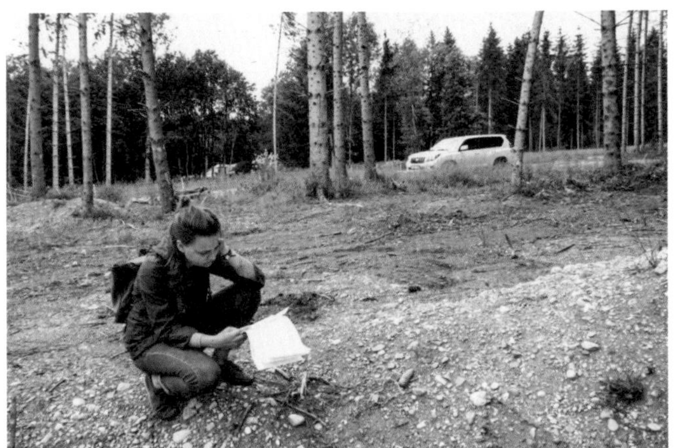

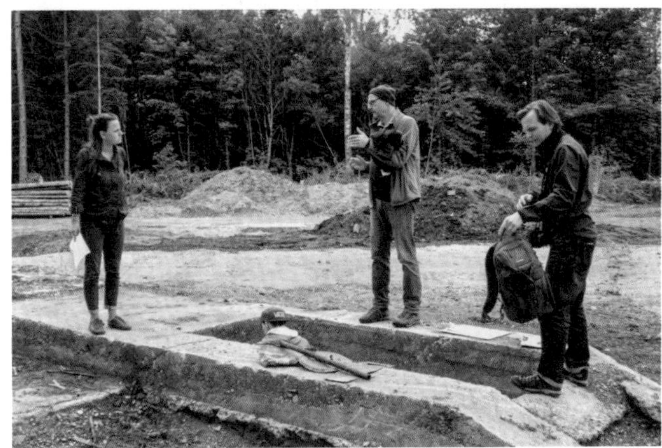

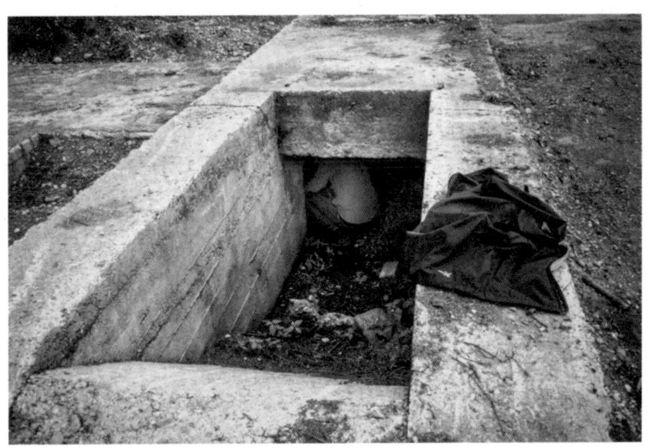

Bilder der *Ortsanalyse I*
Images of *Site Analysis I*

From Camp to Campus
Video, 10 Min., 2019, Stills
Mit Monika Schuck, Sprecherin: Verena Rendtorff
Video, 10 min., 2019, stills
With Monika Schuck, narrator: Verena Rendtorff

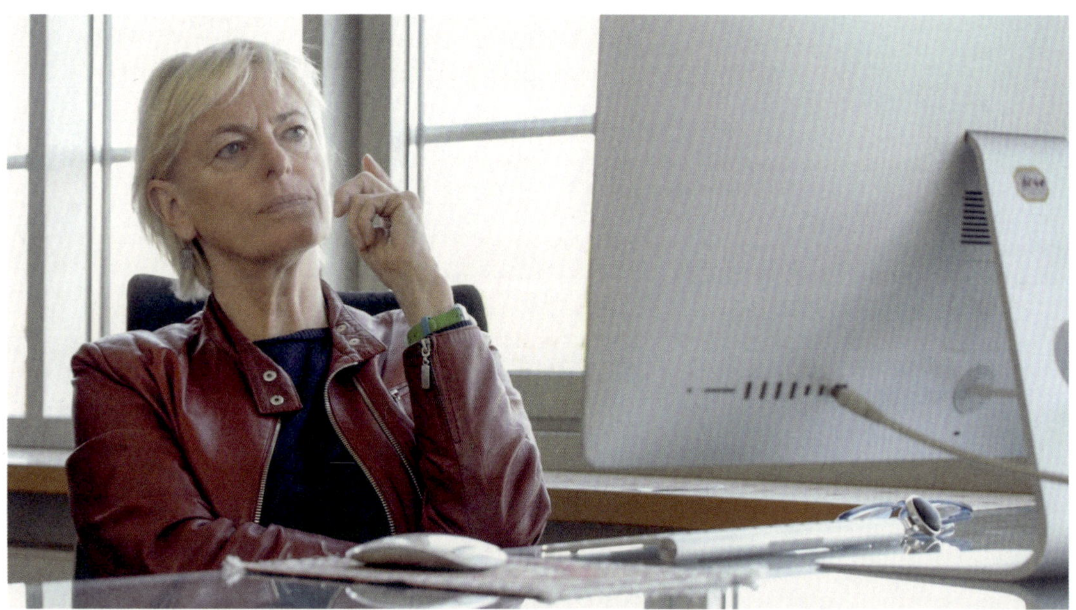

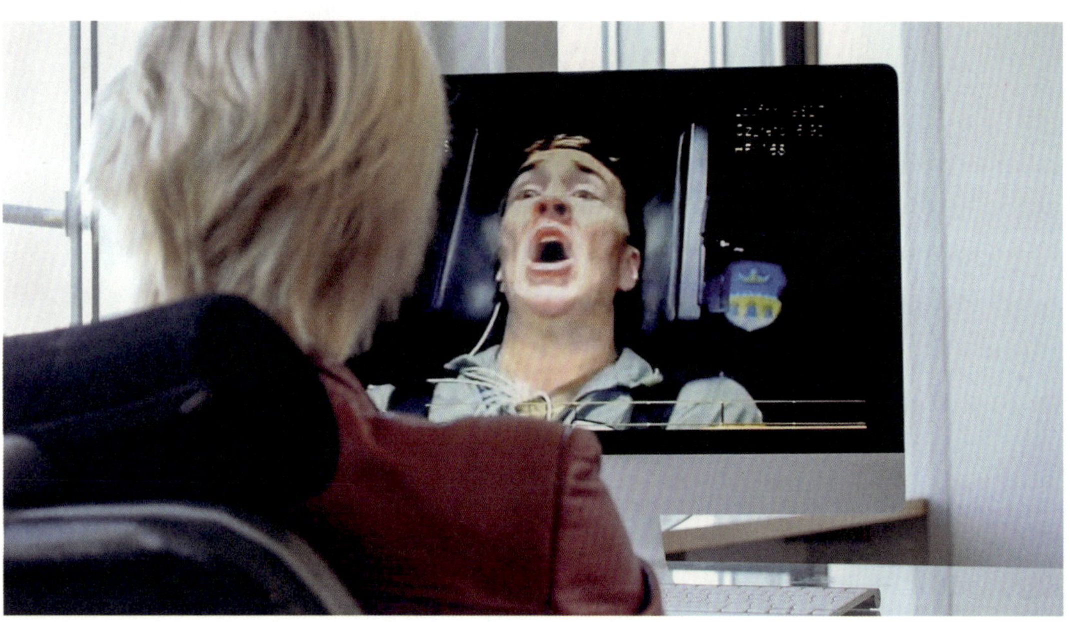

Der Film *From Camp to Campus* setzt die Begriffe „Camp“ und „Campus“ in Beziehung. Unter der Bezeichnung „Luftfahrtforschungsanstalt“ installierte das NS-Regime in einem Waldstück bei München ein Rüstungszentrum. Bis in die Gegenwart wird dort militärisch geforscht und produziert. Die Einbeziehung staatlicher Hochschulen machte den Ort zu einem „Campus“. 2013 wurde der Komplex nach dem NS-Ingenieur Ludwig Bölkow benannt. Zum Bau der „Luftfahrtforschungsanstalt“ wurden Zwangsarbeiter*innen eingesetzt. Die Fundamente und Kellerräume des früheren Arbeitslagers liegen in unmittelbarer Nähe des Campus im Wald. Während die baulichen Dokumente des Gefangenenlagers bereinigt werden, etabliert die Bayerische Staatsregierung am Ort der früheren Zwangsarbeit ihre Luft- und Raumfahrtstrategie „Bavaria One“.

The film *From Camp to Campus* shows the relationship between the terms “camp” and “campus.” Under the name Aeronautical Research Institute, the Nazi regime installed an armaments center in a small section of forest near Munich. Military research and production is still conducted there today. The inclusion of state universities turned the site into a “campus.” In 2013, the complex was named after the engineer Ludwig Bölkow, who developed armaments for the Nazi regime. Forced labor was used to build the Aeronautical Research Institute. The foundations and basement rooms of the former labor camp are in the immediate vicinity of the campus in the forest. While the structural documents of the prisoners’ camp are being expurgated, the Bavarian State Government is establishing its aeronautics and space strategy “Bavaria One” on the site of the former forced labor.

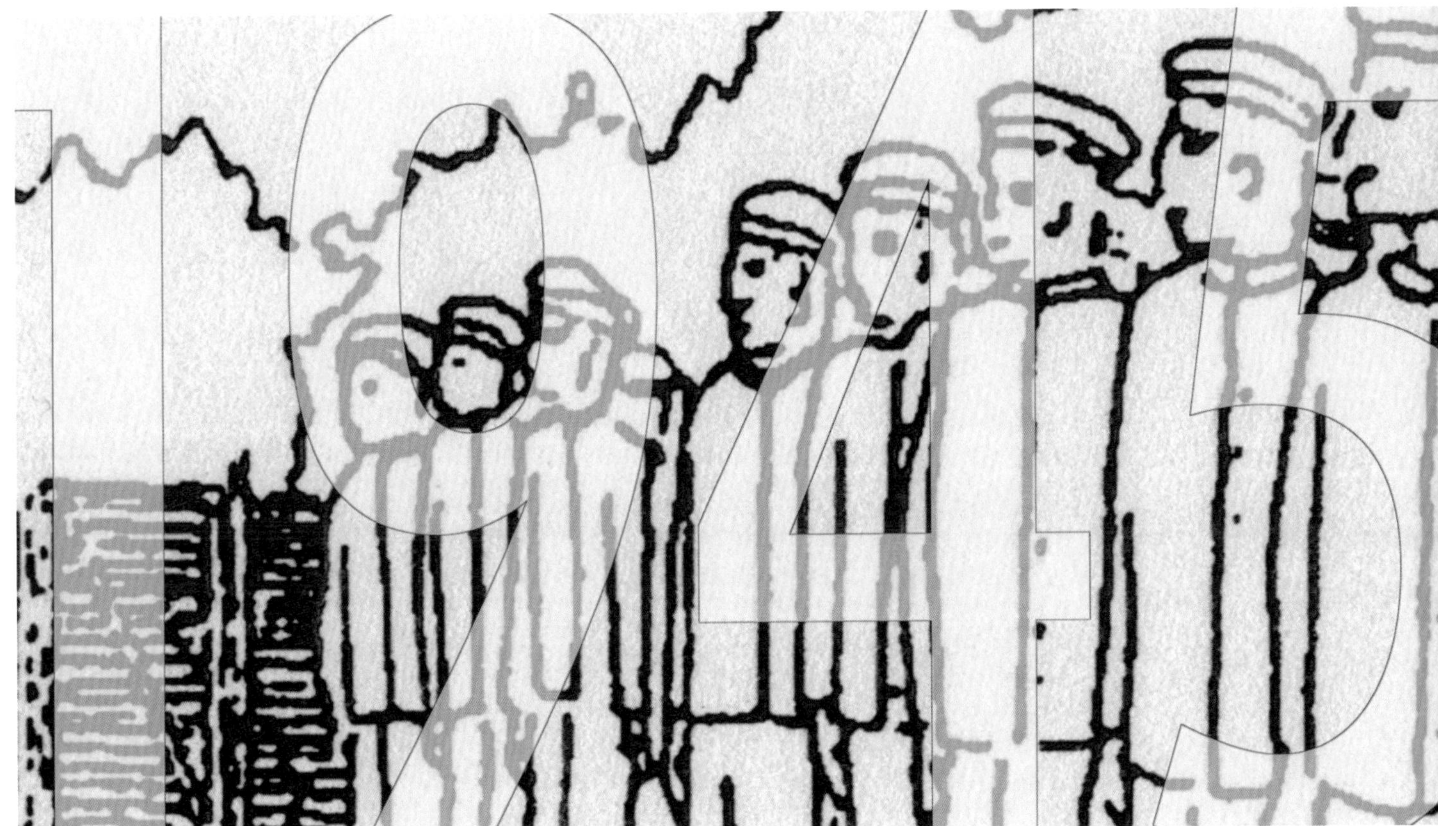

Bereinigung I, szenischer Text, 2019

2017
Der neue Besitzer kann seinen Besitz nicht fassen. Das Gelände des früheren Zwangsarbeitslagers gehört jetzt ihm. Zu einem guten Preis hat er den Waldgrund in Ottobrunn übernommen, der Ludwig-Bölkow-Komplex hat seine NS-Geschichte an ihn entsorgt. Seinen Ruhestand nutzt er, um seinen Besitz von den baulichen Resten zu bereinigen. Als er uns sieht, schwenkt er den Schaufelarm seines Baggers, sodass er uns den Weg versperrt. Wir sagen ihm, dass wir die Fundamente und Kellerräume mit einer Kamera dokumentieren.

— Hier gibt es nichts zu dokumentieren, Bilder machen rentiert sich nicht. Verlassen Sie mein Grundstück!
— Der Wald ist öffentlich. Die Geschichte der Verbrechen, die hier begangen wurden, ist öffentlich.
— Das sind nur Reste von alten Wohnanlagen, die Mauern werden jetzt alle herausgerissen.
— Das sind die Mauern eines Arbeitslagers. Es gibt Luftbilder der Alliierten und Texte von Sabine Schalm und Martin Wolf.

Mit einer fahrigen Handbewegung schwenkt er die Baggerschaufel in unsere Richtung, so als wäre sie die mechanische Verlängerung seiner Perspektive.

— Alle hier haben das gewusst mit dem Lager. Es ist mein Besitz, es ist alles Recht.

Auf seinem Grund treffen die Zeiten aufeinander und hinterlassen ihn eingeschlossen.

Decontamination I, scenic text, 2019

2017
The new owner is unable to grasp that he owns the property. The site of the former forced labor camp now belongs to him. He acquired the wooded land in Ottobrunn for a favorable price; the Ludwig-Bölkow complex disposed of its Nazi history by handing it over to him. He is making good use of his retirement by clearing his property of the remains of the buildings. When he sees us, he swivels the shovel arm of his excavator so that it blocks our path. We tell him that we are going to document the foundations and cellar rooms with our camera.

— There is nothing here to document; it's not worth taking any pictures. Leave my property at once!
— The wood is public land. The story of the crimes which were perpetrated here is public knowledge.
— These are only remains of old housing estates; the walls are going to be torn down.
— They are the walls of a labor camp. There are aerial photos taken by the Allies and texts by Sabine Schalm and Martin Wolf.

With an agitated gesture, he swings the excavator bucket toward us as if it were the mechanical extension of his point of view.

— Everyone here knew about the camp. It's my property, it's all perfectly legitimate.

Here on his land, he is caught between different eras and is left with his hands tied.

Seite / Pages 41, 45, 47
Bilder der *Ortsanalyse I*, 2017
Images of *Site Analysis I,* 2017

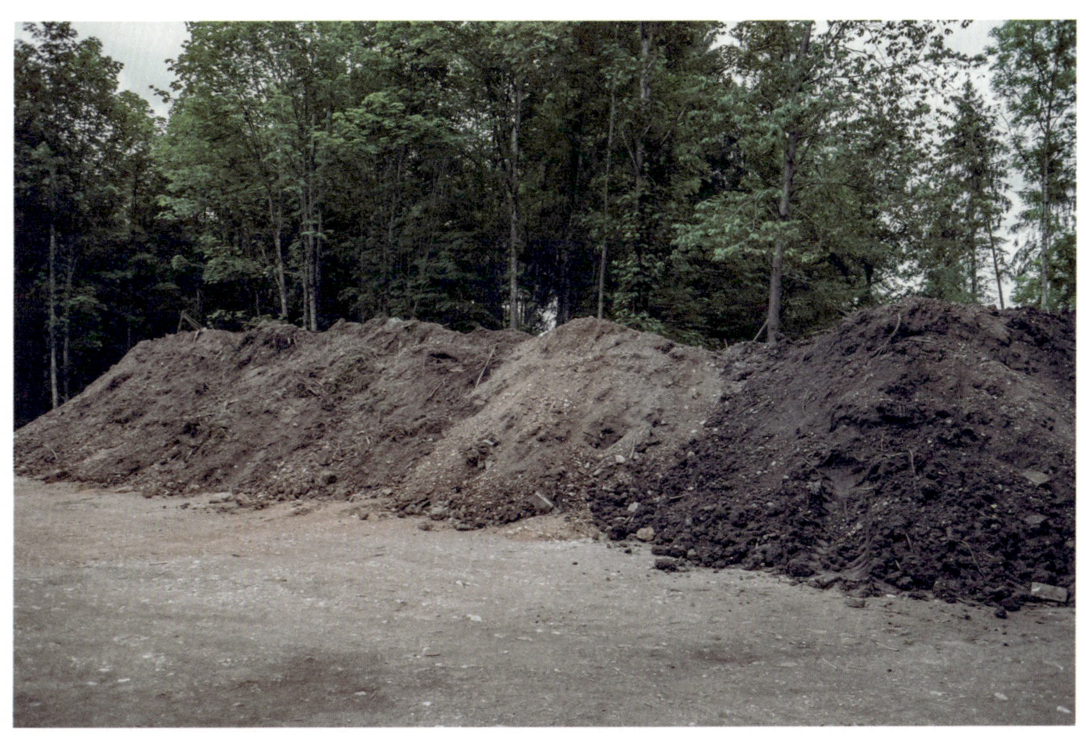

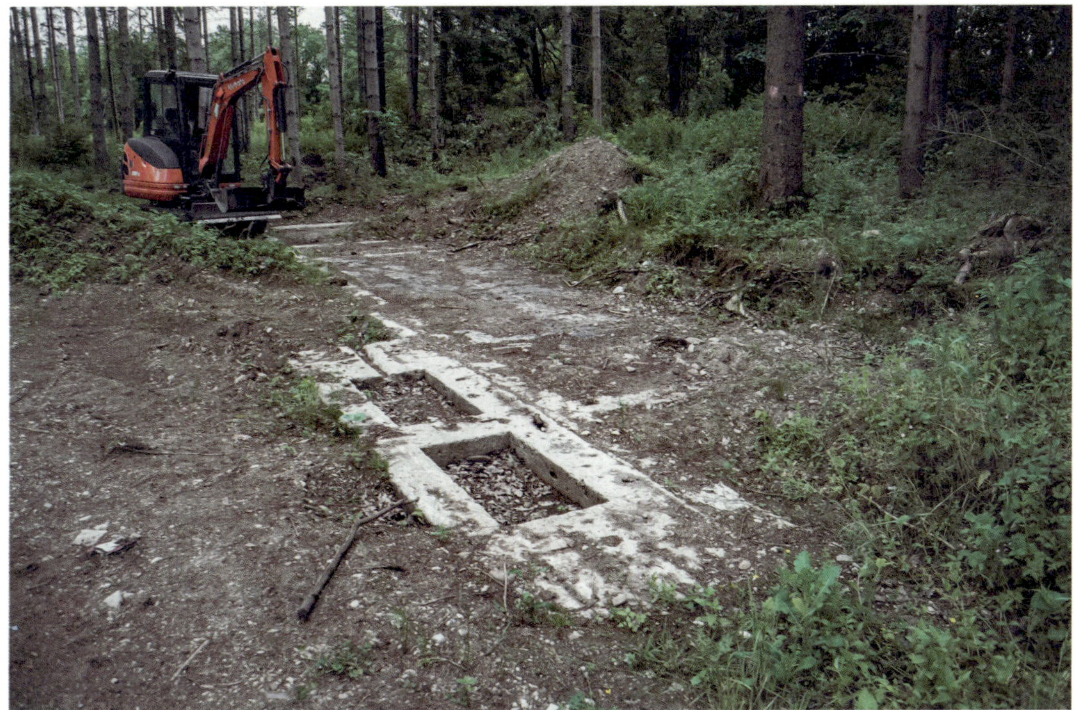

Bereinigung II, szenischer Text, 2019

2017/18
Korrespondenz mit dem Bayerischen Landesamt für Denkmalpflege und der Unteren Denkmalschutzbehörde

2017

– Sind die erhaltenen Fundamente und Kellerräume des nationalsozialistischen Arbeitslagers am Ludwig Bölkow Campus von öffentlichem Interesse?
– Wir danken für Ihr Interesse. Ein berechtigtes Interesse für die von Ihnen erwünschten Auskünfte liegt nicht vor.

– Bedeuten die baulichen Dokumente einen gesellschaftlichen, historischen oder kulturellen Wert?
– Für die betroffenen Flächen besteht derzeit die begründete Vermutung, dass es sich um Bodendenkmäler handelt.

– Aus welchem Grund werden die Fundamente und Kellerräume entfernt?
– Die bisherigen Freilegungsarbeiten fanden ohne denkmalfachliche Begleitung statt. Ein Antrag auf Erlaubnis liegt bislang nicht vor. Hinsichtlich Ihrer Betretung des Waldgrundes sollte in jedem Fall das Einvernehmen des Eigentümers vorliegen.

2018

– Warum fanden die Freilegungsarbeiten ohne Erlaubnis und ohne denkmalfachliche Begleitung statt?
Wie erlangt man ein berechtigtes Interesse?
Wie wird die Geschichte des NS-Arbeitslagers erzählt?

Seit die Bayerische Staatsregierung am Ludwig Bölkow Campus einen Standort ihrer Luft- und Raumfahrtstrategie „Bavaria One" plant, bleiben die Fragen an die Behörden ohne Antwort.

Decontamination II, scenic text, 2019

2017/18
Correspondence with the Bavarian State Office for Monument Protection and the Lower Historic Monument Protection Authority

2017

– Are the extant foundations and cellars of the National Socialist labor camp near the Ludwig Bölkow Campus of public interest?
– Thank you for your interest. There is no justifiable interest for supplying the information you request.

– Do the architectural remains possess a social, historical, or cultural value?
– There is currently reason to assume that the areas in question are historic monuments.

– What was the reason for demolishing the foundations and cellars?
– The excavations to date have taken place without specialist support from experts for historic monuments. To date, no application for permission has been received. With regard to your entering the woodland, you must definitely have the owner's permission to do so.

2018

– Why did the excavations take place without permission and without specialist support from experts for historic monuments?
How can a justifiable interest be proven?
How will the history of the Nazi labor camp be told?

Ever since the government of the State of Bavaria drew up plans for a location for its aviation and space strategy "Bavaria One" on the Ludwig Bölkow Campus, none of these questions addressed to the authorities has been answered.

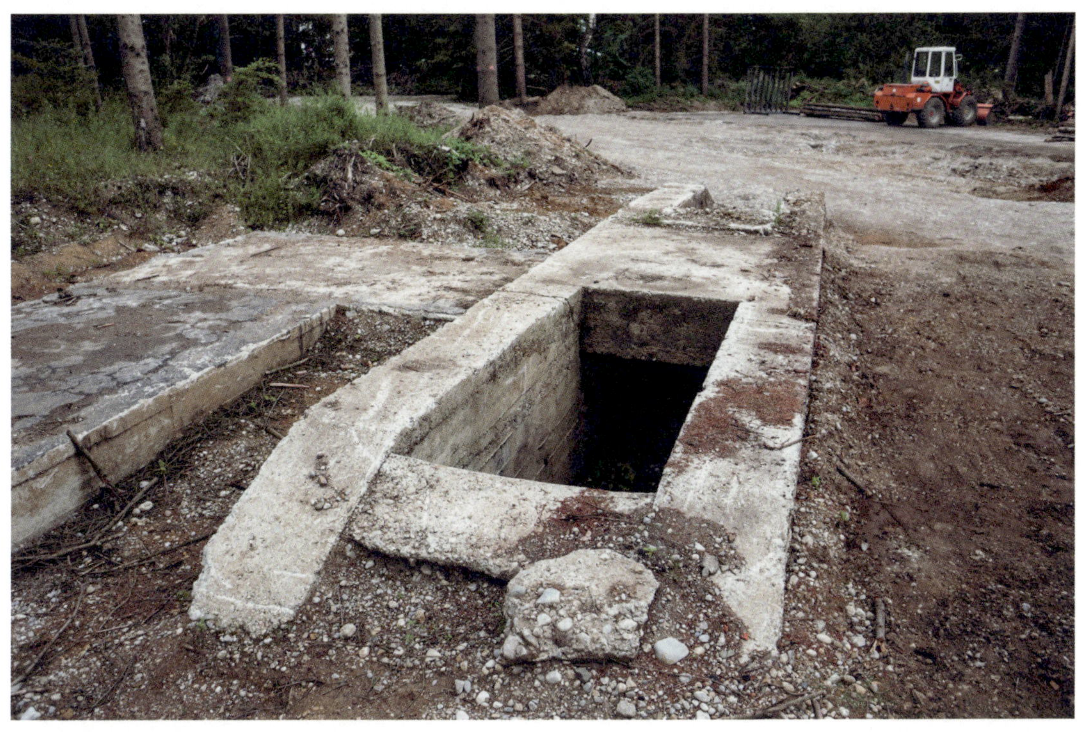

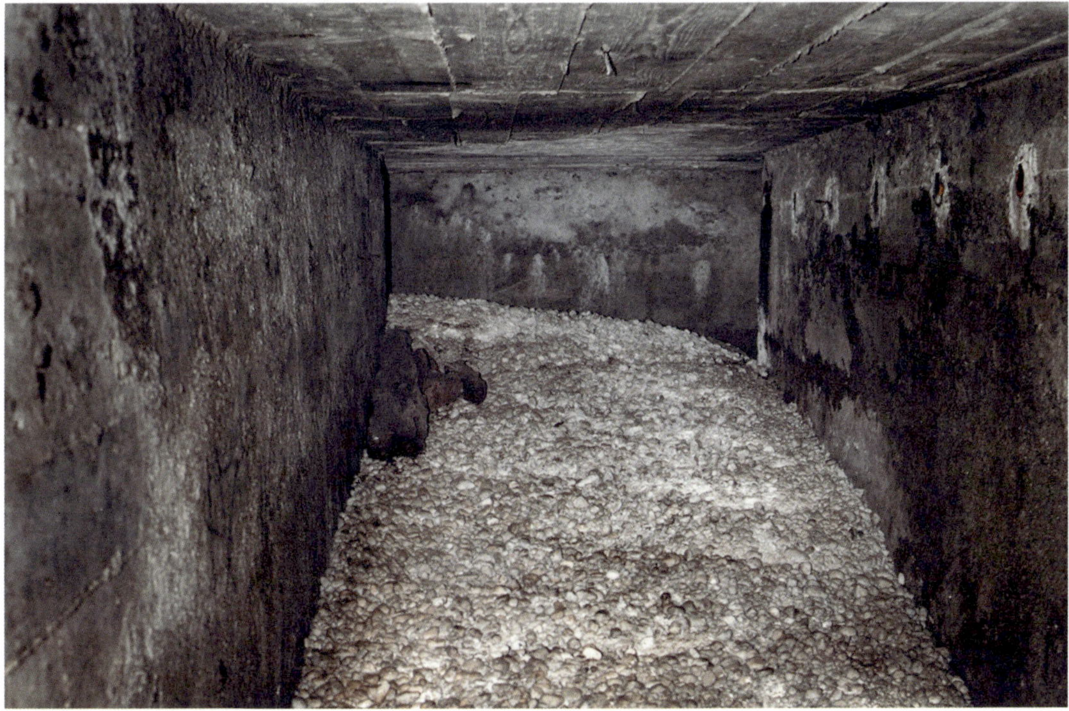

Battle Management Drawing IV

Traumatisierte Soldat*innen sind ein Risiko. Die steigende Zahl verletzter Psychen beim Bund gefährdet den Rückhalt der Bevölkerung für Auslandseinsätze. Um das Image zu glätten und Jugendliche anzuwerben, veröffentlicht die Bundeswehr 2016 auf YouTube die Dokusoap *Die Rekruten*. In der Folge mit dem Titel *22 Pushup Challenge* reiht sich die Truppe in eine massenkulturelle „Gedenkaktion“ ein. Gemeinsam macht man 22 Liegestützen, weil ebenso viele traumatisierte US-Soldat*innen pro Tag Selbstmord begehen. Die Kampagne nutzt die Toten, um Solidarität zu demonstrieren. Der Kriegseinsatz wird zum entpolitisierten Schicksal, das manche umbringt und alle zusammenschweißt.

Traumatized soldiers are a risk. The rising number of injured psyches in the armed forces is jeopardizing the population's support for overseas deployments. To polish its image and encourage adolescents to enlist, the Bundeswehr released a docusoap on YouTube in 2016 called *Die Rekruten* (The Recruits). In the episode titled "22 Pushup Challenge," the troops join the ranks of a mass-cultural "commemoration event." The participants each perform 22 push-ups together—22 being the number of traumatized US soldiers who commit suicide every day. The campaign uses the dead to demonstrate solidarity. War deployment becomes a depoliticized fate, which kills some yet bonds everyone together.

Text in the image:
... for patients and for your career. ... what really counts: ... care and therapy professions in the medical service. German Armed Forces

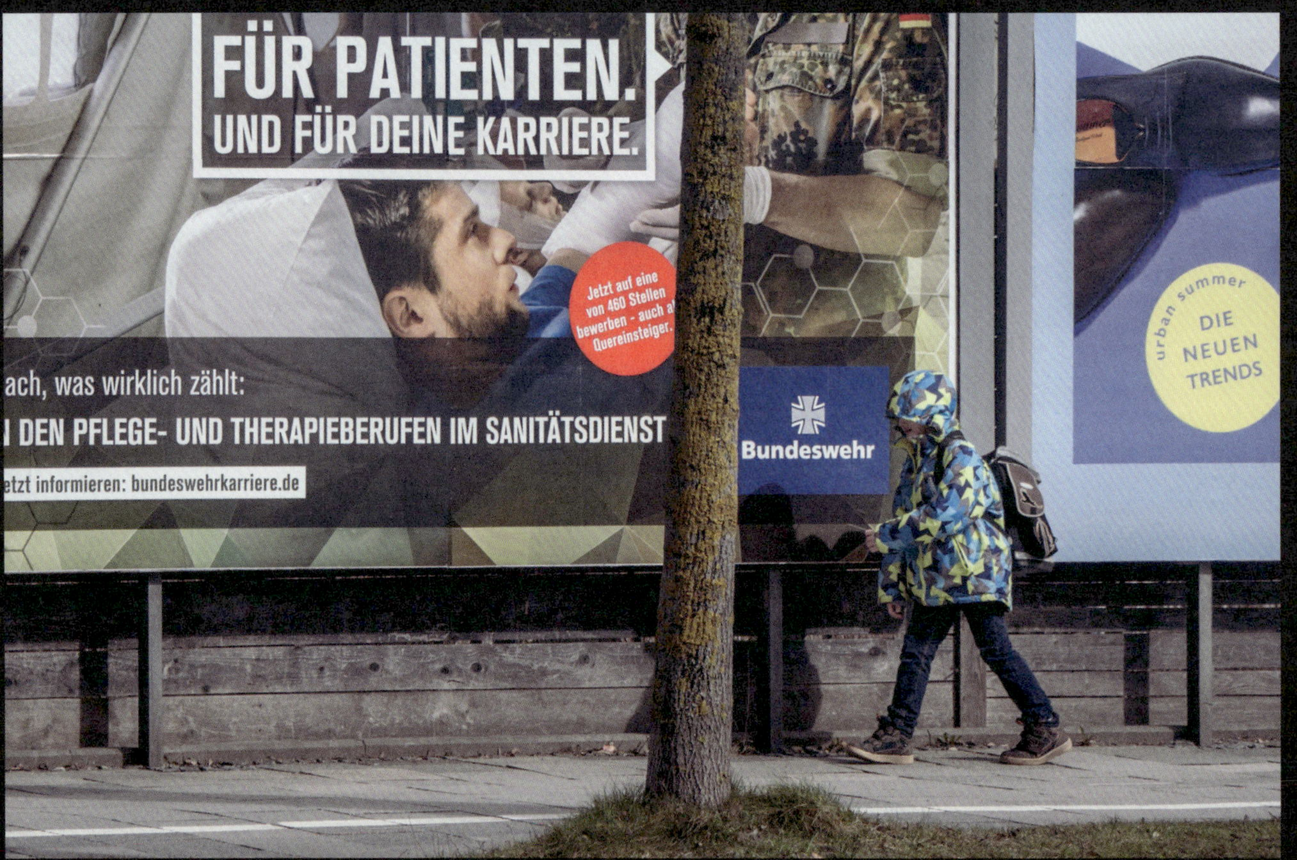

Die Anerkennung eines karrierebedingten Traumas durch das Verteidigungsministerium ist mit hohen Hürden versehen. Wer seine Beschädigung beweisen kann, wird militärpsychologisch behandelt – unter Ausschluss einer Analyse kausaler Zusammenhänge. Im Gegensatz dazu kann eine Therapie nach medizinischen Standards bewirken, dass sich Patient*innen mental entwickeln und vitalen Impulsen folgen. Die Absicht des Bundes ist aber nicht die Lebendigkeit, sondern die Tauglichkeit.

There are major obstacles to overcome before the Ministry of Defense officially recognizes a career-related trauma. Those who can prove that they have suffered damage are given military psychological treatment—to the exclusion of an analysis of causal relationship. In contrast to this, a therapy according to medical standards can induce patients to develop mentally and to follow their vital impulses. However, the aim of the federal ministry is not vitality but fitness.

Text in the image:
Sign 1: Career Center of the German Armed Forces
Sign 2: Federal property. Military area. Transit at your own risk
Memorial inscription: They died for Germany's glory and honor. To the dead of the Bavarian Railroad Troops, 1914–18 World War

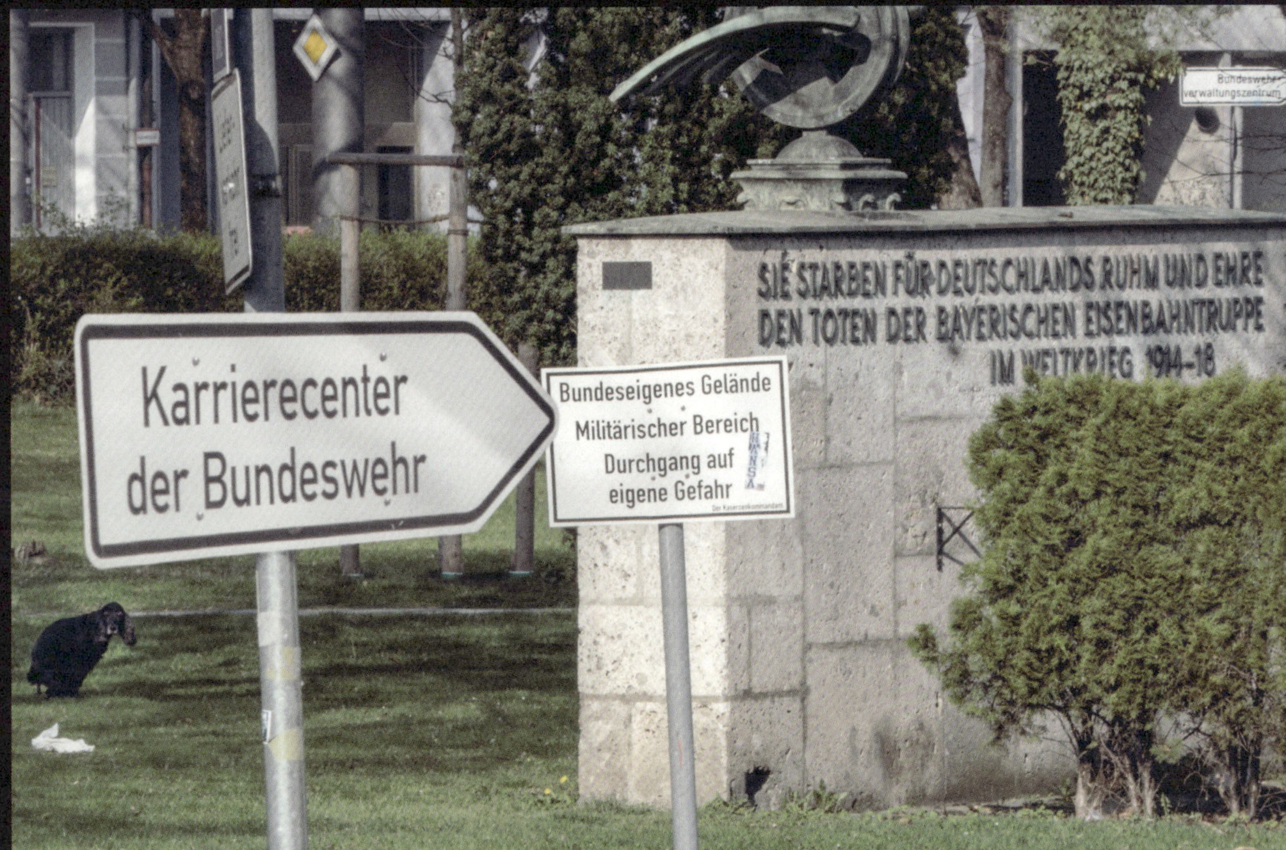

Battle Management Drawing V

Eine *Objektschutzstreife* schützt die Mauer, die Anwohnende in München-Neuperlach vor der Anwesenheit von Flüchtlingen schützen soll. Die abgelehnten Asylsuchenden aus Afghanistan, Mali und dem Kosovo werden in Einsatzgebiete der Bundeswehr zurückgeschickt. Ihre Heimatstaaten sind sicher genug, um sie dorthin abzuschieben, aber zu unsicher, um die deutsche Armee von dort abzuziehen. Mehrheitlich stellt man sich diese Regionen als Krisengebiete und gleichzeitig als ungefährliche Herkunftsländer vor.

An object security patrol protects the wall intended to protect local residents in Munich-Neuperlach from the presence of refugees. The rejected asylum seekers from Afghanistan, Mali, and Kosovo are sent back to theaters of operation in which German military forces are deployed. Their home countries are safe enough to deport people to, but not safe enough to withdraw the German army. Most people imagine these regions to be both areas of conflict and nondangerous countries of origin at the same time.

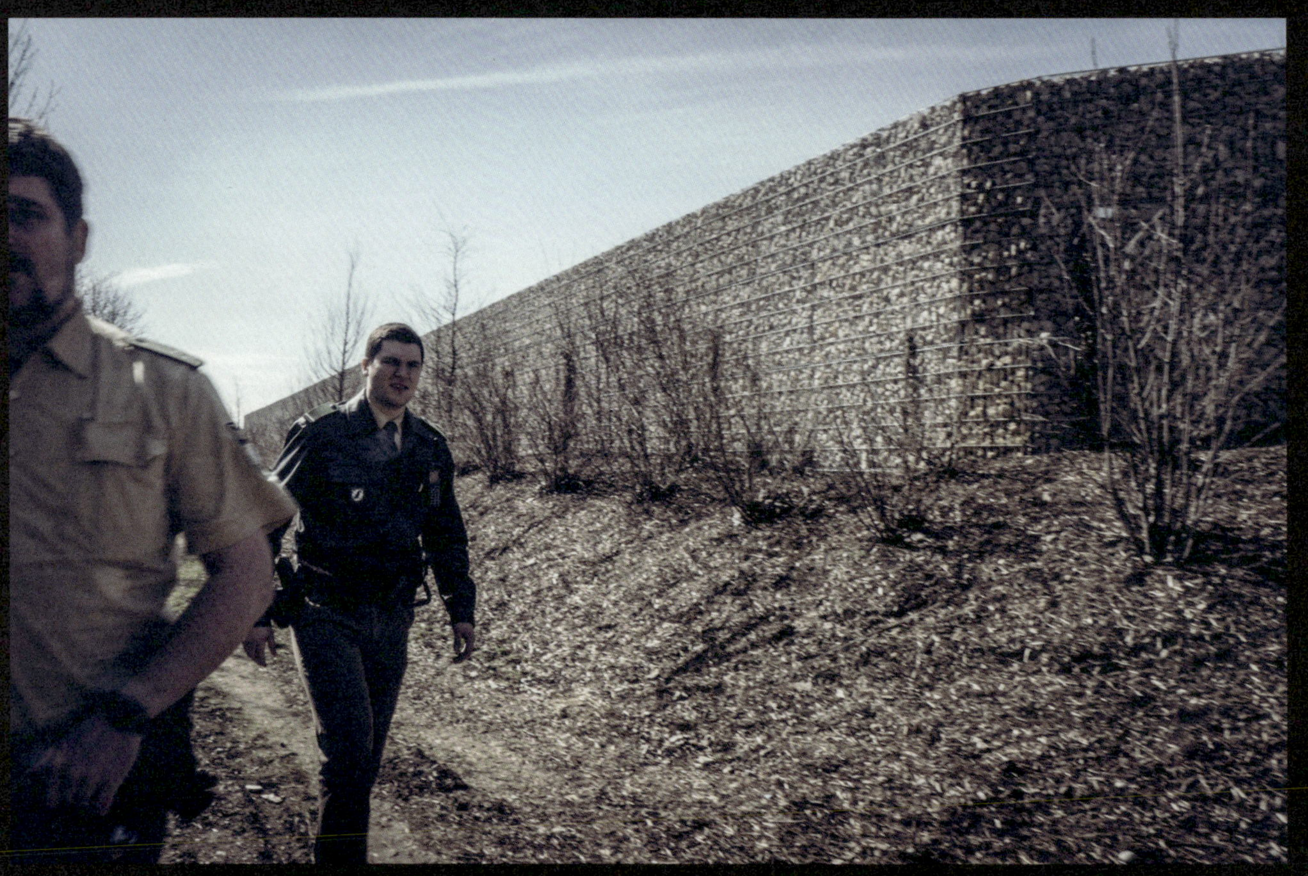

Die Europäische Union blockiert ihre Grenzen auf drei Niveaus: Ein Netz autonomer Sensorbojen erkennt Flüchtlingsboote vom Wasser aus, Drohnen überwachen das Mittelmeer aus der Luft, und Satelliten leisten Fernaufklärung aus dem All. Ein Schaubild versieht Objekte mit Symbolen für detektierte Boote. Der Algorithmus sagt: „Probability of refugees on board: 76 %." Der Bereich für Wehrtechnik der Firma Carl Zeiss, der die optronische Präzision liefert, ist seit 2014 in Airbus integriert. Das Fraunhofer-Institut nutzt das All, den Luftraum und das Meer als Überwachungsschichten und fusioniert die Daten zum *Objekt-Orientierten Weltmodell.*

The European Union blocks its borders on three levels: a network of autonomous sensor-buoys detects refugee boats from the water; drones surveil the Mediterranean from the air; and satellites carry out remote reconnaissance from space. A diagram provides objects with symbols for detected boats. The algorithm reads "Probability of refugees on board: 76%." The Carl Zeiss company's department for military technology, which supplies the optronic precision, has been integrated into Airbus since 2014. The Fraunhofer Institute uses outer space, airspace, and the ocean as surveillance layers and fuses the data into an Object-oriented World Model.

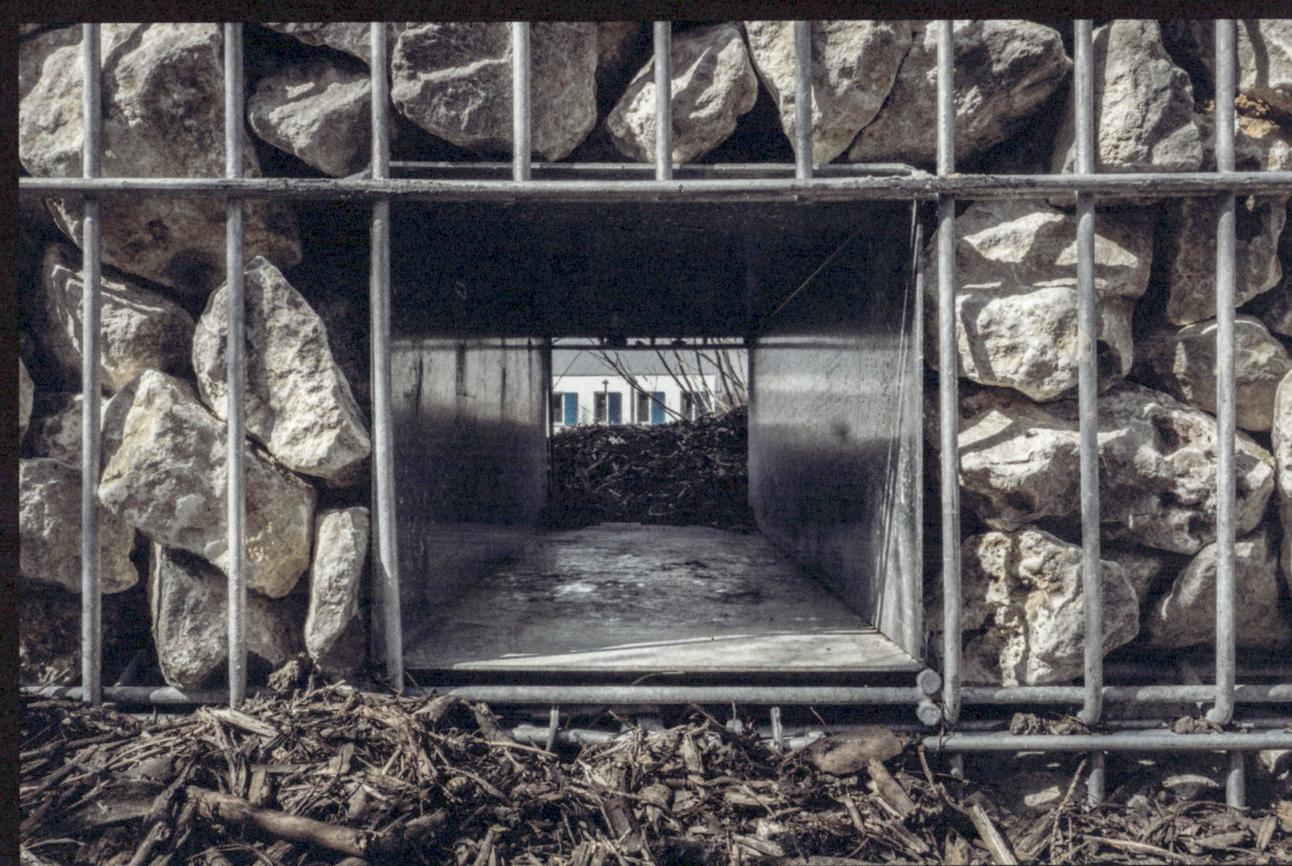

Ortsanalyse II
Öffentliche Raumuntersuchung, Schutzmauer vor einer Flüchtlingsunterkunft
in München-Neuperlach, 18. Juni 2017

Franz Wanner wird mit Interessierten die Orte und Zusammenhänge seiner zur Ausstellung *After the Fact. Propaganda im 21. Jahrhundert* (2017) im Kunstbau des Lenbachhauses entstandenen Arbeiten *Battle Management Drawings* und *From Camp to Campus* aufsuchen, aufzeichnen und verhandeln.

Martina Oberprantacher, Kunstvermittlerin an der Städtischen Galerie im Lenbachhaus und Kunstbau München

Site Analysis II
Public space exploration, protective wall in front of refugee accommodation
in Munich-Neuperlach, June 18, 2017

Franz Wanner will make recordings and negotiate with interested parties during visits to the locations and contexts of his works *Battle Management Drawings* and *From Camp to Campus*; both installations are on display at the Lenbachhaus in the exhibition *After the Fact. Propaganda in the 21st Century* (2017).

Martina Oberprantacher, art educator at the Städtische Galerie im Lenbachhaus und Kunstbau München, Munich

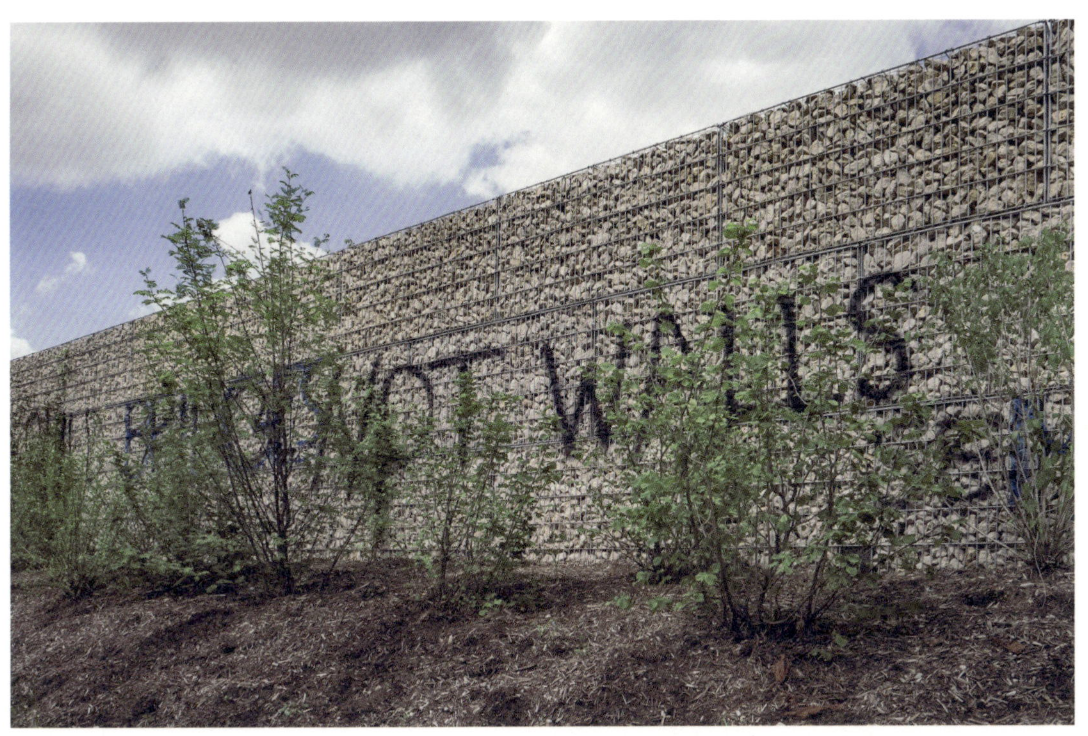

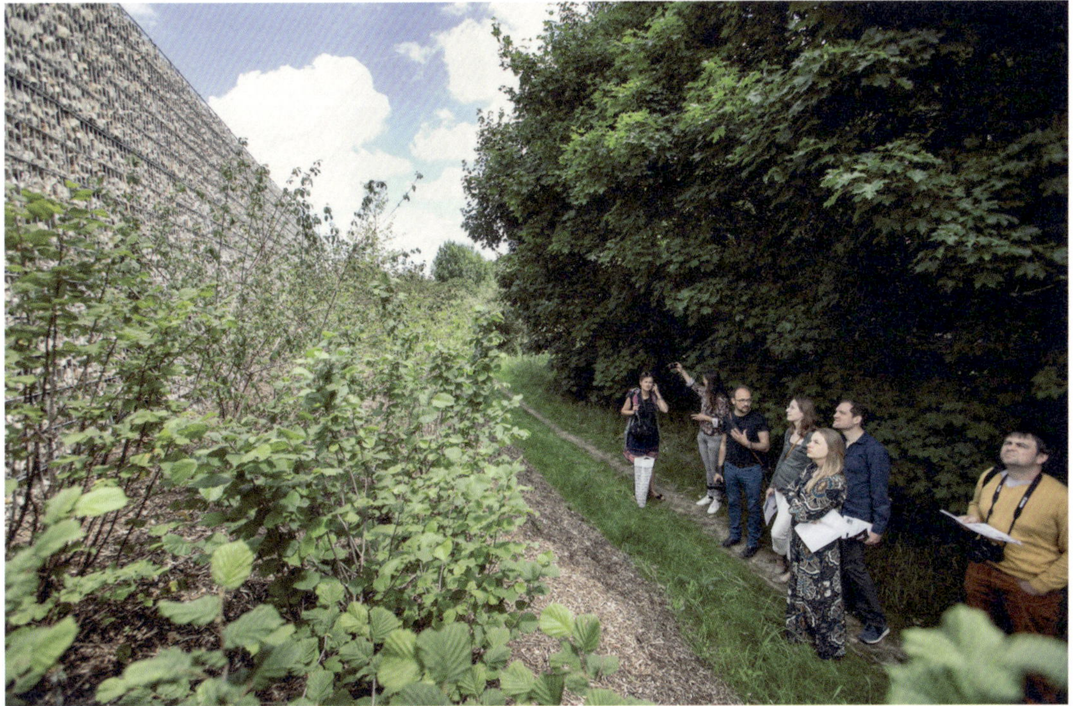

Bilder der *Ortsanalyse II*
Images of *Site Analysis II*

Beschränkung I, szenischer Text, 2019

2017
Ich möchte eines ganz klar sagen: Es ist keine Mauer gegen Flüchtlinge. Und ich lasse nicht zu, dass unser Viertel in Verruf gebracht wird, dass hier eine Mauer gegen Flüchtlinge errichtet wird. Sondern es ist ganz klar eine Schallschutzmaßnahme. Politiker, Bezirksausschuss München-Neuperlach

Es gab eine gerichtliche Auseinandersetzung, und wir haben uns auf diesen Kompromiss geeinigt. Gelingende Integration macht sich nicht an einer Lärmschutzwand fest. Wir haben solche Lärmschutzwände auch bei anderen Einrichtungen in der Stadt, zum Beispiel bei Kindertageseinrichtungen.
Politikerin, Dritte Bürgermeisterin von München

Wir haben die Klage angestrengt, um ein gedeihliches Zusammenleben zwischen den Flüchtlingen und den Anwohnern zu erreichen. Und wenn 160 minderjährige Flüchtlinge hier Fußball spielen, ist das naturgemäß mit Emissionen verbunden. Und wir hätten gern am Feierabend und am Wochenende etwas Ruhe in unseren Gärten. Anwohner, Richter am Landgericht München

– Wie hoch ist der Lärmpegel an der Mauer?
– Auf der Seite der Unterkunft für geflüchtete Jugendliche ist der Geräuschpegel ungewöhnlich niedrig. Er liegt bei 40 dB(A). Das liegt daran, dass in der Unterkunft niemand wohnt.
– Die Unterkunft steht leer?
– Ja, seit ihrem Bau vor mehr als einem Jahr ist sie unbewohnt.
– Und auf der Seite der klagenden Anwohner*innen?
– Auf dieser Seite der Mauer ist der Pegel etwas höher. Die Wohnemission überlagert sich mit gelegentlichen Klagegeräuschen und dem Bellen von Wachhunden in den Gärten. Der Wert liegt bei 55 dB(A).

Wir müssen unsere Emissionsauflagen auch dann einhalten, wenn es um Flüchtlinge geht. Ob das erwachsene oder minderjährige Flüchtlinge sind, ist gleichgültig. Entscheidend ist die Frage, wo Sie heute hinbauen – also auch am Schlachthof und am Viehhof können wir derzeit emissionsbedingt keine Wohnungen bauen. Politiker, Fraktionsvorsitzender im Münchner Rathaus

Wir sind hier nicht „the evil Germans or Krauts". Es ist eine ruhige Nachbarschaft. Es ist nicht gegen die Flüchtlinge. Anwohner, Immigrant aus Griechenland

Alle haben sich als Alterssicherung ein Reihenhäuschen gekauft und haben jetzt natürlich Angst, dass ihr Häuschen an Wert verliert. Ich sag mal, darüber diskutiert keiner, sondern nur über die Toleranz, die abverlangt wird. Anwohner, Reihenhausbesitzer

– Welche Wertminderung erfährt ein Reihenhaus, wenn in der Nähe eine Unterkunft für Geflüchtete gebaut wird?
– Das hängt vom Grad der gemeinschaftlichen Xenophobie ab. Im Gegensatz zum Emissionspegel ist dieser nicht exakt messbar.
– Kann man diesen Grad an der Höhe der Mauer ablesen?
– Genau lässt er sich nicht ablesen. Willkommen scheinen die Geflüchteten aber nicht zu sein, denn die Anwohner*innen haben die Mauer schließlich durch ihre Klage gegen den Lärm der Geflüchteten erzwungen.
– Aber die Unterkunft steht doch leer. Hier leben keine Geflüchteten.
– Ob die Unterkunft bewohnt ist oder nicht, spielt keine Rolle.
– Welche Wertminderung erfährt ein Reihenhaus, wenn davor eine vier Meter hohe Mauer gebaut wird?

Wir sollten eher Mauern abbauen, auch in den Köpfen. Andererseits muss man auch diesen Schutz der Bevölkerung irgendwie sehen. Ich denke, man muss da ganz offen und ehrlich darüber nachdenken, und vielleicht zeigt die Situation, wenn die Flüchtlinge dann da sind, dass man manches wieder abbauen kann. Integrationsbeauftragter der Bayerischen Staatsregierung

Limitation I, scenic text, 2019

2017
I should like to make one thing quite clear: It is not a wall against refugees. And I will not allow our neighborhood to be brought into discredit by claims that we are building a wall against the refugees here. It is, quite definitely, a noise-prevention measure.

Politician, Munich-Neuperlach District Committee

There was a legal dispute and we agreed on this compromise. Successful integration does not stand or fall because of a noise barrier. We have similar noise barriers for other facilities in the city, such as daycare centers.

Politician, third mayor of Munich

We brought the complaint in order to arrive at a positive coexistence between the refugees and the residents. When 160 young refugees play football here, it naturally involves noise. And after work and at weekends, we would like a bit of peace and quiet in our gardens.

Resident, Munich District Court judge

— How high is the noise level by the wall?
— On the side of the accommodation for young refugees, the noise level is unusually low. It's in the region of 40 dB(A). That's because no one is living in the accommodation.
— So the accommodation is empty?
— Yes. It's been empty since building was completed over a year ago.
— And on the side of the residents who lodged the complaint?
— On their side of the wall, the noise level is somewhat higher. There, the sounds that generally emanate from people's homes are occasionally overlaid by the noise of people complaining and the barking of guard dogs in the gardens. The noise level is around 55 dB(A).

We must also comply with emission requirements when refugees are involved. It makes no difference whether they're adult refugees or minors. What matters is the question of where you build today—so at the moment, we cannot build any apartments at the slaughterhouse and at the stockyard because of emission-related issues.

Politician, political group chairman at Munich's Town Hall

We're not "evil Germans or Krauts" here. It's a quiet neighborhood. We've nothing against the refugees.

Resident, Greek immigrant

The residents all bought their row houses as provision for their old age. Of course, now they're afraid that their houses may lose value. What I'm saying is, nobody talks about that, only about the tolerance that's expected of us.

Resident, row house owner

— How much does the value of a row house decrease when refugee accommodation is built in the vicinity?
— It depends on the level of collective xenophobia. Unlike emission levels, that cannot be measured accurately.
— Is it possible to gauge the amount based on the height of the wall?
— That's not something you can determine precisely. However, the refugees don't seem to be welcome, because in the end, it was the residents who compelled the authorities to build the wall by lodging a complaint about the noise made by the refugees.
— But the accommodation is empty. No refugees live there.
— It's irrelevant whether the accommodation is lived in or not.
— How much does a row house depreciate if a four-meter-high wall is built in front of it?

We should be dismantling walls, including those in people's heads. On the other hand, we must also somehow understand this effort to protect the population. I think we must be completely open and think honestly about this, and once the refugees are there, the situation may show that certain things can be taken down again.

Integration commissioner for the government of the State of Bavaria

Beschränkung II, szenischer Text, 2019

Betreff: Schutzobjekt Objektschutz
Datum: 26. Mai 2017 14:56:23 MESZ

Sehr geehrte Polizeihauptkommissarin S.,

um ein paar Fragen zu klären, die der Polizeieinsatz am 26. März 2017 an der Mauer in Neuperlach an der Nailastraße aufwarf, möchte ich mich an Sie wenden. Als mich ihre Kollegen Herr S. und Herr P. an diesem Sonntagvormittag nach meiner Tätigkeit an der Mauer fragten, gab ich Auskunft über meinen Beruf und sie über den ihren als Objektschutzstreife. Die Mauer als Schutzobjekt und die Streife als Objektschutz kombinierte ich daraufhin zu einem fotografischen Motiv. Da die beiden Objektschützer sich in das öffentliche Interesse meiner Aufnahmen zu integrieren weigerten und ich diese nicht beabsichtigte zu löschen, wie mich die beiden Beamten anwiesen, riefen sie Verstärkung. Auch die Mitarbeit der Polizisten Herr F. und Herr R. führte zu keiner Lösung. Erst nachdem als weitere Verstärkung Herr S.2 und Sie zum Ermittlungsteam stießen, konnte der Fall aufgeklärt werden: Die Aufforderung der Objektschutzstreife, meine Fotos zu löschen, der körperliche Einsatz durch die Herrn S. und P., mit dem sie mich von der Mauer entfernten, sowie die Androhung, meine Kamera zu beschlagnahmen, erwiesen sich laut Ihrer finalen Einschätzung am Ermittlungsort als haltlos. Nach einer Stunde, in der ich ohne Angabe von Gründen festgehalten wurde, teilten Sie mir mit, dass nichts gegen mich vorliege und ich meinen Beruf weiter ausüben dürfe. Ihren Äußerungen habe ich entnommen, dass sich der Verdacht als falsch erwiesen hat und die Ermittlungen gegen mich eingestellt wurden.
Nachdem Sie den Ermittlungsort verlassen hatten, kam Oberkommissar S. erneut auf mich zu, um mich zum Löschen meiner Bilder zu drängen. Am nächsten Tag hinterließ Herr P.2 von der Kripo München seine Stimme auf meiner Mailbox und bat um Rückruf. Im Telefongespräch stellte er Fragen zu meinen Absichten an der Mauer in Neuperlach. Die Arbeit Ihres Teams versuchte ich von Anfang an durch die Information zu beschleunigen, dass meine Fotos in der *Städtischen Galerie im Lenbachhaus und Kunstbau München* gezeigt werden, dessen Kuratorium genau wie mir an der Wahrnehmung und Darstellung gegenwärtiger Phänomene und öffentlicher Interessen liegt. Eventuelle Verdächtigungen möchte ich Sie bitten auszuräumen und die in diesem Zusammenhang gespeicherten Personendaten zu löschen. Um ein vielschichtiges Bild zu entwerfen, möchte ich Ihnen die Gelegenheit bieten, sich an der Beleuchtung der Fragen zu beteiligen, die der Polizeieinsatz verursachte:

Geht von dem Schutzobjekt in Neuperlach eine öffentliche Gefahr aus?
Welcher Verdacht führte zu dem verstärkten Polizeieinsatz?
Hat sich der Verdacht als falsch erwiesen oder laufen weiterhin Ermittlungen?
Wann, durch wen und aus welchem Grund wurde die Kripo eingeschaltet?
Welche Abteilung der Kripo hat meine fotografische Tätigkeit auf öffentlichem Gelände untersucht?
Wo und auf welche Art wurden meine Personendaten registriert und gespeichert?
Wer hat die Objektschutzstreife beauftragt und mit welchen Aufgaben ist sie betraut?
Könnten Sie sich vorstellen, die Bedeutung der Mauer als Schutzobjekt und die Aufgaben der Objektschutzstreife in einer öffentlichen Veranstaltung im Lenbachhaus zu erläutern?

Zur Ausstellung sind Sie und Ihr Ermittlungsteam herzlich willkommen.

Mit den besten Grüßen,
Franz Wanner

E-Mail-Anhang:

„WE POSE ONLY THOSE QUESTIONS WHOSE ANSWERS ARE THE *PRE-GIVEN CONDITIONS* OF THE QUESTIONS THEMSELVES."

Schön, dass Sie da sind! Wir fotografieren bei dieser Veranstaltung. Bitte informieren Sie uns, wenn Sie nicht möchten, dass Bilder, auf denen Sie erscheinen, veröffentlicht werden.

Die Städtische Galerie im Lenbachhaus und Kunstbau München lädt Sie herzlich ein zur Eröffnung der Ausstellung „After the Fact. Propaganda im 21. Jahrhundert"
Mo, 29. Mai 2017, 19 Uhr Begrüßung und Empfang im Garten des Lenbachhauses
(bei schlechtem Wetter im Atrium)

Sabine Krieger, Stadträtin der Landeshauptstadt München in Vertretung des Oberbürgermeisters
Matthias Mühling, Direktor des Lenbachhauses
Stephanie Weber, Kuratorin der Ausstellung

Betreff: AW: Schutzobjekt Objektschutz
Datum: 29. Mai 2017 15:40:19 MESZ

Sehr geehrter Herr Wanner,

Ihre Email ist für uns nicht verständlich und auch nicht zuzuordnen.
Können Sie uns Ihr Anliegen noch mal formulieren?

Mit freundlichen Grüßen,
H.

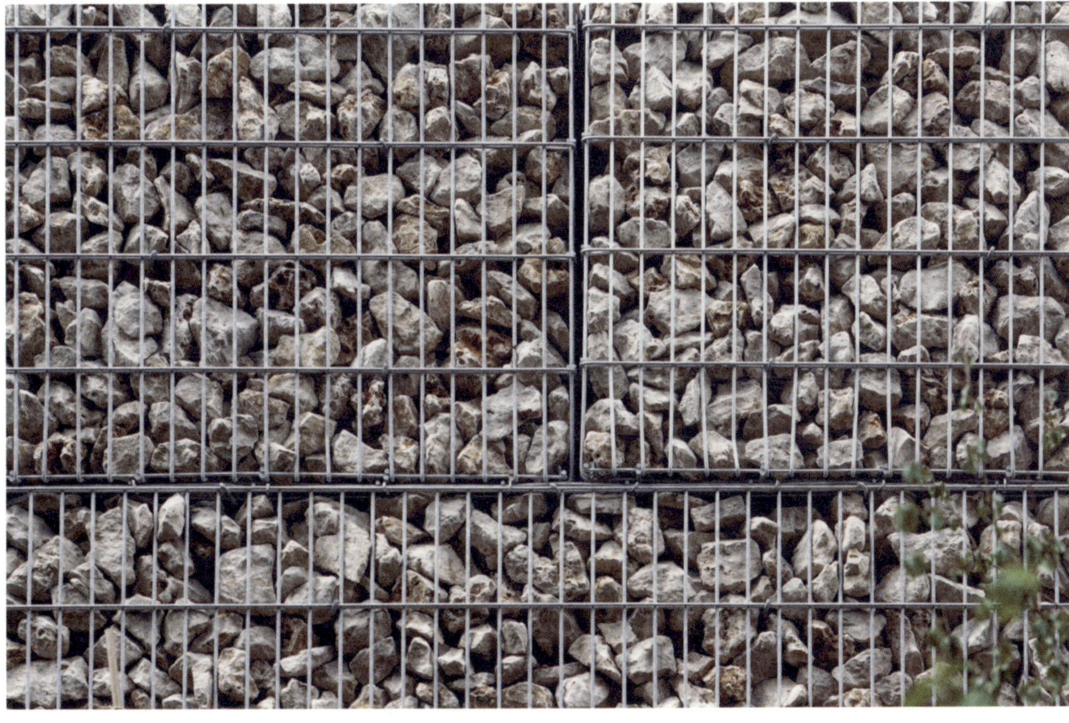

„ES IST NICHT
DAS BEWUSSTSEIN
DER MENSCHEN,
DAS IHR SEIN,
SONDERN
UMGEKEHRT IHR
*GESELLSCHAFTLICHES
SEIN*, DAS IHR
BEWUSSTSEIN
BESTIMMT."

Die Städtische Galerie im Lenbachhaus
und Kunstbau München lädt Sie herzlich
ein zur Eröffnung der Ausstellung

After the Fact
Propaganda im 21. Jahrhundert
Mo, 29. Mai 2017, 19 Uhr
Begrüßung und Empfang
im Garten des Lenbachhauses
(bei schlechtem Wetter im Atrium)

Sabine Krieger
Stadträtin der Landeshauptstadt München
in Vertretung des Oberbürgermeisters

Matthias Mühling
Direktor des Lenbachhauses

Stephanie Weber
Kuratorin der Ausstellung

Schön, dass Sie da sind!
Wir fotografieren bei dieser Veranstaltung.
Bitte informieren Sie uns, wenn Sie nicht
möchten, dass Bilder, auf denen Sie
erscheinen, veröffentlicht werden.

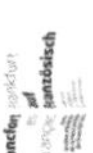

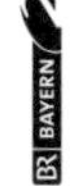

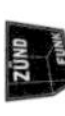

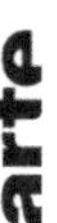

Medienpartner

Zitat: Karl Marx

Städtische Galerie im Lenbachhaus
und Kunstbau Munich cordially
invites you to the opening of

After the Fact
Propaganda in the 21st Century
Mon, May 29, 2017 at 7pm
Words of welcome and reception
in the Lenbachhaus garden
(weather permitting)

Sabine Krieger
Councillor, City of Munich
representing the Lord Mayor

Matthias Mühling
Director of Lenbachhaus

Stephanie Weber
Curator of the exhibition

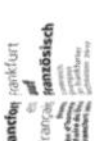

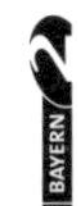

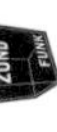

arte

Media Partners

Quote: Alain Badiou

Great to have you here!
May we take your picture?
Please let us know, if you do not
wish that we publish pictures
from the opening in which you appear.

"WE POSE ONLY THOSE QUESTIONS WHOSE ANSWERS ARE THE *PRE-GIVEN CONDITIONS* OF THE QUESTIONS THEMSELVES."

Limitation II, scenic text, 2019

Subject: Protected Object – Site Protection
Date: May 26, 2017 14:56:23 MESZ

E-mail to Police Chief Inspector S.

Dear Ms. S.,

I am taking the liberty of contacting you in order to clarify a few questions arising from the police operation on March 26, 2017 by the wall at Nailastraße in Neuperlach. When your colleagues Mr. S. and Mr. P. asked me on that Sunday morning what I was doing there, I informed them of my occupation and they told me that they were patrolling the site in the interests of security. I then created a subject for a photograph by combining the patrolling guards as a site security measure and the wall as the object of their protection. In their role as security guards, the two policemen then summoned reinforcements because they refused to allow me to incorporate them into my photos, which are of public interest, and because I had no intention of deleting them, as the two policemen instructed me to do. The assistance offered by the police officers Mr. F. and Mr. R. also did not lead to a solution. Only after further reinforcements joined the investigation team in the person of Mr. S.2 and yourself was it possible to resolve the issue. According to your final assessment at the scene of the incident, there were no grounds for the police patrol's insistence that I delete my photos, for the physical involvement of Mr. S. and Mr. P., who removed me from the wall, or for the threat that my camera would be confiscated. After I had been detained for an hour without being given a reason, you informed me that there was no evidence against me and that I was free to continue my work as a photographer. I took your comments to mean that the police officers' suspicions had proved to be baseless and that the investigation against me was being dropped.
After you had left the scene of the incident, I was once again approached by Detective Sergeant S., who urged me to delete my photos. The next day, Mr. P.2 from Munich's Criminal Investigation Division (CID) left a message on my voicemail and asked me to call him back. During our telephone conversation, he questioned me about my intentions at the wall in Neuperlach. From the start, I endeavored to speed up the work of your team by informing them that my photos were to be exhibited at the Städtische Galerie im Lenbachhaus und Kunstbau München, whose advisory board, like myself, values the perception and representation of contemporary phenomena and matters of public interest. May I ask you to dispel any suspicions that may have arisen and to delete any personal data that has been stored in this context. In order to create a balanced picture, I would like to offer you the opportunity to help clarify the questions that led to the police operation:

Does the object of protection in Neuperlach represent a public danger?
What suspicions led to the increased police operation?
Did those suspicions prove to be groundless or are you continuing your investigations?
When was the CID brought in, by whom, and for what reason?
Which section of the CID was in charge of the investigations into my activities as a photographer on public land?
Where and how were my personal data registered and stored?
Who instructed the security patrol and what were their duties?
Would you be prepared to consider explaining the importance of the wall as an object in need of protection and the tasks of the security patrol at a public event at the Lenbachhaus?

You and your team of investigators are most welcome to visit the exhibition.

Yours sincerely,
Franz Wanner

E-mail attachment:

“WE POSE ONLY THOSE QUESTIONS WHOSE ANSWERS ARE THE *PRE-GIVEN CONDITIONS* OF THE QUESTIONS THEMSELVES.”

It’s good to see you! We’ll be taking photographs during this event. Please let us know if you do not wish us to publish photos on which you appear.

The Städtische Galerie im Lenbachhaus und Kunstbau München cordially invites you to the opening of the exhibition *After the Fact. Propaganda in the 21st Century*
Monday, May 29, 2017, 7:00 p.m. Welcome and reception in the garden of the Lenbachhaus (in the atrium in the case of inclement weather)

Sabine Krieger, Munich City Councillor, representing the Mayor of Munich
Matthias Mühling, Director of the Lenbachhaus
Stephanie Weber, Curator of the exhibition

Subject: Protected Object – Site Protection
Date: May 29, 2017, 15:40:19 (CEST)

Dear Mr. Wanner,

We do not understand the reason for your e-mail and are unable to assign it appropriately. Would you kindly explain your concern again?

Yours sincerely,
H.

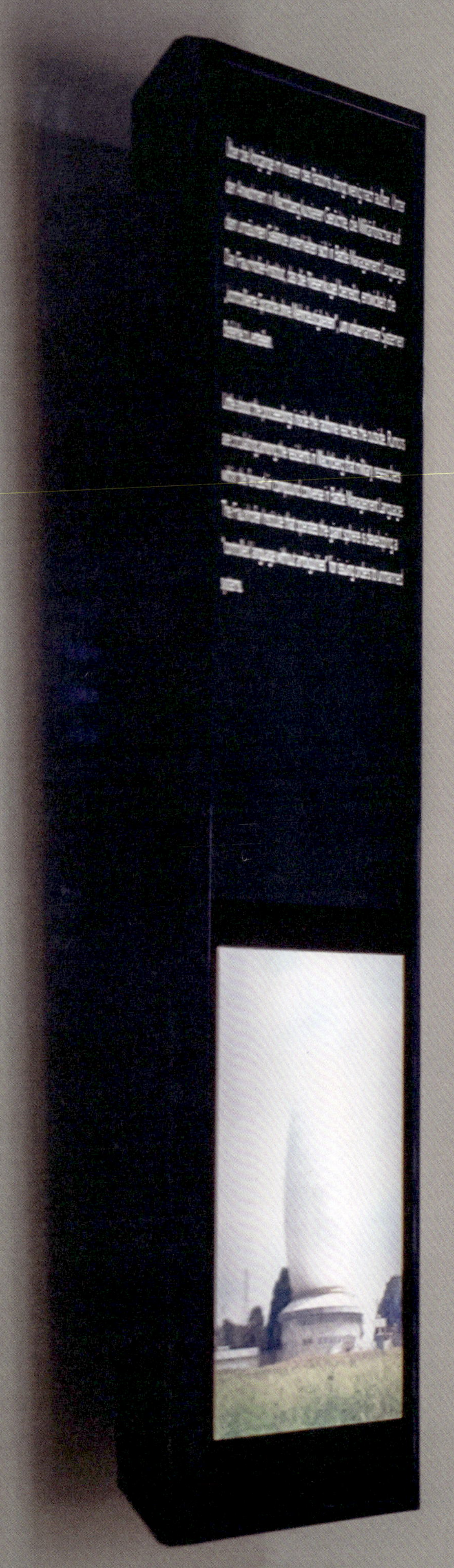

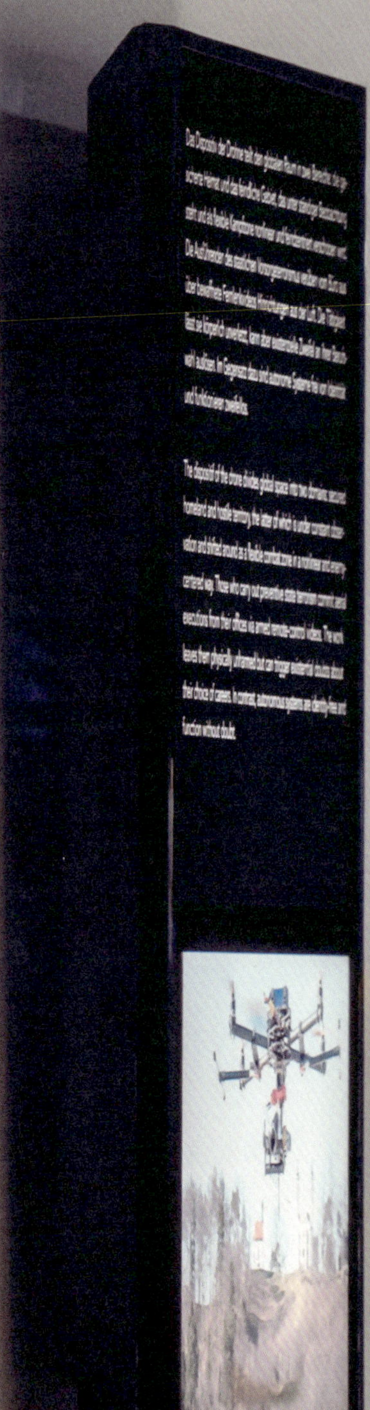

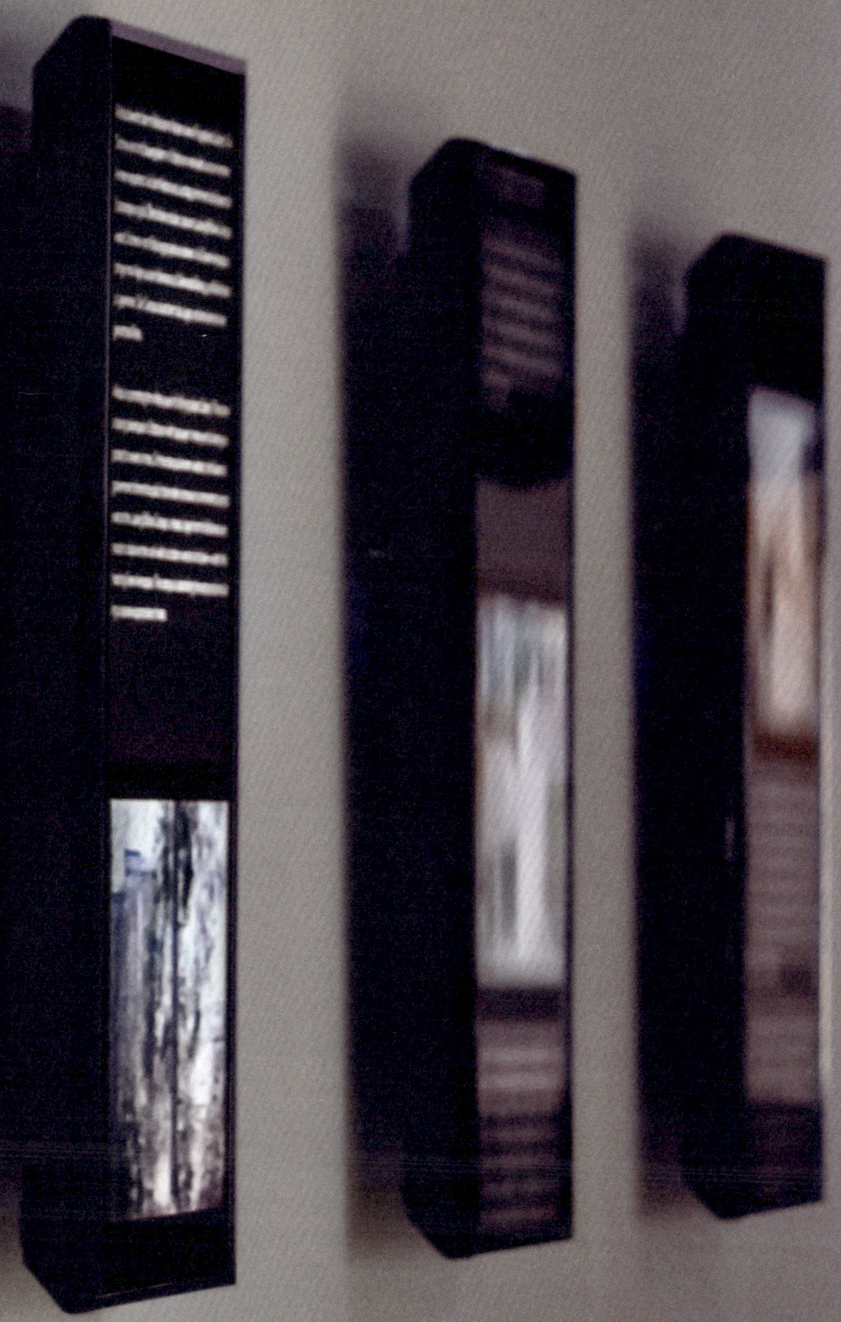

Installation *Battle Management Drawings I–V*, Ausstellung *After the Fact. Propaganda im 21. Jahrhundert*, Städtische Galerie im Lenbachhaus und Kunstbau München, 2017
Installation *Battle Management Drawings I–V*, exhibition *After the Fact. Propaganda in the 21st Century*, Städtische Galerie im Lenbachhaus und Kunstbau München, Munich, 2017

SECRET SITES

Die Befragung

Situativer Loop für drei Schauspieler*innen und zwei Teilnehmende
Münchner Kammerspiele, *X Shared Spaces* / Public Art Munich
Premiere: 19. Juli 2018, Preview: 18. Juli 2018, Aufführungen: 19.–22. Juli 2018

Der Geheimdienst der Bundesrepublik Deutschland ist älter als die Bundesrepublik. Unter US-Kontrolle wurde er 1946 als „Organisation Gehlen" gegründet. Zu einem großen Teil bestand er aus ehemals ranghohen Nationalsozialisten. 1956 benannte er sich um in „Bundesnachrichtendienst" (BND). Neben den Zentralen in München-Pullach und Berlin betreibt der BND weltweit etwa 200 geheime Dienststellen, die Hälfte davon in Deutschland. Sie tragen Tarnnamen wie „Bundesvermögensverwaltung, Abteilung Sondervermögen" und erfüllen unterschiedlichste Funktionen – von der Herstellung falscher Papiere bis zur Observation von Journalist*innen und der Einrichtung getarnter Funkkreise, deren Sende- und Empfangsanlagen an signifikanten Orten wie dem nördlichen Glockenturm der Münchner Frauenkirche untergebracht sind.

Der situative Loop *Die Befragung* behandelt das Befragungswesen des BND. Die Einheit verfügt über eigene Außenstellen und vernimmt dort Asylsuchende. Wenn sie kooperieren und Informationen liefern, wird ihnen eine Aufenthaltsgenehmigung in Aussicht gestellt. Die Praxis der geheimdienstlichen „Abschöpfung" von Geflüchteten wurde 2015 für beendet erklärt und die zuständige „Hauptstelle für Befragungswesen" geschlossen. Seitdem werden die Befragungen an anderen Orten fortgesetzt. Die Theaterinszenierung stellt keine tatsächliche Befragung nach, sondern simuliert eine Übung im Rahmen der Agent*innenausbildung. Die Teilnehmenden (Publikum) werden als BND-Auszubildende adressiert. Die Befragungsleitung weist sie an, sich in rhetorischen Methoden zu üben, die darauf abzielen, den inneren Ausnahmezustand und die rechtsfreien Zonen, als deren institutionalisierte Form der Geheimdienst gelesen werden kann, als normal und notwendig zu verstehen. Das Einüben von Normalisierungstechniken, die hier exemplarisch vorgeführt werden, ermöglicht ein internalisiertes Handeln im Sinne der Sicherheit. Die performative Situation, die an der Oberfläche wie das Reenactment einer Schulung erscheint und immersive Momente aufruft, zeigt die Verhandelbarkeit dokumentarischer Wahrheitsgehalte und möglicher Konstellationen von Wirklichkeitsfragmenten.

__Personen

Befragungsleitung: Lena Lauzemis
Schulungsbetreuung: Christophe Vetter
Coding Developer*innen (und Abläufe Backstage): Mariella Maier, Michaela Andrae
BND-Auszubildende (verkörpert durch zwei Personen, die das Publikum bilden)

__Rahmen

Pro Aufführung (je zehn Minuten Dauer) werden zwei Personen eingelassen. Sie werden von der Befragungsleitung und der Schulungsbetreuung als BND-Auszubildende adressiert. In dieser Rolle der Geheimdienstlehrlinge, in der sie sich mit ihrem Eintritt in das Stück wiederfinden, erhalten sie eine Lektion in Befragungstechniken. Am Ende der Schulungseinheit werden sie verabschiedet und die beiden nächsten Teilnehmenden in die Handlung involviert. Der *situative Loop* läuft mehrere Stunden ohne Unterbrechung. Die Aufführungen finden an mehreren Tagen statt. Das Publikum wird durch genaue Zeitangaben auf der Eintrittskarte über den jeweiligen Einstiegszeitpunkt informiert.

__Skript

Die Teilnehmenden klingeln an der Tür mit der Aufschrift „Südtechnik", die Schulungsbetreuung öffnet.

Guten Tag. Bitte treten Sie ein. Wenn Sie Ihre Mobiltelefone bitte hier ablegen wollen.

Die Schulungsbetreuung hält den Teilnehmenden eine Plastikbox entgegen.

Die Geräte werden sicher verwahrt. Wenn Sie mir bitte folgen wollen.

Die Schulungsbetreuung führt die Teilnehmenden über einen Flur zum Schulungsraum. Dort bittet sie eine*n der beiden an der Tür zu warten, während der*die andere aufgefordert wird einzutreten.

Bevor wir beginnen, möchte ich Sie bitten, nacheinander auf dem Monitor ein paar kurze Hinweise zu lesen. Wenn Sie fertig sind, tippen Sie Ihren Namen bitte in das vorgesehene Feld.

Die Schulungsbetreuung wendet sich an eine*n der beiden Teilnehmenden.

Wenn Sie anfangen würden.

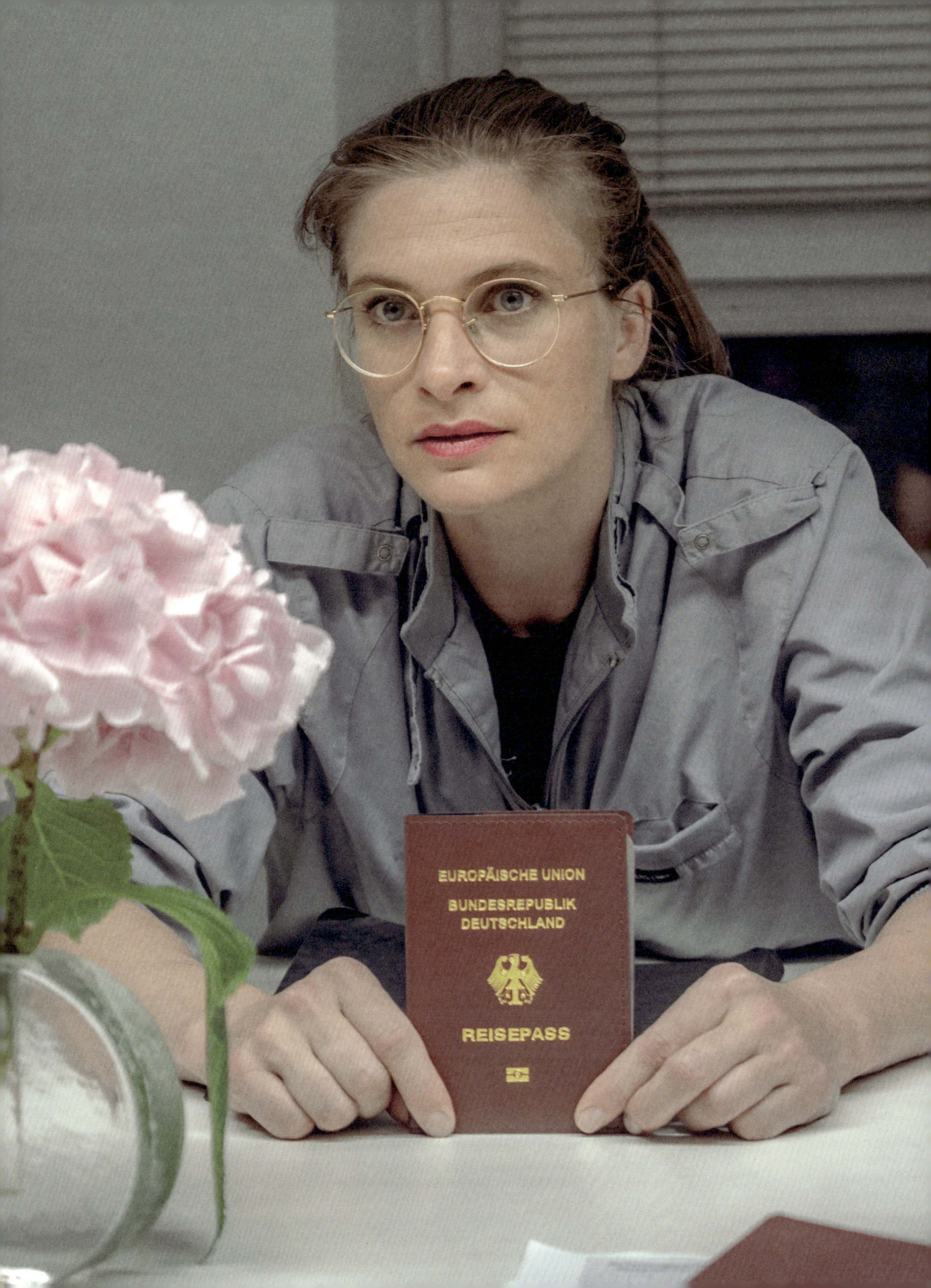
EUROPÄISCHE UNION
BUNDESREPUBLIK
DEUTSCHLAND
REISEPASS

Eine*r der beiden tritt in den Schulungsraum ein und liest den Text auf dem Monitor. Die*der andere wartet so lange an der offen stehenden Tür, bis auch sie*er hereingebeten wird, um den Text zu lesen:

*Sie befinden sich an einem Schulungsort des Bundesnachrichtendienstes. Im Rahmen Ihrer geheimdienstlichen Ausbildung geht es heute um das Befragungswesen. Ziel der Schulung ist es, Ihr psychologisches Einfühlungsvermögen zu steigern. Dadurch erhöhen Sie die Effizienz Ihrer künftigen Tätigkeit als Befrager*in. Zu Ihrer eigenen Sicherheit verhalten Sie sich absolut normal und unauffällig. Wenn Sie das verstanden haben, tragen Sie Ihren Namen bitte hier ein:*

______________.

Während die Teilnehmenden nacheinander den Text auf dem Bildschirm lesen und ihre Namen eintragen, wird ohne ihr Wissen über die Monitorkamera ein Foto von ihnen aufgenommen. Ihre Porträtfotos werden backstage ausgedruckt und in Tarnausweise eingeschoben (dafür stehen den Coding Developer*innen etwa vier Minuten zur Verfügung). Nachdem beide Teilnehmende den Text gelesen und mit ihrem Namen bestätigt haben, werden sie gebeten, Platz zu nehmen.

Sie haben soweit alles verstanden? Dann würde ich Sie bitten, hier Platz zu nehmen.

Die beiden Teilnehmenden setzen sich nebeneinander an den großen Tisch in der Mitte des Raums. Der gegenüberstehende Stuhl bleibt leer. Die Schulungsbetreuung händigt die Befragungsbogen aus.

Hier sind Ihre Befragungsbogen. Die Beispielfragen prägen Sie sich bitte ein. Sie bilden die Basis, von der ausgehend Sie später in der Praxis Ihre eigenen Fragen entwickeln werden.

Die Schulungsbetreuung deutet auf den freien Platz gegenüber den beiden Teilnehmenden.

Die Befragungsleitung wird gleich bei Ihnen sein. Bis dahin haben Sie Zeit, sich die Fragen anzusehen.

Auf dem behördlichen Formular sind folgende Fragen zu lesen:

Möchten Sie mit Ihrer Familie zusammen in Deutschland leben?
Die Versorgungslage in Ihrem Heimatland gilt als schwierig. Würden Sie das bestätigen?
Können Sie mir Informationen über Ihren Schwiegervater geben?
Würden Sie mir seine Handynummer bitte diktieren?
Wären Sie bereit, gegen Bezahlung in Ihr Herkunftsland zu reisen und ihm Fragen zu stellen?
Können Sie auf dieser Karte den Standort der Chemiefabrik zeigen, in der er arbeitet?
Bitte markieren Sie die richtige Stelle mit einem Fähnchen!
Waren Sie in militärische Konflikte verwickelt?
Wie lange warten Sie bereits auf Ihre Anerkennung?
Würden Sie folgenden Satz bitte in Ihrer Muttersprache in dieses Mikrofon sprechen:
„Es ist ein schöner Tag, und die Sonne scheint."
Vielen Dank. Falls wir weitere Fragen haben, kommen wir noch einmal auf Sie zu.
Auf Wiedersehen.

Während die Teilnehmenden die letzten Fragen lesen, betritt die Befragungsleitung den Raum. Sie setzt sich ihnen gegenüber, legt ihre Unterlagen bereit, wartet ab und beginnt dann unvermittelt:

Im Befragungswesen geht es um das Abschöpfen von Quellen. Das Bundesamt für Migration nimmt die persönlichen Daten der neu Angekommenen auf und schickt sie Ihnen wöchentlich zu. Jeden Montag erhalten Sie die neu erhobenen Daten. Die Namen auf diesen „Montagslisten" gehen Sie konsequent durch. Das heißt im Klartext: Sie bestellen die Befragungsquellen zu einem Termin und schöpfen sie ab.

Wenn Sie sich von Anfang an genau an alle Vorgaben halten, haben Sie eine solide Basis von der aus Sie Ihre eigene Arbeit entwickeln können. Deshalb würde ich Sie bitten, Ihr Gegenüber anzuweisen, alle seine bzw. ihre Ortsangaben mit einem Fähnchen exakt auf der Karte zu markieren – also zum Beispiel so:

Die Schulungsbetreuung tritt in den Projektionsstrahl der Weltkarte, auf der bestimmte Staaten farblich hervorgehoben sind, und markiert einen Ort mit einem Fähnchen.

Kontrollieren Sie zur Sicherheit die Angaben Ihres Gegenübers zusätzlich mit der Sprachanalyse-Software.

Die Schulungsbetreuung zeigt auf das Mikrofon und den Monitor, die auf dem Tisch installiert sind. Auf dem Bildschirm ist eine grafische Pegelanzeige für die Frequenzbereiche der menschlichen Stimme zu sehen, die in Echtzeit auf die Stimmen im Raum reagiert.

Die Sprachanalyse-Software erkennt den Dialekt und weist dadurch die Herkunft des Gegenübers zu. Die Algorithmen sind neutral und lassen sich nicht täuschen. Im Gegensatz zu menschlichen Aussagen, die oft fehlerhaft sind, liefern die Algorithmen sichere Ergebnisse.

Die Sicherheit ist unsere Kernaufgabe. Das heißt: die Sicherheit unseres Staates und der Schutz unserer Truppen im Ausland. Lassen Sie die Befragten zu deren eigener Sicherheit im Glauben, die Befragung sei ein üblicher Behördenakt im Asylverfahren. Das Auftragsprofil der Bundesregierung zielt auf Angehörige folgender Staaten:

Das Deckenlicht geht aus; die Befragungsleitung zeigt auf die hell leuchtende Projektion der Weltkarte, auf der bestimmte Länder und Gebiete rot hervorgehoben sind:

Russland, Mittlerer und Naher Osten, Balkanstaaten, Iran, Irak, Afghanistan, Syrien und Somalia.

Sie müssen sich darüber im Klaren sein, dass Sie die Befragung im Namen der Bundesregierung durchführen, jedoch unter Umständen mit einer Mitarbeiterin oder einem Mitarbeiter eines befreundeten Geheimdienstes, also mit US-amerikanischen, britischen oder französischen Agentinnen und Agenten.

Sie finden heraus, in welchem der relevanten Bereiche die „Qubef" – also die Quelle des Befragungswesens – etwas wissen könnte. Die für uns relevanten Bereiche sind: Wirtschaft, Militär, Politik, Proliferation sowie Technologie, Terrorismus, Medizin und die Versorgungslage der jeweiligen Länder.

Die abgeschöpften Informationen stehen nicht nur uns zur Verfügung, sondern auch unseren Verbündeten. Allerdings ist die Einbindung anderer Geheimdienste rechtlich nicht vorgesehen, weshalb es unbedingt notwendig ist, dass sich alle Befragenden zu jedem Zeitpunkt als Deutsche ausweisen können.

Die Coding Developerin betritt den Raum und übergibt der Schulungsbetreuung die Tarnpapiere mit den Porträtfotos der Teilnehmenden.

Hier sind die Tarnpapiere.

Die Schulungsbetreuung gibt die Tarnpapiere weiter an die Befragungsleitung, die sie mit einem Blick kontrolliert und dann über den Tisch hinweg den Auszubildenden überreicht.

Hier sind Ihre Tarnpapiere.

Die Auszubildenden bekommen einen Augenblick Zeit, um die ihnen noch nicht bekannten Fotos ihrer eigenen Gesichter in den Tarnausweisen zu betrachten.

Die Coding Developerin stellt einen Blumenstrauß auf den Tisch:

Hortensien.

Geht ab.

Um Sie nicht mit neuen Codes zu überfordern, gehen wir zunächst von einer Standardsituation aus.

Deutet auf den Fragebogen:

Die Fragen, die wir Ihnen vorgelegt haben, sind deshalb noch recht einfach gehalten.

Später in der Praxis kommt es auf Sie an. Sie werden Ihre Fragen weiter präzisieren und in der Befragung konsequent nachhaken.

Fragen, die Sie sich stellen müssen: Wie stellen Sie Ihre Fragen so, dass Ihr Gegenüber relevante Informationen preisgibt? Und: Wie können Sie sicher sein, ob jemand die Wahrheit sagt?

Kann man das lernen? Oder braucht man dafür eine ganz spezielle Begabung?

Wenn Sie sich an die Vorgaben halten, ist es ganz einfach.

Die Teilnahme an der Befragung muss in jedem Fall als „freiwillig" darstellbar sein – auch wenn Sie Druck aufbauen oder Minderjährige befragen. Deuten Sie an, dass ein kooperatives Verhalten zu einer Aufenthaltsgenehmigung führen kann. Die theoretische Nutzbarkeit von Handynummern für die Zielerfassung von Kampfdrohnen ist selbstverständlich mit absoluter Verschwiegenheit zu behandeln. Wenn Ihnen manche Fragen ungewohnt vorkommen, machen Sie sich bewusst, dass Ihre Arbeit dem Vorsorgeterrorismus dient und für unser Staatswohl von allerhöchstem Nutzen ist.

Die Schulungsbetreuung steht auf, holt die Lernpakete mit der Aufschrift „Secret Guide" und übergibt sie der Befragungsleitung. Die Befragungsleitung überreicht sie den Auszubildenden und weist sie an, den darin enthaltenen Bewertungsbogen anzukreuzen:

Hier ist Ihr Lernpaket mit dem Bewertungsbogen. Kreuzen Sie bitte jetzt eine der drei Optionen an.

__Auswertung

Die Befragung ist für die Sicherheit und das Staatswohl der Bundesrepublik Deutschland und ihrer Verbündeten

☐ *von hohem Nutzen – Effizienz: 80 %*
☐ *von besonders hohem Nutzen – Effizienz: 90 %*
☐ *von allerhöchstem Nutzen – Effizienz: 100 %*

Vielen Dank für Ihre Auswertung. Im Rahmen der Lektion wurden fotografische Bilder von Ihnen hergestellt. Würden Sie einer Speicherung zustimmen? Die Fotos würden dann für Schulungszwecke und zur Dokumentation verwendet.

Seite / Pages 67, 70, 73–75, 86, 91–93
Die Befragung, Szenenansichten
Scenes from *The Interrogation*

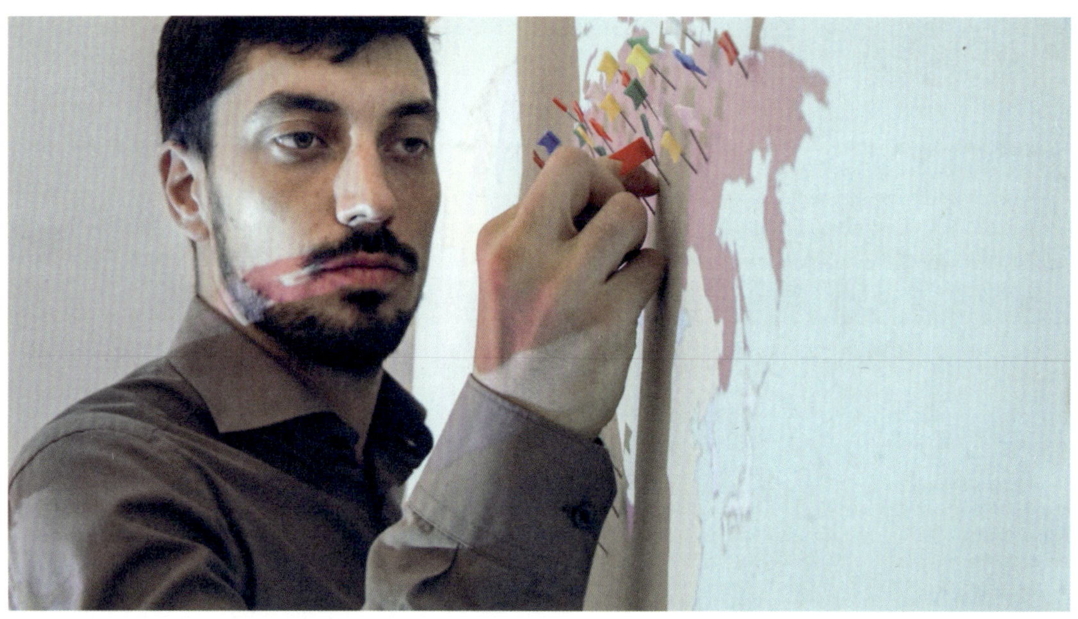

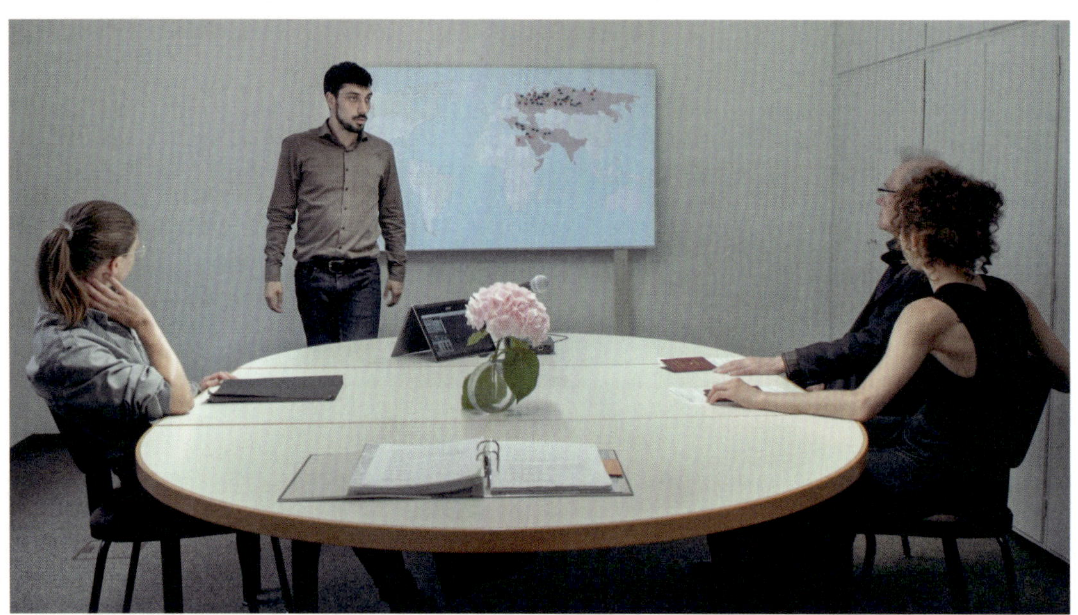

Die Auszubildenden geben ihre Zustimmung oder Ablehnung.

Die Ausweise und die Fragebogen geben Sie zurück, Ihr Lernpaket nehmen Sie bitte mit. Bis zur nächsten Lektion prägen Sie sich alle Informationen gründlich ein. Kommende Woche sehen wir uns wieder, dann befassen wir uns eingehend mit unseren Außenstellen. Bis dahin und auf Wiedersehen.

Ich bringe Sie noch zur Tür. Ihre Handys erhalten Sie unbeschadet zurück.

Die Schulungsbetreuung gibt die Handys zurück und begleitet die Auszubildenden zur Tür.

Über den nächsten Termin werden wir Sie zeitnah informieren. Auf Wiedersehen.

Die Auszubildenden verlassen den Spielort, und die nächsten Teilnehmenden werden in die Situation involviert. Die Handlung beginnt von Neuem.

Secret Guide

Der Faltplan *Secret Guide* enthält:

__Stadtplan von München, in dem 125 geheimdienstliche Außenstellen (Org und BND) von 1946 bis 2018 verzeichnet und mit Bildern und Angaben versehen sind (Adresse, Tarnbezeichnung, Funktion, Datierungen usw.);

__Fleurop-Liste

Blumennamen, die der BND intern für andere Staaten und Geheimdienste verwendet:

Hortensie__USA
Aster__Großbritannien
Narzisse__Frankreich
Schneeglöckchen__Italien
Mammutbaum__Russland
Ibis__Israel
Mangrove__Simbabwe
Raps__Zypern
Melisse__Griechenland
Hanf__Türkei
Weißdorn__Portugal
Koriander__Niederlande
Pfingstrose__Belgien
Eisenhut__Luxemburg
Iris__Finnland
Dahlie__Schweden
Gladiole__Norwegen
Begonie__Dänemark
Chrysantheme__Österreich
Anis__Schweiz
Rotdorn__Kanada

__Glossar

Qubef__ Quelle(n) des Befragungswesens (zum Beispiel Asylsuchende)
Abschöpfung__ Informationsgewinnung durch eine Quelle
Rezeptive Befragung__ Vorhandene Information der Quelle wird direkt abgeschöpft
Operative Befragung__ Quelle aktualisiert ihren Wissensstand durch Reise und/oder Treffen mit weiteren Personen und wird dann abgeschöpft
Dislozierung__ Verteilung von Dienststellen mit unterschiedlichen Aufgaben auf den Stadtraum
Tarnfirma__ Real existierende Firma, deren Strukturen geheimdienstlich genutzt werden
Scheinfirma__ Firmenfassade, die zur Tarnung geheimdienstlicher Tätigkeit aufgebaut wird, hinter der aber keine reale Firma existiert
Org__ Abkürzung für die Organisation Gehlen (1946 gegründet, 1956 in Bundesnachrichtendienst umbenannt)
Die Namen der Scheinfirmen der Org begannen meist mit den Buchstaben S und T. Der Kontaktmann des Geheimdienstes in der Münchner Verwaltung, der die Firmen ins Handelsregister eintrug, war nur für diese beiden Buchstaben zuständig, sodass die Namenswahl beschränkt blieb.

Schulungsunterlagen Befragungswesen
Interrogation Training Materials

Lektion Nr. 3 – Die Befragung Lesson No. 3 – The Interrogation	- Nur für den Dienstgebrauch - - For Internal Use Only -	Quellennummer / Source Number

Zeile

Möchten Sie mit Ihrer Familie zusammen in Deutschland leben?
Do you wish to live in Germany with your family?

Die Versorgungslage in Ihrem Heimatland gilt als schwierig. Würden Sie das bestätigen?
The supply conditions in your home country are difficult. Would you agree with this?

Können Sie mir Informationen über Ihren Schwiegervater geben?
Würden Sie mir seine Handynummer bitte diktieren?
Can you give me any information about your father-in-law?
Would you please dictate his cellphone number for me?

Wären Sie bereit, gegen Bezahlung in Ihr Herkunftsland zu reisen und ihm Fragen zu stellen?
Would you be prepared to travel back to your country of origin and ask him questions in return for payment?

Können Sie auf dieser Karte den Standort der Chemiefabrik zeigen, in der er arbeitet?
Bitte markieren Sie die richtige Stelle mit einem Fähnchen!
Can you show me on this map where the chemicals factory he works for is located?
Please mark the correct location with a little flag.

Waren Sie in militärische Konflikte verwickelt?
Were you involved in military conflicts?

Wie lange warten Sie bereits auf Ihre Anerkennung?
How long have you been waiting for recognition already?

Würden Sie folgenden Satz bitte in Ihrer Muttersprache in dieses Mikrofon sprechen:
„Es ist ein schöner Tag, und die Sonne scheint."
Would you please speak the following sentence into this microphone in your mother tongue:
"It's a beautiful day and the sun is shining."

Datum / Date

Vielen Dank. Falls wir weitere Fragen haben, kommen wir noch einmal auf Sie zu. Auf Wiedersehen.
Thank you very much. We will contact you again in case of further questions. Goodbye.

- 1/1 -

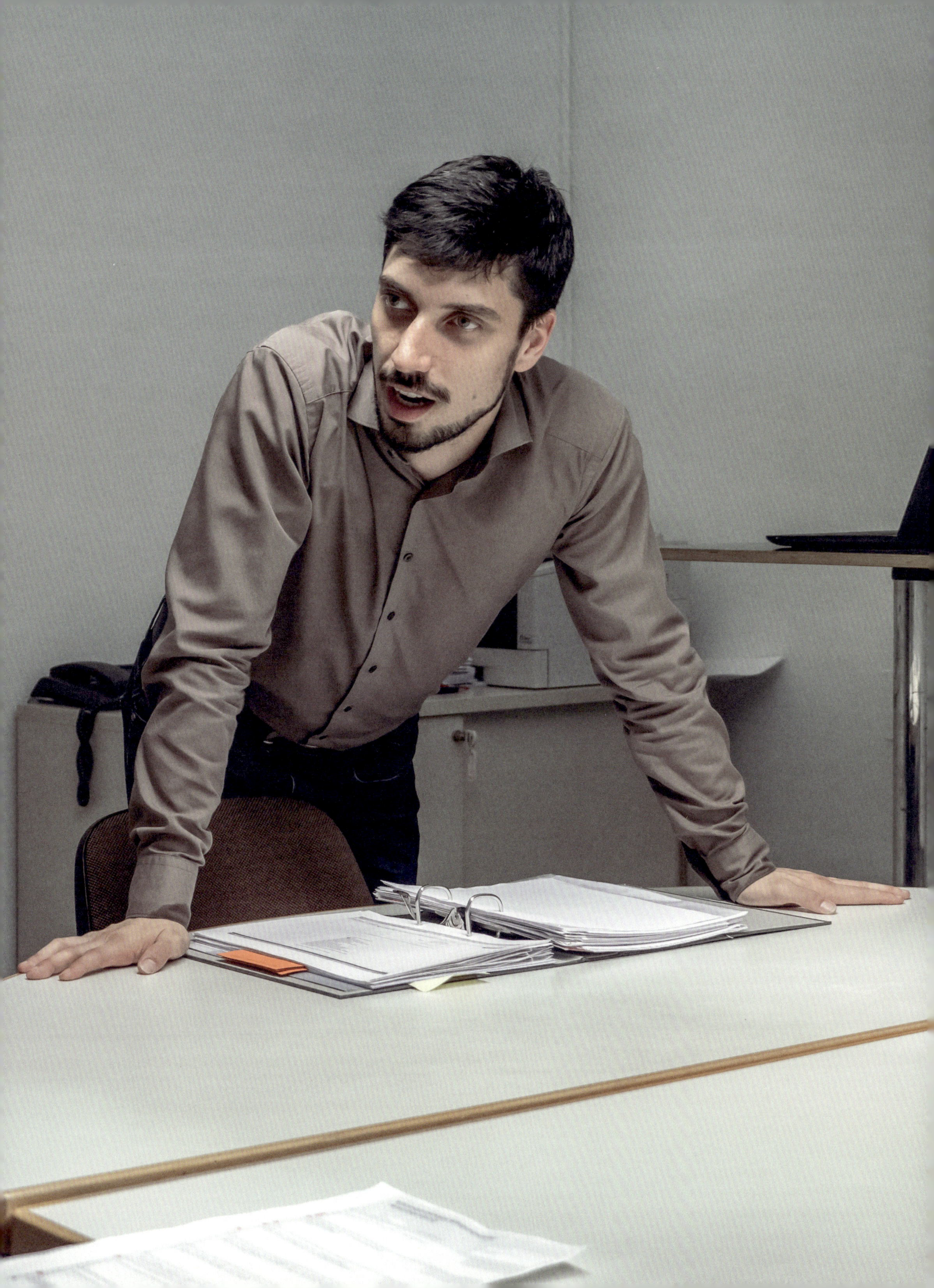

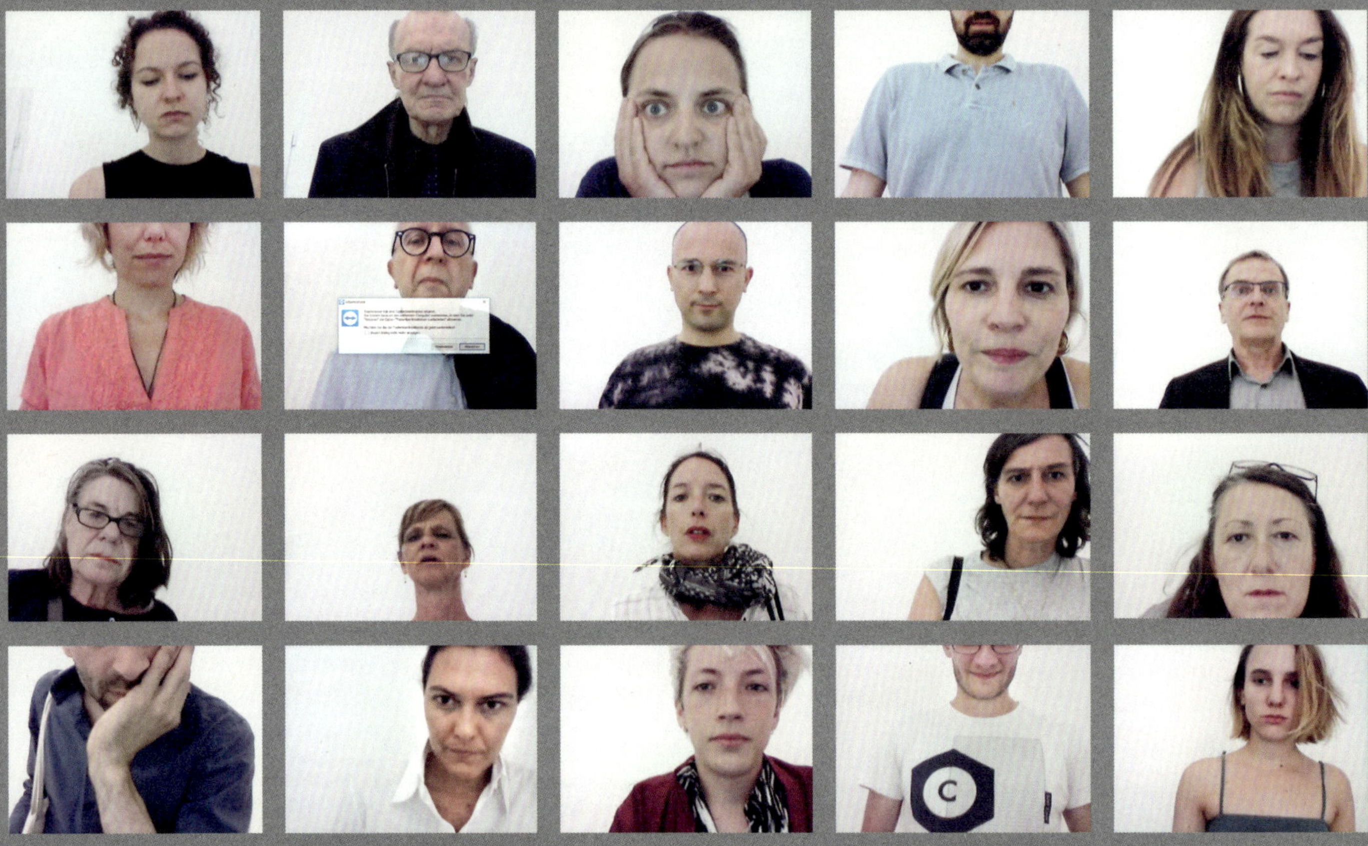

Sie befinden sich an einem Schulungsort des Bundesnachrichtendienstes. Im Rahmen Ihrer geheimdienstlichen Ausbildung geht es heute um das Befragungswesen. Ziel der Schulung ist es, Ihr psychologisches Einfühlungsvermögen zu steigern. Dadurch erhöhen Sie die Effizienz Ihrer künftigen Tätigkeit als Befrager*in. Zu Ihrer eigenen Sicherheit verhalten Sie sich absolut normal und unauffällig. Wenn Sie das verstanden haben, tragen Sie Ihren Namen bitte hier ein: ____________________.

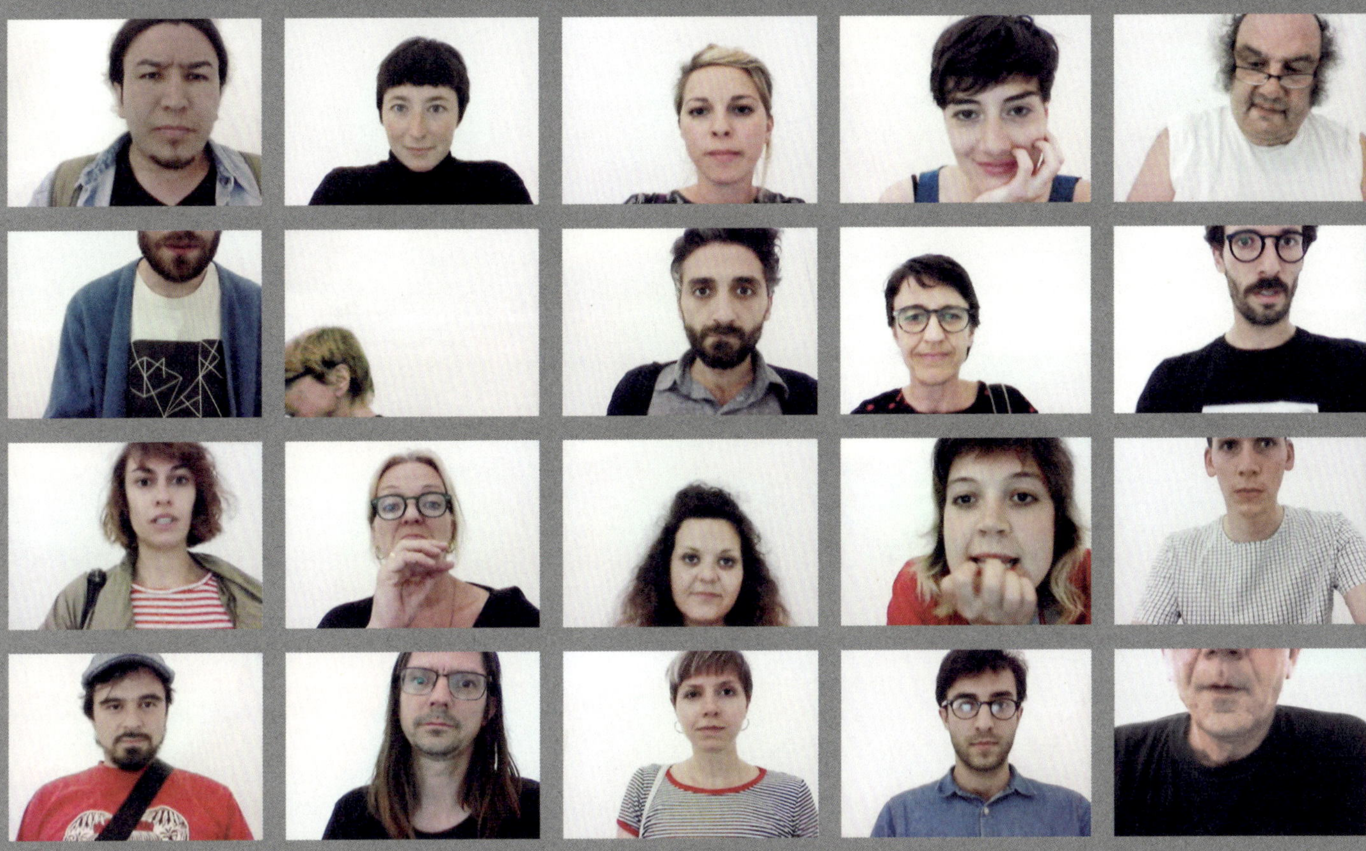

You are at a training location of the BND (Intelligence Service of the Federal Republic of Germany). Your intelligence lesson today is about interrogation. The aim of the training is to increase your psychological empathy. This will increase the efficiency of your future work as an interrogator. For your own safety, please behave absolutely normally and inconspicuously. If you have understood this, please enter your name here: ____________________.

The Interrogation

Situational loop for three actors and two participants
Munich Kammerspiele, *X Shared Spaces* / Public Art Munich
Premiere: July 19, 2018; Preview: July 18, 2018; Performances: July 19–22, 2018

The secret service of the Federal Republic of Germany is older than the Federal Republic itself. It was founded in 1946 under the control of the United States as the "Gehlen Organization," which consisted largely of former high-ranking National Socialists. In 1956, it renamed itself the "Bundesnachrichtendienst" (BND)—the Federal Intelligence Service. In addition to its headquarters in Munich-Pullach and Berlin, the BND also operates some 200 secret offices worldwide, half of them in Germany. They have cover names like "Bundesvermögensverwaltung, Abteilung Sondervermögen" (Federal Property Management Division, Special Assets Department) and fulfill a wide range of functions—from the production of false documents to the surveillance of journalists and the establishment of concealed radio stations, whose transmission and receiving installations are housed in important locations, such as the north bell tower of Munich's cathedral: the Frauenkirche.

The situational loop *The Interrogation* deals with the interrogation techniques of the BND. The unit has a number of outposts where it questions asylum seekers, who are told that they may be granted a residence permit if they cooperate and provide information. In 2015, it was declared that the secret service practice of "siphoning off" refugees for information had been terminated and that the "Main Office of Interrogation," which had been responsible for the process, had been closed down. Since then, the interrogations have continued at other locations. This theatrical presentation does not reconstruct an actual interrogation, but shows an exercise in a BND instructional context. The participants (the audience) are addressed as BND trainees. The person in charge of the interrogation instructs the participants to practice rhetorical methods which are intended to make the internal exceptional state and the extralegal zones be perceived as normal and necessary—the Secret Service being construable as their institutionalized form. Rehearsing the normalization techniques shown here by way of example permits an internalized course of action in terms of security. The performative situation, which on the surface looks like the reenactment of a training session and which evokes its immersive moments, shows the negotiability of documentary veracity and possible constellations of fragmented reality.

__Cast List

Head of Interrogation: Lena Lauzemis
Training Supervisor: Christophe Vetter
Coding Developers (and backstage procedures): Mariella Maier, Michaela Andrae
BND trainees (represented by two people who form the audience)

__Background

Two people are admitted to each performance (each lasting for ten minutes). They are addressed as BND trainees by the Head of Interrogation and the Training Supervisor. In their role as Secret Service trainees, in which they find themselves when they enter the play, they receive a lecture on interrogation techniques. At the end of the training unit, they leave and the next two participants are introduced into the action. The *situational loop* runs for several hours without interruption. The performances take place over several days. The precise times given on the entrance cards inform the participants when they have to show up.

__Script

The participants ring at the door with the "Südtechnik" company sign. The Training Supervisor opens the door.

Good morning. Please come in. Please be so good as to leave your cellphones here.

The Training Supervisor holds out a plastic box.

We'll take good care of them. Please follow me.

The Training Supervisor leads the two participants along a corridor to the training room, and asks one of them to wait by the door while the other is asked to enter.

Before we start, I'll ask you to read some brief instructions on the monitor, one after the other. When you've finished, please type your name into the box.

The Training Supervisor turns to one of the two participants.

Would you start, please?

One of the participants enters the training room and reads the text on the monitor. The other

waits by the open door until he or she is also asked to enter the room in order to read the text:
You are at a training center for the Federal Secret Service. Today, as part of your Secret Service training, we will be studying interrogation techniques. The aim of the training session is to increase your psychological intuition. In this way, you will raise the efficiency of your future activities as an interrogator. For your own safety, please behave absolutely normally and unobtrusively. If you have understood this, please enter your name here: ____________.

While the participants are reading the text on the screen and entering their names one after the other, a photo is taken of them without their knowledge via the monitor camera. Their portrait photos are printed out backstage and inserted into counterfeit IDs (the Coding Developers have about four minutes to complete this task). Once both participants have read the text and confirmed the fact with their names, they are asked to take a seat.

Have you understood everything so far? Then please take a seat.

The two participants sit down side by side at the big table in the middle of the room. The chair on the opposite side of the table remains empty. The Training Supervisor hands them the questionnaires.

Here are your questionnaires. Please take note of the specimen questions. They form the basis on which you will develop your own questions in practice later on.

The Training Supervisor indicates the empty chair opposite the two participants.

The Head of Interrogation will be with you in a minute. Until then, you have time to study the questions.

The form is laid out in the style of an official document and contains the following questions:
Do you wish to live in Germany with your family?
The supply situation in your home country is regarded as difficult. Would you confirm that this is the case?
Can you give me any information about your father-in-law?
Would you please dictate his cellphone number for me?
Would you be prepared to travel back to your country of origin and ask him questions in return for payment?
Can you show me on this map where the chemicals factory he works for is located? Please mark the correct location with a little flag.
Were you involved in military conflicts?
How long have you been waiting for recognition already?
Would you please speak the following sentence into this microphone in your mother tongue: "It's a beautiful day and the sun is shining."
Thank you. We will get back to you if we have any further questions. Goodbye.

While the participants are reading the last questions, the Head of Interrogation enters the room. She sits down opposite them, lays out her papers on the table, waits for a moment, and then begins without preamble:

Interrogation is a question of sounding out sources. The Federal Office for Migration records the personal data of new arrivals and sends them to you every week. Every Monday, you will receive the latest data. You should check the names on these "Monday lists" systematically. To put it plainly: Summon the interrogation subjects to an appointment and sound them out.

If you follow all the instructions precisely from the outset, you will have a solid basis from which to develop your own work. Which is why I ask you to instruct the person you are questioning to mark all the relevant locations accurately on the map with a flag—like this, for example:

The Training Supervisor steps forward into the projection beam of the world map, on which certain countries have been marked in color. He marks a location with a flag.

Please use the speech analysis software to double-check the information you are given.

The Training Supervisor points at the microphone and the monitor installed on the table. Its screen shows a graphic level indicator for the frequency levels of the human voice, which reacts in real time to the voices in the room.

The speech analysis software recognizes the interviewee's dialect and thus indicates his or her place of origin. Unlike human statements, which are often incorrect, the algorithms will supply reliable and secure results.

Security is our core mission. That means: the safety of our country and the protection of our troops abroad. In the interests of their own security, let the people you are questioning believe that the interrogation is part of the normal official procedures for asylum-seekers. The Federal Government has focused its assignment profile on citizens of the following countries:

The ceiling light is switched off, and the Head of Interrogation points to the brightly illuminated projection of the world map, where certain countries and regions have been highlighted in red:

Russia, the Middle and Near East, the Balkan countries, Iran, Iraq, Afghanistan, Syria, and Somalia.

You must always be aware of the fact that you are conducting the interrogation in the name of the Federal Government, in some situations, however, together with a representative of a friendly secret service—in other words, with American, British, or French agents.

Your aim is to find out in which of the relevant areas the subject of the interrogation might know something. The areas that are relevant for us are: the economy, the military, politics, proliferation, as well as technology, terrorism, medicine, and the supply situation in the countries concerned.

The information we obtain is available not only to us, but also to our allies. However, there is no legal provision for the involvement of other secret services, so it is absolutely necessary that those carrying out the questioning can prove at all times that they are Germans.

The Coding Developer enters the room and gives the Training Supervisor the counterfeit IDs with the portrait photos of the participants.

Here are the cover identity papers.

The Training Supervisor gives the cover papers to the Head of Interrogation. She examines them quickly and passes them across the table to the trainees.

Here are your cover identity papers.

The trainees have a moment to look at the photos of their own faces in the cover documents, which they have not previously seen.

The Coding Developer places a bunch of flowers on the table:

Hydrangeas.

Exits.

In order not to overtax you with the new codes, we are going to begin with a standard situation.

Points to the questionnaire:

The questions we have given you are therefore still very easy at this stage.

Later, in practice, it will be up to you. You will have to phrase your questions more precisely and follow them up systematically during the interrogation.

The questions you will have to ask yourselves are: How can I phrase my questions in a way that will induce the person being interviewed to reveal relevant information? And: How can I be sure whether someone is telling the truth?

Is that something one can learn? Or does it require a special talent?

If you follow the instructions you have been given, it is quite easy.

In all cases, it is important to present the other person's participation in the interrogation as "voluntary"—even if you exert pressure or question minors. You should imply that cooperative behavior could lead to a residence permit. The theoretical possibility of using cellphone numbers to record the targets of combat drones must obviously be a matter of absolute secrecy. If some of the questions seem unusual to you, remember that your work is in the interests of preventive terrorism and immensely important for the well-being of the state.

The Training Supervisor stands up, picks up the study packages labeled SECRET GUIDE, and gives them to the Head of Interrogation. The Head of Interrogation hands them to the trainees and instructs them to put a cross on the assessment sheet they contain:

Here is your study package with the assessment sheet. Now please put a cross beside one of the three options.

__Assessment

For the safety and the public good of the Federal Republic of Germany and its allies, the interrogation is

☐ *Extremely useful – Efficiency: 80 %*
☐ *Exceptionally useful – Efficiency: 90 %*
☐ *Of the greatest possible use – Efficiency: 100 %*

Thank you for your assessment. During the course of this training session, photos have been taken of you. Do you consent to their being stored? The photos will then be used for training purposes and documentation.

The trainees indicate whether they consent or not.

Return the IDs and the questionnaires, and please take your study package with you. Make a careful note of all information before the next training session. We will meet again next week for an in-depth study of our branch offices. Goodbye until then.

Let me show you the way out. Your cellphones will be returned to you undamaged.

The Director of Training gives back the cellphones and accompanies the trainees to the door.

We will inform you about the next appointment nearer the time. Goodbye.

The trainees leave the performance space and the next participants become involved in the situation. The action begins all over again.

Secret Guide

The *Secret Guide* folding plan contains:

__City map of Munich, listing 125 secret service outposts (Org and BND) from 1946 to 2018, along with pictures and information (addresses, cover names, functions, dates, etc.)

__Fleurop List

Flower names that the BND (Intelligence Service of the Federal Republic of Germany) uses internally for other countries and secret services:

Hydrangea__USA
Aster__Great Britain
Daffodil__France
Snowdrop__Italy
Sequoia__Russia
Ibis__Israel
Mangrove__Zimbabwe
Rapeseed__Cyprus
Melissa__Greece
Hemp__Turkey
Hawthorn__Portugal
Cilantro__The Netherlands
Peony__Belgium
Wolf's Bane__Luxembourg
Iris__Finland
Dahlia__Sweden
Gladiola__Norway
Begonia__Denmark
Chrysanthemum__Austria
Anise__Switzerland
Pink Hawthorn__Canada

__Glossary

Qubef__interrogation sources, for example asylum seekers (Quellen des Befragungswesens)
Siphoning off__acquisition of information through a source
Receptive interrogation__a source's available information is siphoned off directly
Operative interrogation__a source updates his/her level of knowledge through travel and/or meeting with additional persons and is then siphoned off
Dislocation__distributing offices with various functions throughout the urban area
Front company__an actual company whose structures are used by intelligence services
Bogus company__a company facade constructed to disguise intelligence activities, but behind which no real company exists
Org__abbreviation for the Gehlen Organization (founded in 1946, renamed Bundesnachrichtendienst [Federal Intelligence Service] in 1956)

The names of the bogus companies of Org usually began with the letters S and T. The intelligence agency's contact man in the Munich administration, who entered the companies into the trade register, was responsible for these two letters alone, so that the choice of names remained limited.

Franz Wanner

SECRET GUIDE

Grundkurs Geheimdienst
Basiswissen für Agent*innen

Lektion 3__Die Befragung
Lektion 4__Die Außenstellen

Franz Wanner

SECRET GUIDE

Intelligence 101
Basics for Agents

Lesson 3_The Interrogation
Lesson 4_The Outposts

Faltplan, 59 x 95 cm, Maßstab 1:25 000, siehe Seite 87
Folding map, 59 x 95 cm, scale 1:25,000, see page 87

Die Befragung
Video, 7 Min., 2019, Stills
Filmische Adaption der gleichnamigen Theaterperformance mit Lena Lauzemis und Christophe Vetter
The Interrogation
Video, 7 min., 2019, stills
Film adaption of the theater performance of the same name with Lena Lauzemis and Christophe Vetter

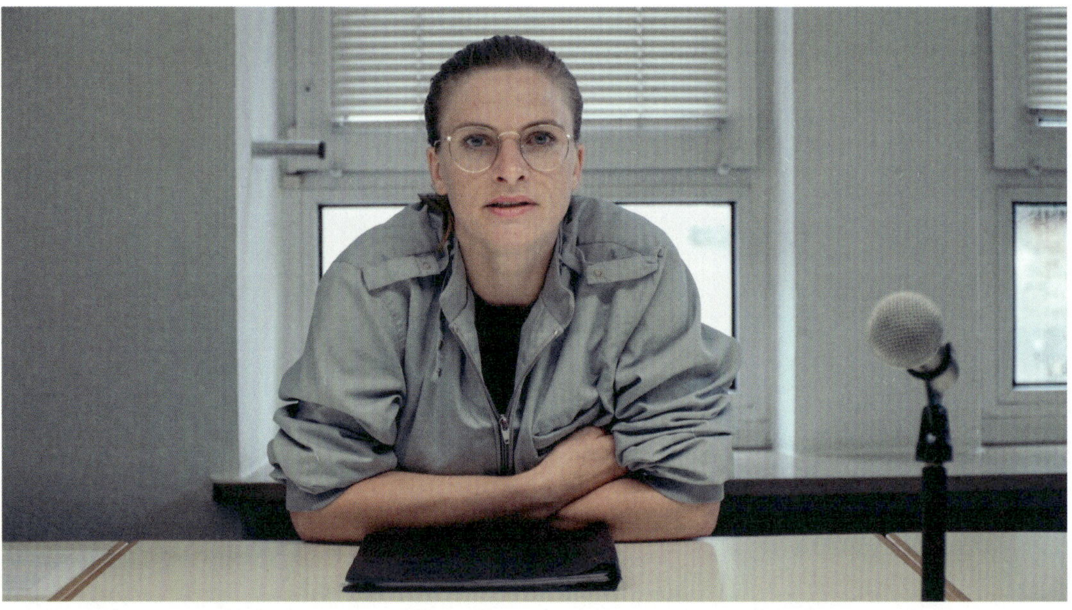

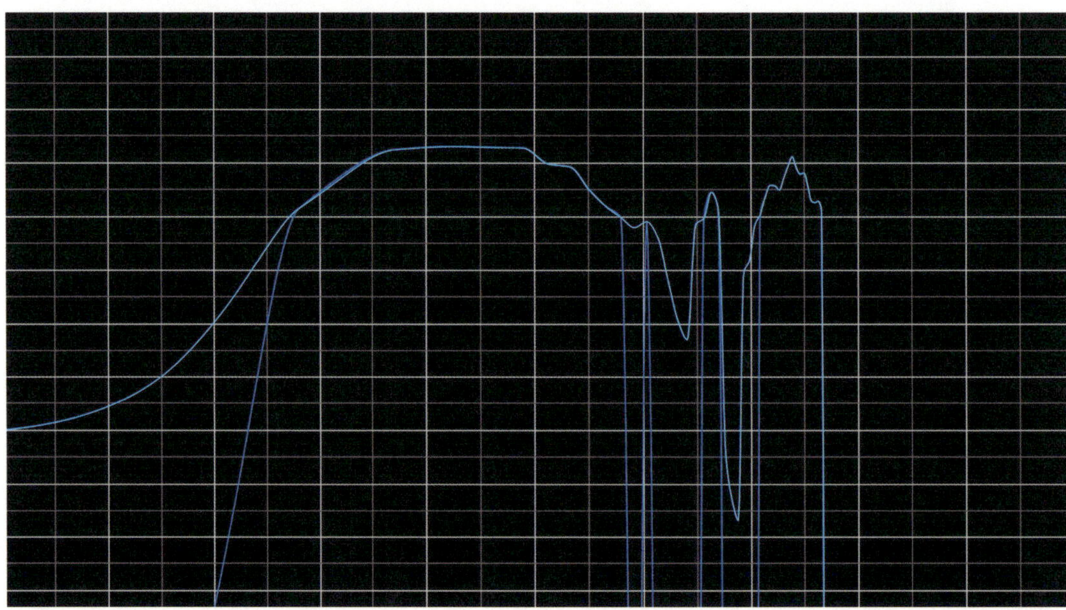

Maria Muhle und Franz Wanner

Die Befragung – ein Gespräch

Muhle__ In deiner Arbeit geht es um Geheimdienstfragen, ein Thema, das natürlich für viel Aufsehen sorgt, das bei dir aber auf seine konkreten Mechanismen, Operationen und Techniken beziehungsweise Verfahren befragt wird. Man könnte sagen, dass du so etwas wie eine gemeindienstliche Kulturtechnik in den Blick nimmst. Eine solche vielleicht etwas ungewöhnliche Kulturtechnik beruht auf Begriffen wie dem des Staatsgeheimnisses und des Ausnahmezustands und könnte als eine Art Wahrheitsproduktionsmaschine beschrieben werden, deren Aufgabe es vorgeblich ist, verdeckte Wahrheiten aufzudecken, die dabei aber eben auch gleich ihre eigenen Wahrheiten mitproduziert. Ich würde daher gerne einsteigen mit der Frage nach der Art der Dokumente, die für dich wichtig waren, und zugleich fragen, wie du diese Dokumente in den performativen Ablauf der Arbeit eingebaut hast? Du hast gesagt, dass der Abschlussbericht des NSA-Untersuchungsausschusses eine Quelle für dich war, aber es gab ja auch noch andere Quellen. Die Frage wäre also, was für eine Logik des Dokumentarischen hinter dieser Arbeit steckt und inwiefern sie mit der spezifischen Inszenierungslogik der Arbeit zusammengeht?

Wanner__ Zum einen interessieren mich Dokumente wie das von dir genannte oder auch das CIA-Dokument „Memorandum for the Record. Subject: CATIDE Cover Firms", das geheimdienstliche Orte offenlegt, oder parlamentarische Anfragen, Dokumente also, die meist öffentlich zugänglich sind. Man muss nicht immer einbrechen oder geleakte Informationen verwenden, sondern es gibt allgemeine Zugänge, die man findet, wenn man ein Interesse verfolgt. Zum anderen spreche ich mit Leuten, die verschiedene Perspektiven auf das Thema haben, an dem ich gerade arbeite. Im Entstehungsprozess von *Die Befragung* (2018) waren das Leute, die Befragungen erlebt haben, oder Jurist*innen, die Geflüchtete vertreten. Public Art Munich hat im Rahmen meiner Arbeit zusätzlich einen Geheimdienstexperten engagiert, der weiteres Material für mich recherchiert hat, wie etwa Schulungsunterlagen des Bundesnachrichtendienstes (BND). Die recherchierten Dokumente als solche spielen in der Inszenierung aber keine Rolle. Stattdessen habe ich versucht, einzelne Fragmente daraus neu zusammenzustellen und eine narrative Struktur zu entwickeln. Am Beispiel der Tarnpässe, die den Teilnehmenden während des Stücks ausgehändigt werden, lässt sich die Inszenierungslogik gut veranschaulichen: Laut Abschlussbericht des NSA-Untersuchungsausschusses haben Angehörige ausländischer Geheimdienste im Namen der Bundesrepublik und im Wissen des BND Asylsuchende befragt. Weil Geheimdienste dazu angehalten sind, die Interessen des eigenen Staats zu vertreten, und es deshalb offiziell nicht im Interesse der Bundesregierung liegen kann, dass Geheimdienste anderer Staaten im Namen Deutschlands selbstständig Befragungen durchführen, stellte der BND den französischen, britischen und US-amerikanischen Befrager*innen deutsche Tarnpässe aus. Während des Stücks erhalten auch die Rezipient*innen in der Rolle der BND-Auszubildenden spezielle Tarnpässe, in denen sie dann auf den Passfotos ihre eigenen Gesichter entdecken. Geheimdienstliche Praktiken wie diese habe ich recherchiert und einen Lehrplan für BND-Auszubildende zusammengestellt, auf dem die inszenierte Schulung basiert. Mir geht es dabei nicht um das Moment des Enthüllens dieser Praktiken, sondern zunächst darum, überhaupt einen Zugang zu schaffen und die Dinge zu benennen, unabhängig davon, ob die Dokumente offenliegen oder durch Whistleblowing öffentlich werden. Erst dann ist es möglich, Zusammenhänge erzählbar zu machen und in einen diskursiven Raum zu stellen. Es interessiert mich nicht so sehr, durch zugänglich gemachte „echte" Fakten einen höheren Wahrheitsgehalt zu erzielen. Ich versuche stattdessen, Fragmente in Beziehung zu setzen und Schichtungen zu erzeugen, um damit eine Komplexität zu erfassen, die ich in dieser als normal geltenden Konstellation sehe, in der wir leben: eine Gemeinschaft, die versucht, eine nationale Sicherheit herzustellen, indem sie auf Wissen verzichtet und dieses einem Rechtsstaat überlässt, der im Interesse des Staatswohls rechtsfreie Zonen einrichtet und dort Asylsuchende als Informationsquellen benutzt. Diese Konstruktion ziehe ich in Zweifel.

Muhle__ Du sprichst auch von dem sehr spektakulären sogenannten „Curveball"-Fall, in dem genau diese Geheimdiensttechnik der Befragung von Geflüchteten tatsächlich einen globalen Einfluss entfaltet, insofern die Befragung dieses Asylsuchenden, der den Decknamen „Curveball" erhielt und dann in einer Münchner BND-Tarnfirma arbeitete, dazu geführt hat, dass die US-Armee die Ergebnisse dieser Befragung als Begründung für ihren Angriff auf den Irak verwendete.

Wanner__ Ja, das finde ich deshalb so bezeichnend, weil die Aussagen von Curveball eben falsch waren, aber trotzdem oder gerade deshalb geheimdienstlich relevant. Die Begründung der USA für einen militärischen Angriff auf den Irak bezieht sich auf Aussagen, die faktisch keine Verbindung zur Realität zeigen. Der dann folgende Krieg ist aber real. Die gemeindienstliche Kulturtechnik als Wahrheitsproduktionsmaschine, die ihre eigenen Wahrheiten produziert, wie du es beschrieben hast, zeigt sich hier sehr deutlich.

Muhle__ Eine andere spektakuläre Aufdeckung im Rahmen deiner Recherchen ist die Geschichte mit den Funkanlagen am Marienplatz, in der Frauenkirche. Das ist ja auch sofort aufgenommen worden von der Presse. Ich glaube, man sollte unbedingt unterscheiden zwischen dieser Aufdeckungs- oder Aufklärungslogik und deiner Arbeit, die sehr viel subtiler vorgeht und der es eben nur zweitrangig um Offenbarungen geht. Es ist natürlich interessant und medienwirksam, sich zu fragen, was die katholische Kirche von dieser Abhöranlage wusste. Und die Gemüter regen sich – auch zu Recht – darüber auf. Aber ich glaube wie gesagt, dass man zwei Zugriffe auf den Geheimdienstkomplex unterscheiden muss. Auf der einen Seite den des BND-Experten, der sich eben mit Geheimdienstfragen auskennt, und, wie du sagst, „Leute von innen" kennt. Hier scheint es einen ganz spezifischen Anspruch zu geben, dass etwas „aufgedeckt" wird, im Sinne von „Schaut mal, unter unseren Augen! Und dann auch noch im Kirchturm." Das führt zu einem gewissen Aha-Effekt und daran anschließend zum Glauben daran, dass man diese Missstände beheben kann und muss. Das hat beispielsweise ein *tz*-Artikel sehr deutlich veranschaulicht, in dem es um „Münchens Spitzelorte" geht, und oben auf der Seite kommt dann auch noch die „Kunstaktion" vor. Das ist also ein spektakularisierender Zugang, der diesen Enthüllungscharakter stärker in den Vordergrund stellt. Im Gegensatz dazu hat deine Arbeit einen anderen Anspruch, denke ich.

Wanner__ Ja, das stimmt. Trotzdem kann es natürlich Spaß machen, sich ein Spektakel auszudenken. Als „enthüllt" wurde, womit bis dahin wirklich niemand rechnen konnte, nämlich dass Gläubige durch Institutionen in ihrem Vertrauen missbraucht werden, gab es kurzfristig einen hohen Druck auf die Kirche und den BND. „Mein Gott, im Kirchturm sind geheime BND-Funkanlagen", und aus einer Panik heraus wurde die Ansage laut: „Sofort abbauen! Sofort abbauen!" So wurde in einer Nacht im März 2018 der ganze Nordturm der Frauenkirche abgebaut. Als sich das Missverständnis zeigte, wurde der Turm noch vor Tagesanbruch wieder hochgezogen. Das Foto, das ich von dem falschen Wahrzeichen mit nur einem Turm aufgenommen habe, habe ich nicht in meine Arbeit integriert, würde es aber exklusiv der Presse anbieten.
Ich habe mich in meiner Inszenierung gegen die Frauenkirche entschieden und stattdessen die „Hauptstelle für Befragungswesen" gewählt – einen Ort, an dem die Begrifflichkeiten, die mir als realitätsprägend erscheinen, viel deutlicher zutage treten. Dort treffen Geflüchtete, die Schutz suchen, auf einen Staat, der ein demokratisches Image pflegt. Die Asylsuchenden, auch Minderjährige, werden vom Geheimdienst in einem rechtsfreien Raum vernommen, in dem keine demokratischen Regeln gelten. Es werden Informationen zur nationalen Sicherung auf der einen Seite gegen eine Aufenthaltsgenehmigung und eventuell die Chance auf ein Leben auf der anderen Seite eingesetzt.

Muhle__ Ja, ich denke auch, das ist das viel grundlegendere Problem. Aber gerade um auf diesen Unterschied zwischen zwei Zugriffen hinzuweisen, finde ich das Spiel mit dem Spektakulären, das du inszenierst, so pointiert. Denn du thematisierst ja auch den Spektakelcharakter, den Traum von der Enthüllung geheimdienstlicher Operationen, aber man hat den Eindruck, dass deine Arbeit genau vor dieser Versuchung durch das Spektakel abbiegt, dass sie dieses also vor allem im Hintergrund mitlaufen lässt, um dann aber konkret auf die rassistischen und damit auch lebensgefährlichen Techniken des BND gegenüber Schutz suchenden Geflüchteten hinzuweisen. Es geht dir nicht um die Aufdeckung einer geheimdienstlich vernebelten Wahrheit, sondern darum zu zeigen, wie der Geheimdienst in diesem Fall mit Wahrheiten arbeitet, wie er sie operationalisiert. Wie Dinge einmal als wahr und dann wieder als unwahr dargestellt werden, um so mit ihnen arbeiten zu können; als „Wahrheit und Lüge im außermoralischen Sinne" (Friedrich Nietzsche), wenn man das bemühen möchte. Ich fand das sehr interessant, wie sich diese Divergenz auch in der Presselandschaft noch mal abgebildet hat. Auf der einen Seite gab es einen Beitrag der *tz*, die unter dem Motto arbeitet: „Tauchen Sie ein in die Welt der Spione." Und auf der anderen Seite einen *taz*-Artikel, der versucht, sich dem Thema über die Lektüre des Buchs *Die Kunst der Revolte* von Geoffroy de Lagasnerie (2015) zu nähern.

Wanner__ Der *taz*-Artikel von Luise Glum ist eine ernsthafte Auseinandersetzung, sie zeigt die Möglichkeit, sich an einem Diskurs zu beteiligen. Den *tz*-Artikel zu lesen, habe ich noch nicht geschafft, weil ich nicht weiß, wo ich einsteigen soll. Das Layout hat versucht, mich abzuwehren.

Muhle__ Ich würde gerne noch mal spezifisch auf die ästhetische Strategie zurückkommen, und ich denke, das verbindet sich auch mit der Frage nach den unterschiedlichen Zugriffen – also einem aufklärerisch-spektakulären versus einen fragmentarisch-dokumentarischen. Man könnte ja tatsächlich sagen, dass es sich um ein Reenactment handelt oder um eine Nachstellung einer Übungssituation. Und dann würde man klassischerweise sagen, dass Reenactments oder Nachstellungen ästhetische Praktiken sind, die immersive Situationen herstellen, in denen man sich mit dem, was passiert, identifizieren kann, etwas erneut durchleben und dadurch eine einfachere und klarere Kenntnis dessen bekommen kann, was da passiert ist. Bei dir ist das Gegenteil der Fall. Hier wird auf ästhetischer Ebene nochmals ein Bruch eingeführt, insofern eine quasi-immersive Strategie benutzt, nicht um Identität herzustellen, sondern um Ent-Identifizierung oder Fragmentarisierung hervorzurufen. Das gilt natürlich auch für die interaktiven Elemente in der Situation. Man wird quasi dazu gedrängt, immer wieder Rekontextualisierungen vorzunehmen, aus den Fragmenten, die einem präsentiert werden, aus den verschiedenen Anknüpfungspunkten unterschiedliche Narrationen zu bauen, die sowohl die Funktion des Geheimdienstes im Allgemeinen, aber auch die spezifischen Informationen betreffen, die einem in der nachgestellten Situation mitgeteilt werden, beispielsweise über die Verwendungsmöglichkeiten von Handynummern für die Zielvorgaben von Kampfdrohnen.

Wanner__ Um die Inszenierung auf diese Art zu realisieren, hat es mir geholfen, erst einmal bestimmte normalisierte Abläufe und Mechanismen zu beobachten und dann auseinanderzunehmen. Eine der Methoden der Inszenierung würde ich darin sehen, die recherchierten Komponenten, die in einer gewohnten Zusammensetzung einem mehrheitlich als normal empfundenen Zustand entsprechen – wie zum Beispiel der Annahme, nicht transparente Staatsstrukturen wären notwendig, um vor Gefahr zu schützen –, auf eine Art zu montieren, die diese tradierte Vorstellung um ihre Selbstverständlichkeit bringt. Ein bestimmtes Verhältnis aus Demontage und neuer Anordnung als nicht geschlossene Erzählzone, die die Zuschauer*innen auf eine bestimmte Art involviert, kann diese sogenannte Normalität als fragwürdige Konstruktion aufscheinen lassen. Mich interessiert es, darüber sprechen zu können, wer Teil der produzierten Wahrheiten ist und wer ausgeschlossen bleibt. Mich interessiert die Frage, in wessen Interessen eine Wahrheit produziert wird.

Muhle__ Das ist eben ein grundlegender Unterschied. Es geht natürlich auch hier um Wahrheit, es geht auch hier um Dokumente, die einen spezifischen Wahrheitsgehalt haben, aber was genau dieser Wahrheitsgehalt ist und wie er produktiv erzeugt wird, ist verhandelbar. Das ist es, was in dieser Arbeit ausgestellt wird. Das Operieren dieser Wahrheitsproduktion, darin würde ich das kritische Moment oder auch das ästhetisch-politische Moment der Arbeit verorten, insofern hier eine mögliche Konstellation von Wirklichkeitsfragmenten vorgeführt wird, die eben auch immer anders konstelliert werden können.
Zuletzt würde ich gerne fragen, warum du eine Schulungssituation darstellst. Die Arbeit heißt *Die Befragung*, aber es wird keine Befragung dargestellt, sondern die Übung zu einer Befragung. Es wird also quasi eine weitere Metaebene oder Medialisierung, damit auch eine weitere mediale Verunsicherung eingezogen. Ich musste an Harun Farockis *Immersion* (2009) denken. Bei *Immersion* ist es ja so, dass man erst zum Schluss versteht, dass es eine Übungssituation ist. Man hat eigentlich die ganze Zeit den Eindruck, das wäre die „reale" Situation, es ist aber eine Übungssituation. Und hier – und das fand ich bei dir eigentlich besser gelöst – ist es von Anfang an klar, dass es eine Übung ist, und daher gibt es auch nicht diesen Aha-Effekt, der so eine Arbeit dann letztendlich doch immer wieder in einen Aufklärungsmodus einschreibt.

Wanner__ Das ist ein Moment, das mich früher sehr gereizt hat, dieses Behaupten, und dann stimmt es nicht. Aber das verwende ich mittlerweile kaum noch. Ich habe eine Schulungssituation deshalb ausgewählt, weil in ihr deutlich wird, welche Form von Wahrheit, von Exklusivität und Realitätsproduktion dort erlernt werden soll. Denn nach der erfolgreich absolvierten Schulung wird es darum gehen, das Gelernte als Normalität anzuwenden. Ein großer Teil der Gesellschaft würde diese geheimdienstliche Arbeit erst mal als normal anerkennen und sie als Schutz empfinden. Diese Wahrnehmung von Normalität ist nicht angeboren, so wie auch eine Nationalität nicht angeboren ist, sondern beide werden hergestellt. Leute zu inszenieren, die diese Herstellung von nationaler Normalität lernen und lehren, ist zur Analyse gut geeignet, weil ihre Konstruiertheit dabei anschaulich wird. In der Inszenierung gibt es diese Stelle, die du schon erwähnt hast, in der davon gesprochen wird, dass die theoretische Nutzbarkeit von Handynummern zur Zielerfassung von Kampfdrohnen mit absoluter Verschwiegenheit zu behandeln sei. Für Neulinge kann das verstörend wirken oder Zweifel hervorrufen. Diese labile Stelle im Konstrukt wird von der Schulungsleitung sofort didaktisch aufgefangen: „Wenn Ihnen manche Fragen ungewohnt vorkommen, machen Sie sich bewusst, dass Ihre Arbeit dem Vorsorgeterrorismus dient und für unser Staatswohl von allerhöchstem Nutzen ist." Das Staatswohl zeigt sich als der letzte gerade noch als demokratisch haltbare Knotenpunkt in einem Netz, das ab dort in einer „trüben Zone" (de Lagasnerie) verschwindet, in der kein Bezug mehr möglich ist – das Ende der Transparenz, das Ende der Demokratie, mitten im Deutschland der Gegenwart.

Muhle__ Ja, das ist genau der Punkt, an dem die Normalisierungstechniken einsetzen. Das finde ich extrem spannend, die Einsicht, dass eben nicht Spektakularisierung das Problem der Stunde ist, sondern vielmehr die Normalisierung – vor allen wenn man sieht, was alles „normal" gesagt werden kann, wird deutlich, wie gefährlich diese Produktion von Normalitäten und damit von Annehmbarkeiten sein kann. Deswegen finde ich es sowohl ästhetisch als auch politisch viel interessanter, auf diese Banalisierungs- und Normalisierungsstrategien von Ausnahmemomenten hinzuweisen, anstatt sie zu re-spektakularisieren.

Die Befragung, Szenenansicht, 2018, siehe Seite 66
Scene from *The Interrogation*, 2018, see page 76

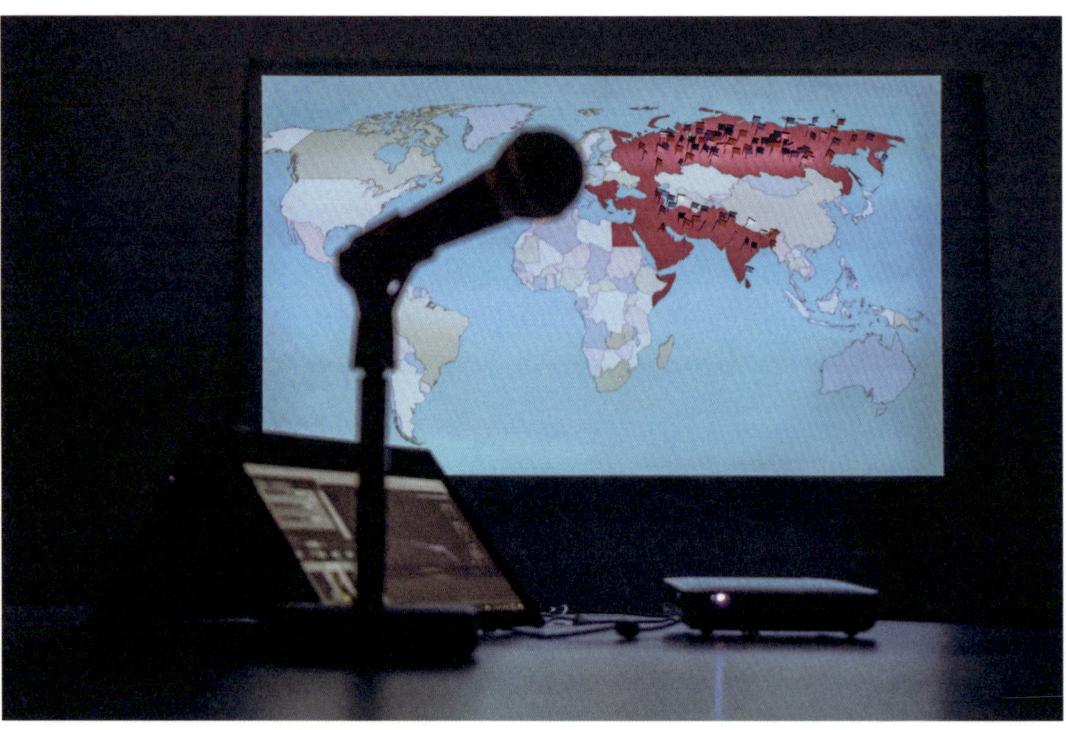

Maria Muhle and Franz Wanner

The Interrogation – A Conversation

Muhle__ Your work is concerned with questions regarding the Secret Service, a topic that inevitably arouses a great deal of concern. In your work, however, you investigate the Secret Service with regard to its concrete mechanisms, operations, and techniques and/or procedures. We could say that you focus your attention on what might be considered everyday Secret Service cultural techniques. A cultural technique of this kind is perhaps somewhat unusual and relies on expressions like "state secrets" and "state of emergency." It could be described as a sort of machinery for the production of truth, whose task is ostensibly to reveal concealed truths but which also produces its own truths at the same time. I would therefore like to start with a question regarding the type of documents that were important for you, and also ask how you built these documents into the performance processes of your work? You said that the final report of the NSA investigation committee was one of your sources, but that you had other sources as well. So my question would be: What kind of documentary logic lies behind this work, and to what extent is it combined with the specific presentation logic of the work?

Wanner__ On the one hand, I'm interested in documents like the one you referred to, but also the CIA document "Memorandum for the Record. Subject: CATIDE Cover Firms," which reveals Secret Service locations, as well as parliamentary questions, in other words, documents that are mostly in the public domain. It isn't always necessary to stage a break-in or use leaked information, but there are general ways of approaching this which one finds when pursuing a subject of interest. And then I also speak with people who have different viewpoints on the subject I'm currently working on. During the process in which *The Interrogation* (2018) was taking shape, these were

Gürsoy Doğtaş, Kurator des diskursiven Programms von Public Art Munich 2018, bei der Einführung zum Künstlergespräch zwischen Maria Muhle und Franz Wanner, 20. Juli 2018, Café-Bar 404–page not found, München

Gürsoy Doğtaş, curator of the discursive program of Public Art Munich 2018, during the introduction to the artist talk between Maria Muhle and Franz Wanner, July 20, 2018, Café-Bar 404–page not found, Munich

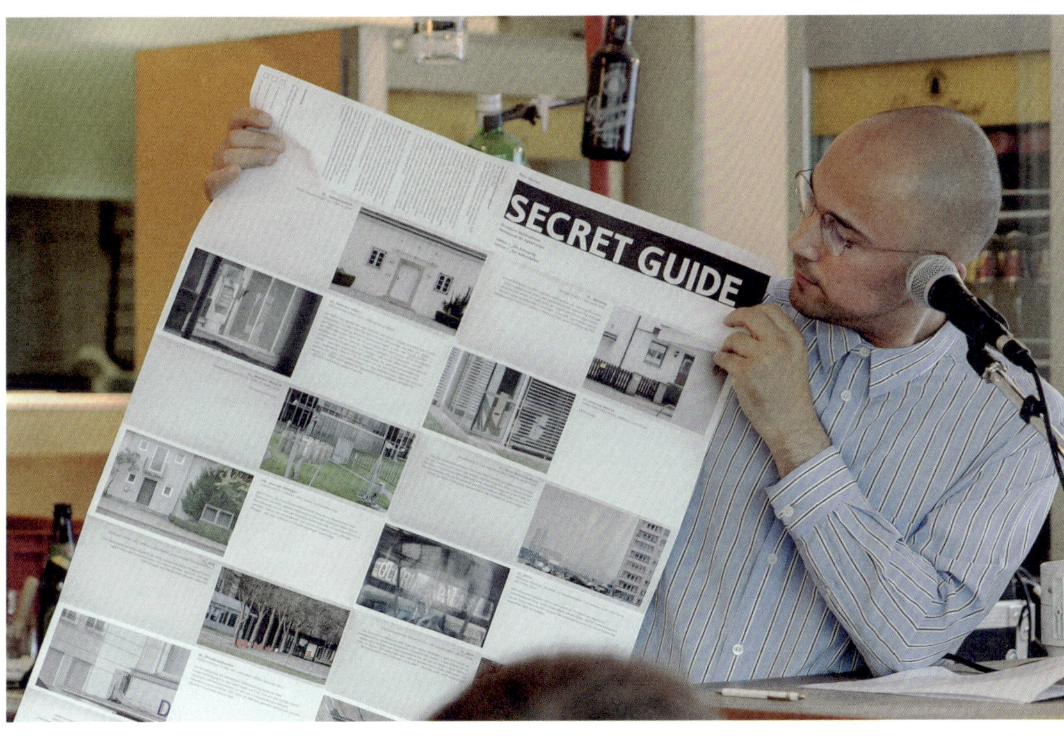

people who had experienced interrogations, or lawyers who represent refugees. Within the framework of my work, Public Art Munich also engaged a secret service expert who researched additional material for me, such as training documents of the Federal Intelligence Service (BND). The documents that were researched as such do not play a part in the dramatization, however. Instead, I tried to extract individual fragments and to reassemble them in order to develop a narrative structure. By using the example of the cover passports given to the participants during the play, it's possible to show the logic behind the dramatization quite clearly: according to the final report of the NSA investigation committee, members of foreign secret services interrogated asylum seekers in the name of the German Federal Republic and with the knowledge of the BND. Because secret services are called upon to represent the interests of their own state, and it therefore cannot officially be in the interest of the Federal Government for secret services of other countries to carry out independent interrogations in Germany's name, the BND provided the French, British, and American interrogators with German cover passports. During the play, the recipients playing the part of BND trainees are given special cover passports whose photos feature their own faces. I researched secret service practices like this and drew up a teaching plan for BND trainees, on which the dramatized training session is based. I'm not concerned here about the moment of revelation of these practices; my main aim is to create access and to name things, independently of whether the documents are publicly available or become public as a result of whistleblowing. Only then is it possible to create a narrative about the connections and place them in a discursive context. I'm not really that interested in achieving a higher degree of truth through "real" facts which have been made accessible. Instead, I try to put the fragments within a context and to create layers so as to record a complexity I see in this constellation in which we live, and which is regarded as normal: a community trying to create national security by dispensing with knowledge and leaving it to a state of law that establishes extralegal zones in the interests of the public good and uses asylum seekers as sources of information. It is this construction that I call into question.

Muhle__ You also speak about the highly spectacular, so-called Curveball case, in which precisely this secret service technique for the interrogation of refugees actually developed a global influence. The interrogation of this particular asylum seeker, who was given the cover name Curveball and then worked in a BND cover firm in Munich, actually led to the United States Army using the results of the interrogation as the reason for their attack on Iraq.

Wanner__ Yes, I find it all the more significant because the statements made by Curveball were false, but were nonetheless—or perhaps for that very reason—of relevance to the Secret Service. The US justification for a military attack on Iraq was based on statements that bore no relationship to reality, factually speaking. But the war that followed was very real. Here, we can clearly see the cultural technique of the Secret Service, as you described it, as a machine for the production of truth, albeit one that then produces its own truths.

Muhle__ Another spectacular revelation during the course of your research was the story of the radio installation inside Munich's cathedral, the Frauenkirche, at Marienplatz. That was also taken up immediately by the press. I think we should certainly distinguish between the logic of this exposure or revelation and your work, which proceeds much more subtly and in which the revelations are only of secondary importance. It is, of course, interesting and media-effective to ask oneself what the Catholic Church knew about these listening devices. People are concerned about it—and rightly so. But as I said, I believe that we must distinguish between the two attacks on the Secret Service complex. On the one hand, that of the BND expert who knows about Secret Service matters and, as you said, knows people "on the inside." There seems to be a specific demand here that something should be "exposed," in the sense of "Look! Under our very eyes! And in the church tower, of all things!" That leads to a certain "aha effect" and then consequently to the belief that we can and must eradicate these abuses. That was shown very clearly, for example, in an article in the Munich daily *tz* about "Munich's spy locations," which had a report at the top of the page about the "art action." That's a sensationalizing approach which focuses the spotlight more brightly on the question of exposure. In contrast to that, your work makes other claims, in my opinion.

Wanner__ Yes, that's true. Even so, it can be amusing to think up some spectacle. When the "exposure" took place—something which until then absolutely no one had expected—namely that believers had been abused in their trust by the institutions, there was massive pressure on the Church and the BND for a short while. "My God! The BND has installed secret radio devices in the church tower," and people panicked and the demands became louder: "Take it down! Take it down

at once!" And so, one night in March 2018, the entire north tower of the Frauenkirche was dismantled. When it became clear that there had been a misunderstanding, the tower was rebuilt again before daybreak. In my work, I didn't include the photo I'd taken of the fake landmark with only one tower, but I'd be prepared to offer it exclusively to the press.
I decided against including the Frauenkirche in my dramatizations and chose instead the "Main Office of Interrogation"—a place where the conceptions which seem to me to affect reality can be observed much more clearly. There, refugees seeking protection encounter a state that cultivates a democratic image. The asylum seekers, some of them minors, are questioned by the Secret Service in a legal vacuum, in which democratic rules do not apply. Information affecting the interests of national security on the one hand is employed in exchange for a residence permit and possibly the chance of a life on the other.

Muhle__ Yes, I agree with you that that's the far more fundamental problem. But I find that the game with the sensational revelation that you stage is really pointed, especially when it's a matter of showing the difference between the two attacks. Because you also take up the character of the spectacle, the dream of unmasking Secret Service operations, but then we get the impression that your work turns away when faced with the temptation of the spectacle. In other words, that it allows it to continue to run along mainly in the background in order to point out specifically the racist and also the extremely dangerous techniques of the BND toward refugees seeking protection. You're not concerned with revealing a truth which has been obscured by the Secret Service, but with showing how the Secret Service worked with truth in this particular case, how it uses truth for its own purposes. How things that are seen to be true on one occasion are then declared to be untrue again on another, so that they can be made use of—as "truth and lies in a non-moral sense" (Friedrich Nietzsche), if you like. I found it very interesting how this discrepancy was then presented by the press in general. On the one hand, there was a contribution in the *tz* which ran under the heading "Dive into the world of spies," whereas an article in the Berlin daily *taz* attempted to approach the subject via a reading of Geoffroy de Lagasnerie's book *The Art of Revolt* (2015).

Wanner__ The *taz* article by Luise Glum is a serious examination of the subject and shows the possibility of participating in a discourse. I haven't yet managed to read the *tz* article because I don't know where to start. Its layout prevents me from getting into it.

Muhle__ I'd like to come back specifically to the aesthetic strategy, which I think is also linked to the question regarding the different attacks—in other words, an informal and spectacular one as opposed to a fragmentary and documentary approach. We could indeed say that it's about a reenactment or a repetition of an exercise. Traditionally, we would say that reenactments or repetitions are aesthetic practices that create immersive situations in which we can identify with what is happening, can relive an event and thereby gain a simpler and clearer knowledge of what has happened. For you, the opposite is the case. Here, another caesura is introduced on an aesthetic level, inasmuch as a quasi-immersive strategy is used not to create an identity, but rather to bring about a loss of identification or a fragmentation. That naturally also applies to the interactive elements in the situation. We're compelled, as it were, to repeatedly assign the fragments presented to us to a different context, to construct different narratives from the various points of contact, which apply both to the function of the Secret Service in general and to the specific information communicated to us in the reenacted situation, for example about the possibilities for the use of cellphone numbers to specify the targets of combat drones.

Wanner__ In order to realize the dramatization in this way, it helped me to observe, first of all, certain normalized procedures and mechanisms and then to dismantle them. I would see one of the methods of the dramatization as the way in which it presents the researched components. In a familiar arrangement, they correspond to a situation generally regarded as being normal, such as the assumption that nontransparent state structures are necessary in order to protect us from danger. Here, however, they're presented in such a way that it destroys the naturalness of this traditional image. A certain ratio of dismantling and rearrangement as an open narrative zone which involves the audience in a certain way can reveal this so-called normality to be a dubious construction. I'm interested in being able to speak about who forms part of the truths that have been produced, and who is excluded. I'm interested in the question as to whose interest is being promoted when a truth is produced.

Muhle__ That's a fundamental difference. Here, of course, it's a matter of the truth; here, we're talking about documents that contain a specific truthful content, but precisely what this truthful content is and how it is actually produced is a matter for negotiation. That's what's being shown in this work. I would locate the critical moment or the aesthetic-political momentum of the work in the operation of this production of the truth, inasmuch as a possible constellation of fragments of reality is presented here, but one that can be rearranged into an infinite number of constellations. Finally, I'd like to ask why you present us with a training situation. The work is titled *The Interrogation*, yet what it shows isn't an interrogation as such, but rather an exercise relating to an interrogation. In a way, this means that another meta-level or a medialization and hence a further medial destabilization is introduced. I found myself thinking of Harun Farocki's *Immersion* (2009), in which it's only at the very end that we understand that the scene represents a training situation. We had the impression all the time that it was a "real" situation, although it is in fact an exercise. But here—and I found that you came up with the better solution—it's clear from the very beginning that this is an exercise, and so we don't experience the "aha effect" that occurs when a work like *Immersion* ultimately switches into exposure mode again and again.

Wanner__ That's a moment that I used to find very tempting, making a statement that then turns out not to be true. But I hardly ever make use of it nowadays. I chose a training situation because it makes clear what sort of truth, exclusivity and production of reality is to be learned there. For once the training course has been successfully completed, it will be a matter of employing what has been learned as if it were normality. A large section of society would initially regard this Secret Service activity as normal and feel protected by it. This perception of normality is not something we're born with, in the same way as nationality is not innate; both are imposed by external circumstances. To present people who learn and teach this creation of national normality is well suited to analysis because its artificiality can be clearly seen in this way. In the dramatization, there's this place you've already mentioned in which the interrogator says that the theoretical possibility of using cellphone numbers to specify the targets of combat drones must be treated as a matter of absolute secrecy. For newcomers, that might seem distressing or evoke doubts. This precarious moment in the structure is immediately fielded by the Head of Interrogation in a didactic manner: "If some of the questions seem unusual to you, remember that your work is in the interests of preventive terrorism and immensely important for the well-being of the state." The public good is shown to be the last democratically tenable node in a network which from here on disappears into a "murky zone" (de Lagasnerie), in which no further connection is possible—the end of transparency, the end of democracy, right here in Germany, today.

Muhle__ Yes, that's the precise point at which normalization techniques switch in. I find it fascinating that the problem today is not so much the sensationalizing, but rather the normalization—especially when we see all the things that can be classed as "normal." It becomes clear how dangerous this production of normality and hence of acceptability can be. And that's why I find it much more interesting from both an aesthetic and also a political point of view to draw attention to these strategies of the trivialization and normalization of exceptional moments rather than making them into a spectacle yet again.

Der Spielort der Erstaufführung der Theaterperformance *Die Befragung* (2018) liegt im Münchner Bahnhofsviertel (Landwehrstraße / Goethestraße), wo sich die BND-Scheinfirma „Südtechnik“ zur Ausbildung von Agent*innen befand (siehe Cover, Nr. 61).

The premiere venue of the theatre performance *The Interrogation* (2018) is located in the area around Munich's central railway station (Landwehrstraße / Goethestraße), where the bogus BND company Südtechnik for the training of agents was located (see cover, no. 61).

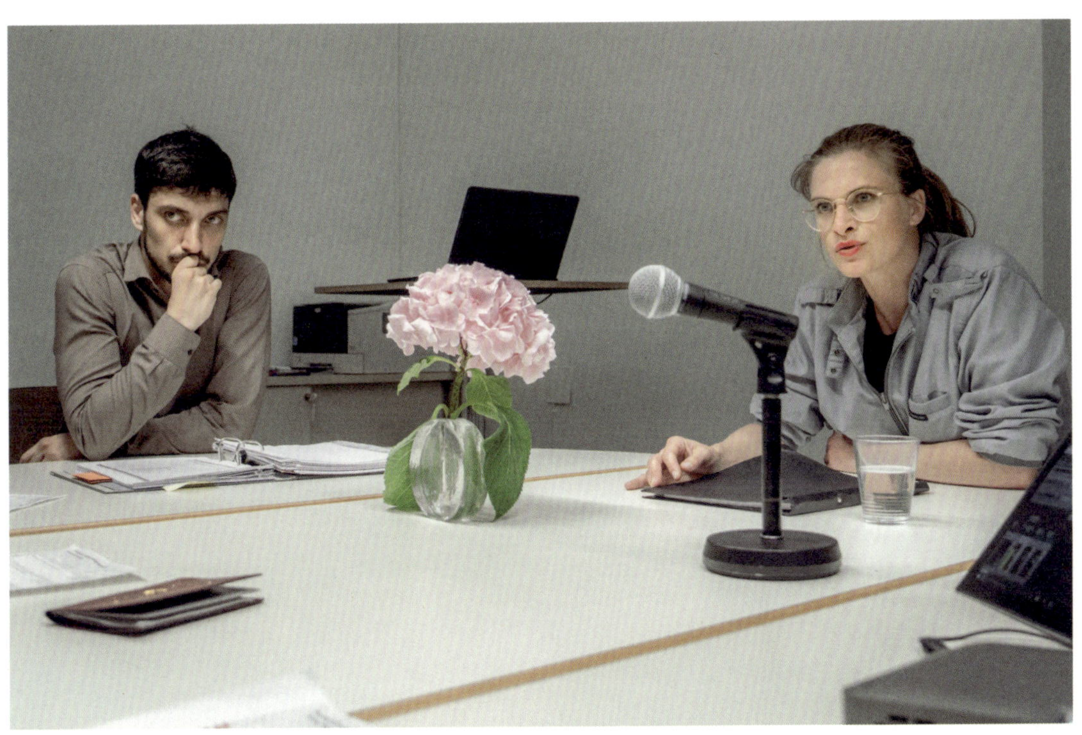

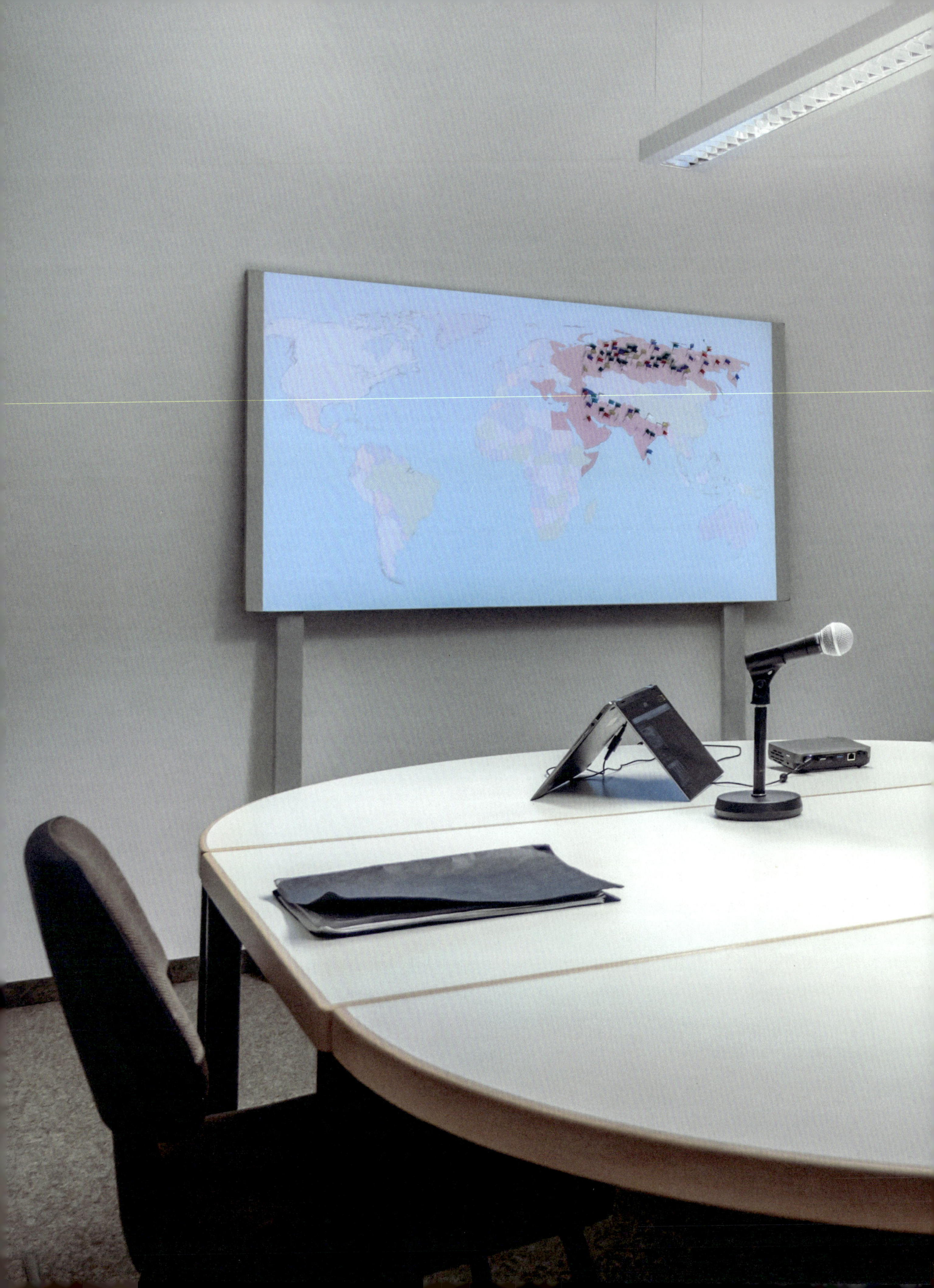

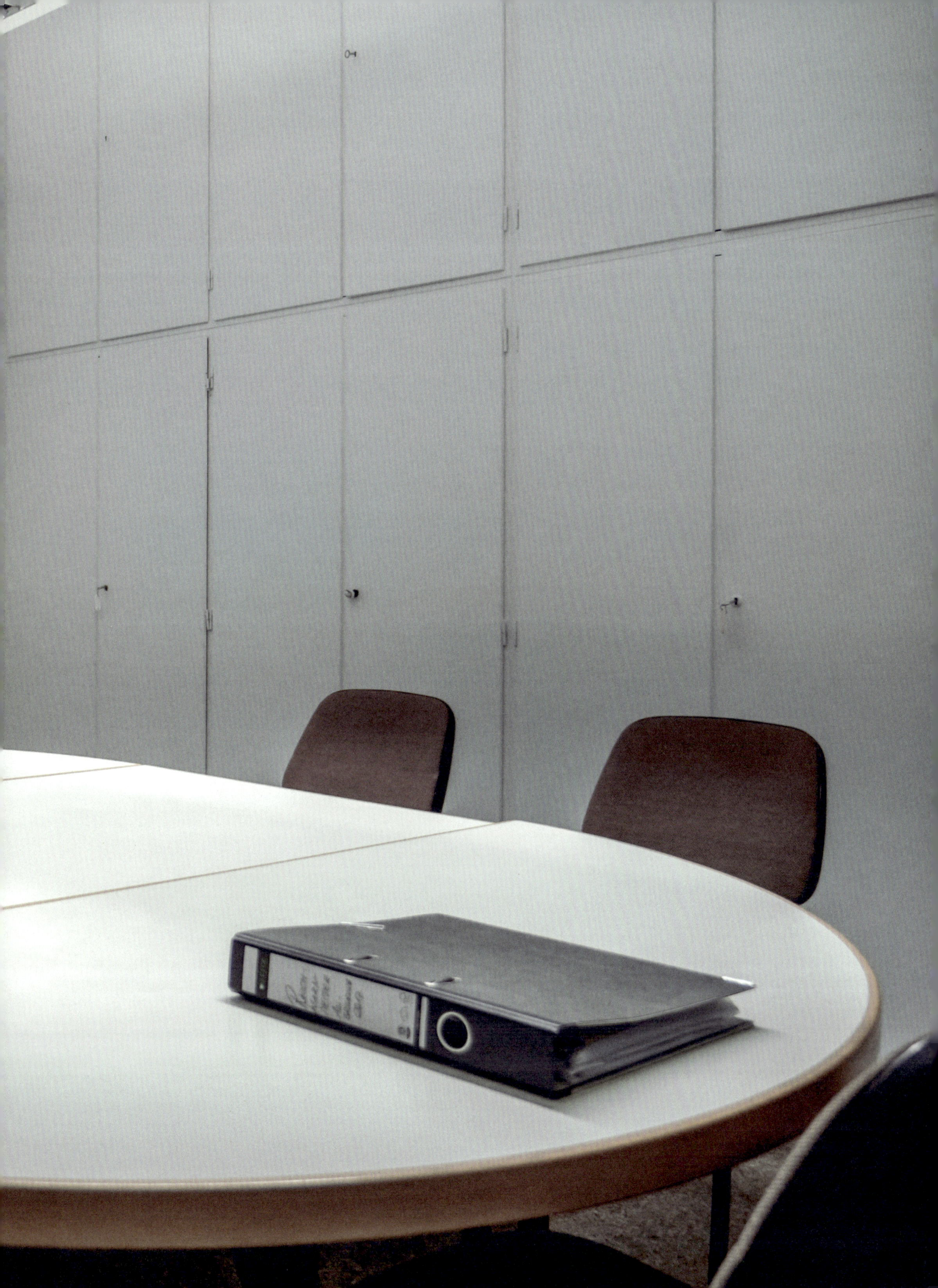

Secret Sites
Fotoreihe, Text-Bild-Konstellation, München, 2018
Photo series, text-image constellation, Munich, 2018

Kunst am Bau, Helene-Weber-Allee 23, *Transparenzoffensive*
Percent for art, Helene-Weber-Allee 23, *Transparency Offensive*

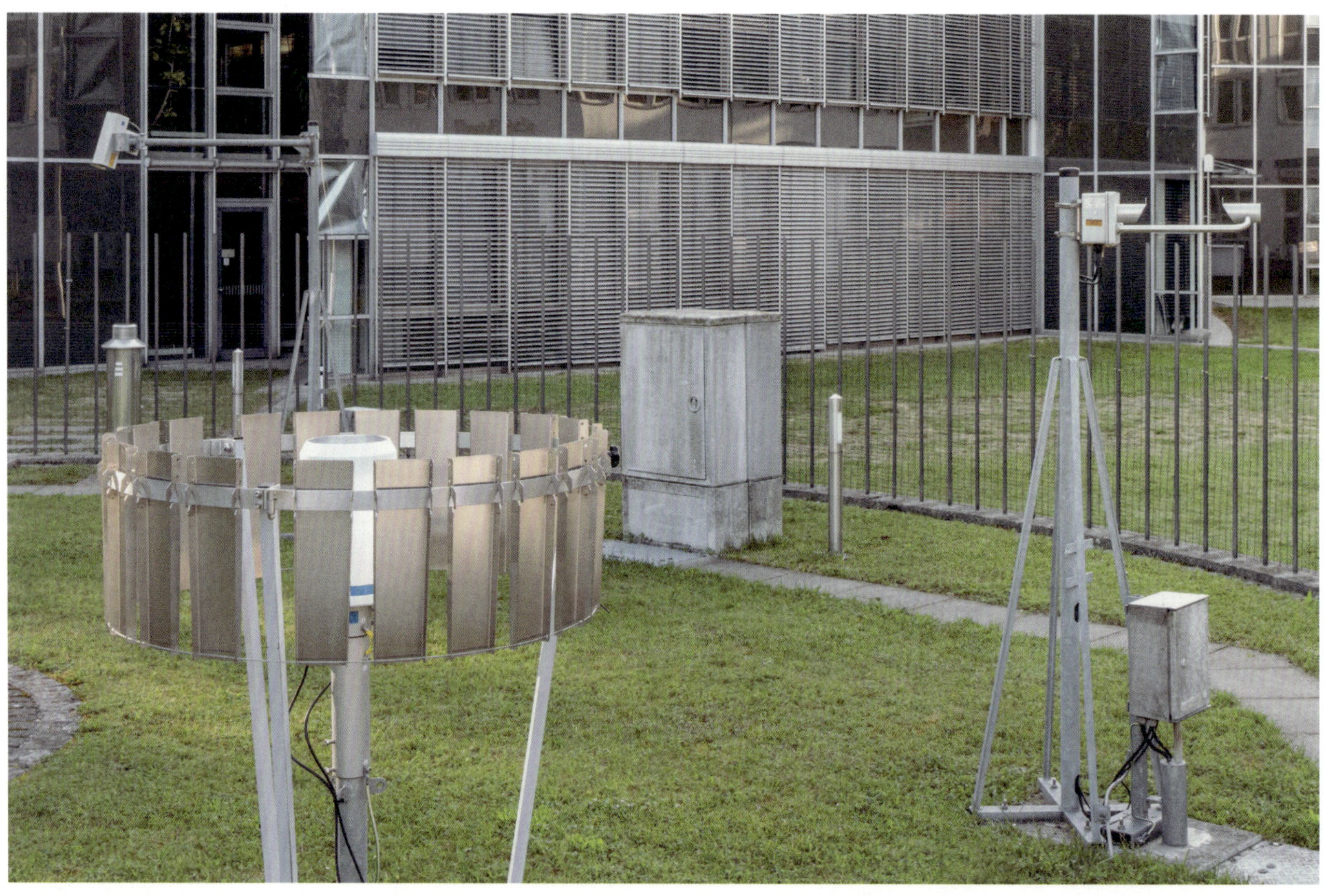

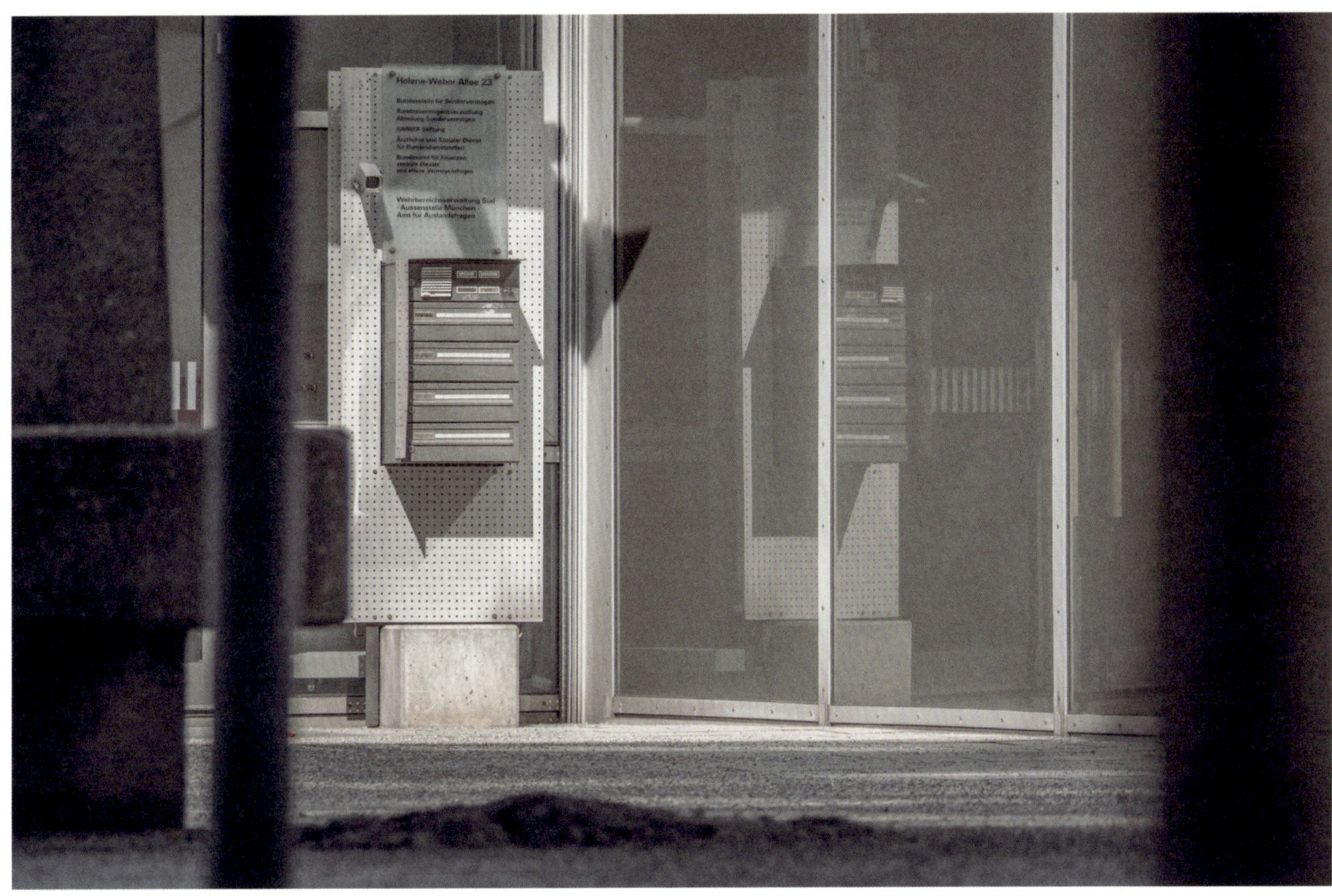

42__Deutsches Wetter
Helene-Weber-Allee 23

Seit ca. 2008
Die Wettermessgeräte vor dem Gebäude sind wie ein Gehege umzäunt. Hinter den spiegelnden Fassaden befinden sich mehrere Dienststellen des BND. Die „Bundesvermögensverwaltung, Abteilung Sondervermögen“ ist eine der Hauptlegenden von BND-Mitarbeiter*innen, die sie auch gegenüber dem Finanzamt als Arbeitgeber angeben. Die „Garner-Stiftung“ finanziert angeworbene Studierende und hilft verhafteten BND-Angestellten. Der „Ärztliche und Soziale Dienst für Bundesdienststellen“ behandelt angeschlagene Agent*innen. Die „Wehrbereichsverwaltung Süd – Außenstelle München“ ist vermutlich ein Sitz des Militärischen Abschirmdienstes. Das „Amt für Auslandsfragen“ ist ein Außenposten, dessen Direktorium um das Jahr 2000 mit Projekten zur Spracherkennung (Software *Sensus* für Europol) in Verbindung gebracht wurde.

42__German Weather
Helene-Weber-Allee 23

Since ca. 2008
The weather instruments in front of the building are fenced in like a compound. Behind the reflective facades are several offices of the BND. The “Federal Property Management Division, Special Assets” (Bundesvermögensverwaltung, Abteilung Sondervermögen) is one of the main covers of BND employees, which they also report as their employer to the tax office. The “Garner Foundation” finances recruited students and assists apprehended BND employees. The “Medical and Social Service for Federal Agencies” treats incapacitated agents. The “Military District Administration South – Branch Office Munich” is presumably a main office of the Military Counter-intelligence Service. The “Office for Foreign Issues” is a BND office whose directorate was connected around the year 2000 to language recognition projects (SENSUS software for Europol).

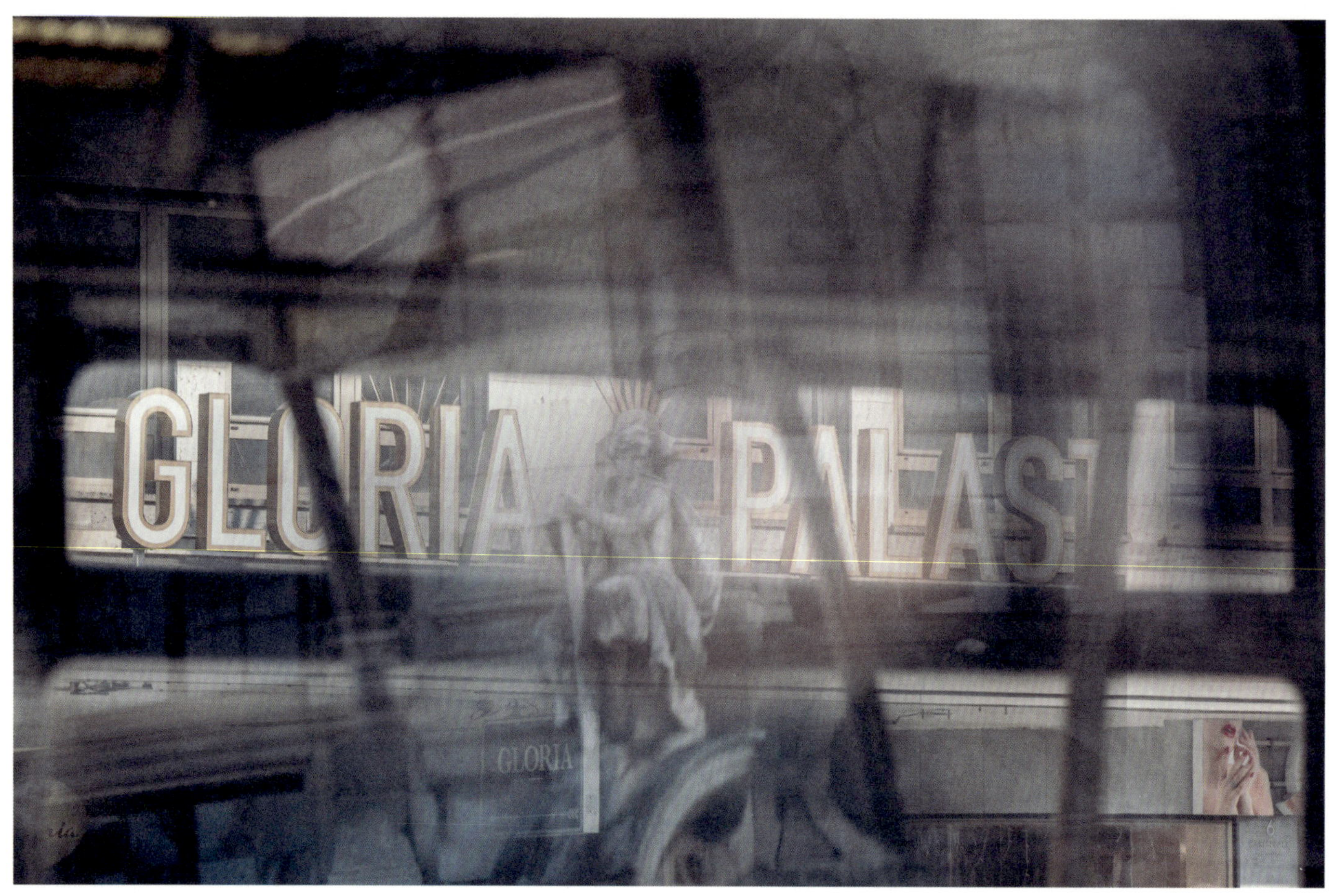

55__08/15
Karlsplatz (Stachus), mit weiteren Büros am Beethovenplatz 2 in Frankfurt am Main

1947 bis in die 1950er-Jahre
Die Central Intelligence Agency (CIA) verzeichnete die Gloria Filmverleih GmbH als Tarnfirma des deutschen Geheimdienstes (Org). Gloria-Heimatfilme wie die Reihe *08/15* liefen erfolgreich, bis der Junge Deutsche Film sie zum Verschwinden brachte. Der Gloria Palast liegt gegenüber dem Justizpalast.

55__08/15
Karlsplatz (Stachus), with further offices at Beethovenplatz 2 in Frankfurt am Main

1947 into the 1950s
The CIA listed the film distributor Gloria Filmverleih GmbH as a front company of the German Intelligence Service (Org). Gloria homeland films like the series "08/15" ran successfully until they were eclipsed by the New German Cinema. The Gloria Film Palace is located across from the Palace of Justice.

69__Befragungswesen
Maria-Theresia-Straße 16

1958 bis 2007
Hauptstelle für Befragungswesen (siehe Seite 66)

69__Interrogation
Maria-Theresia-Straße 16

1958 to 2007
Main Office of Interrogation (see page 76)

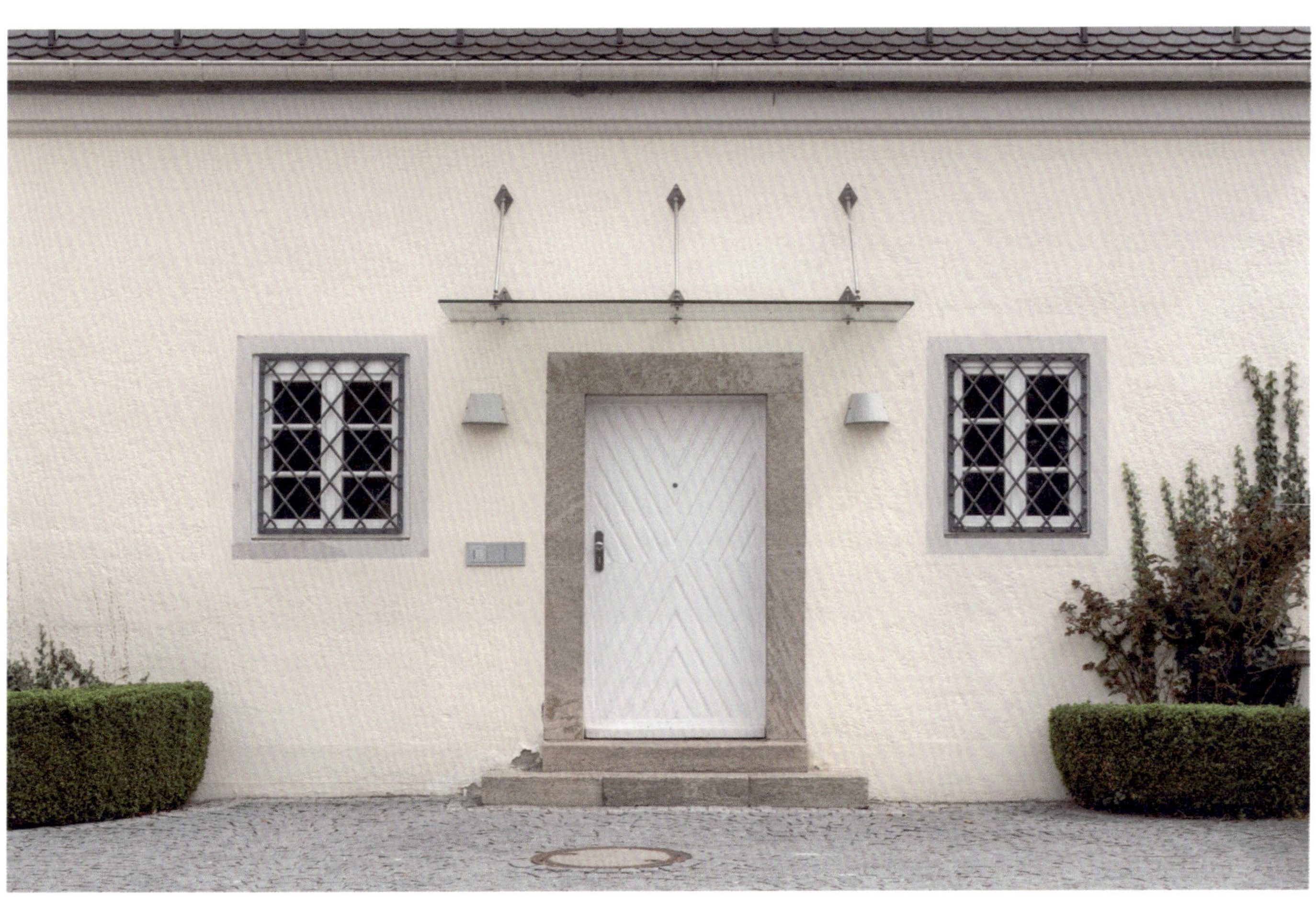

108__Bund der Unfähigen
Tangastraße 22

1981 bis 1994, später am Hauptbahnhof
Agent*innen, die ihren Sicherheitsbescheid etwa durch Alkoholismus oder Spielsucht verlieren, werden Mitglieder im „Bund der Unfähigen“ (BND-interne Bezeichnung). Um sie nicht an feindliche Geheimdienste als Informant*innen zu verlieren, werden sie weiterbezahlt und mit der Auswertung von „offenem Material“, wie dem Abhören von Radiosendungen, beschäftigt.

108__Coalition of the Unable
Tangastraße 22

1981 to 1994, later at the Central Train Station
Agents who lose their security clearance, for example through alcoholism or gambling, become members of the Coalition of the Unable (internal BND designation). In order not to lose them to hostile intelligence services as informants, they continue to be paid and are entrusted with the analysis of “freely available material,” such as listening in to radio transmissions.

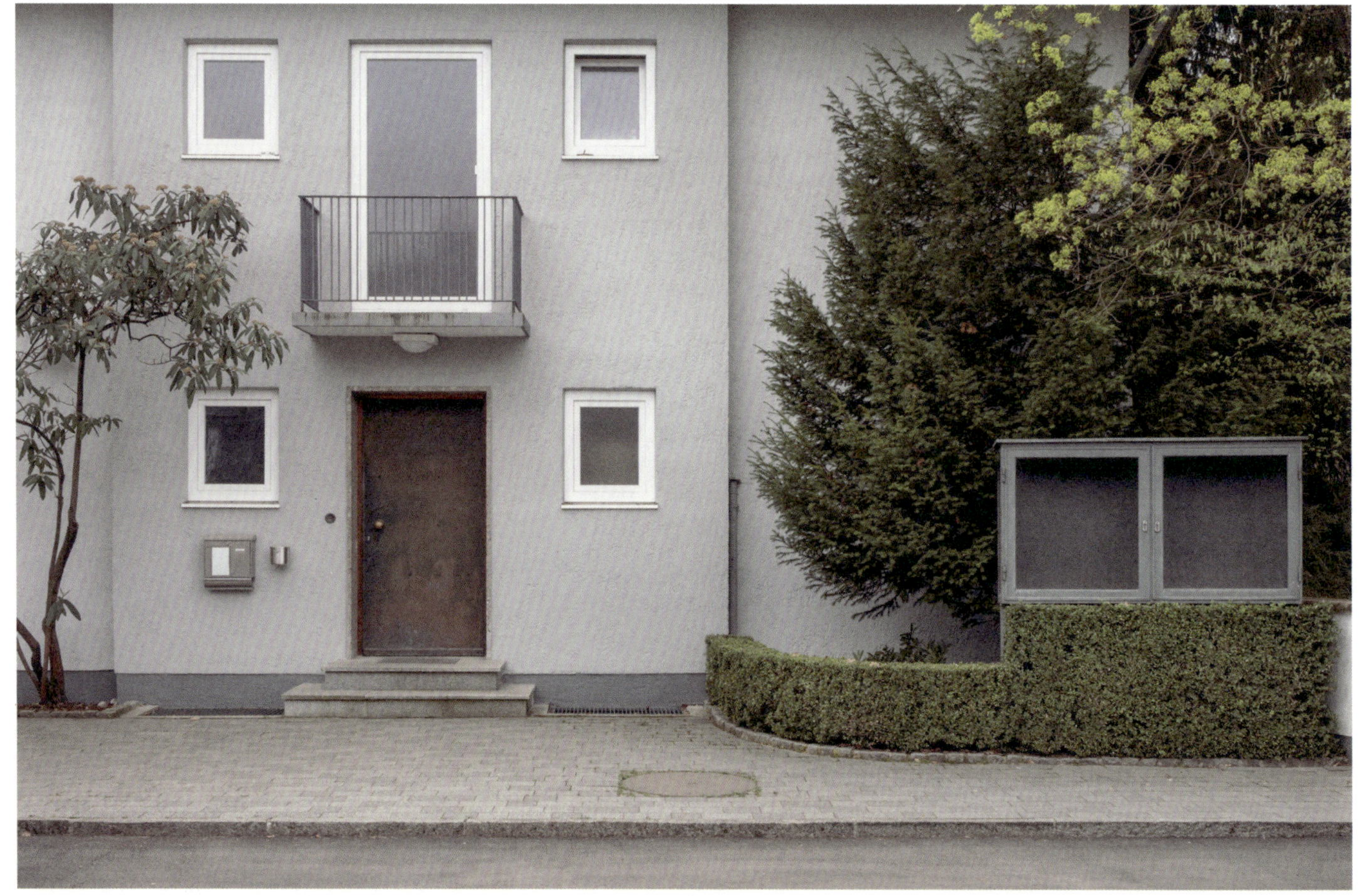

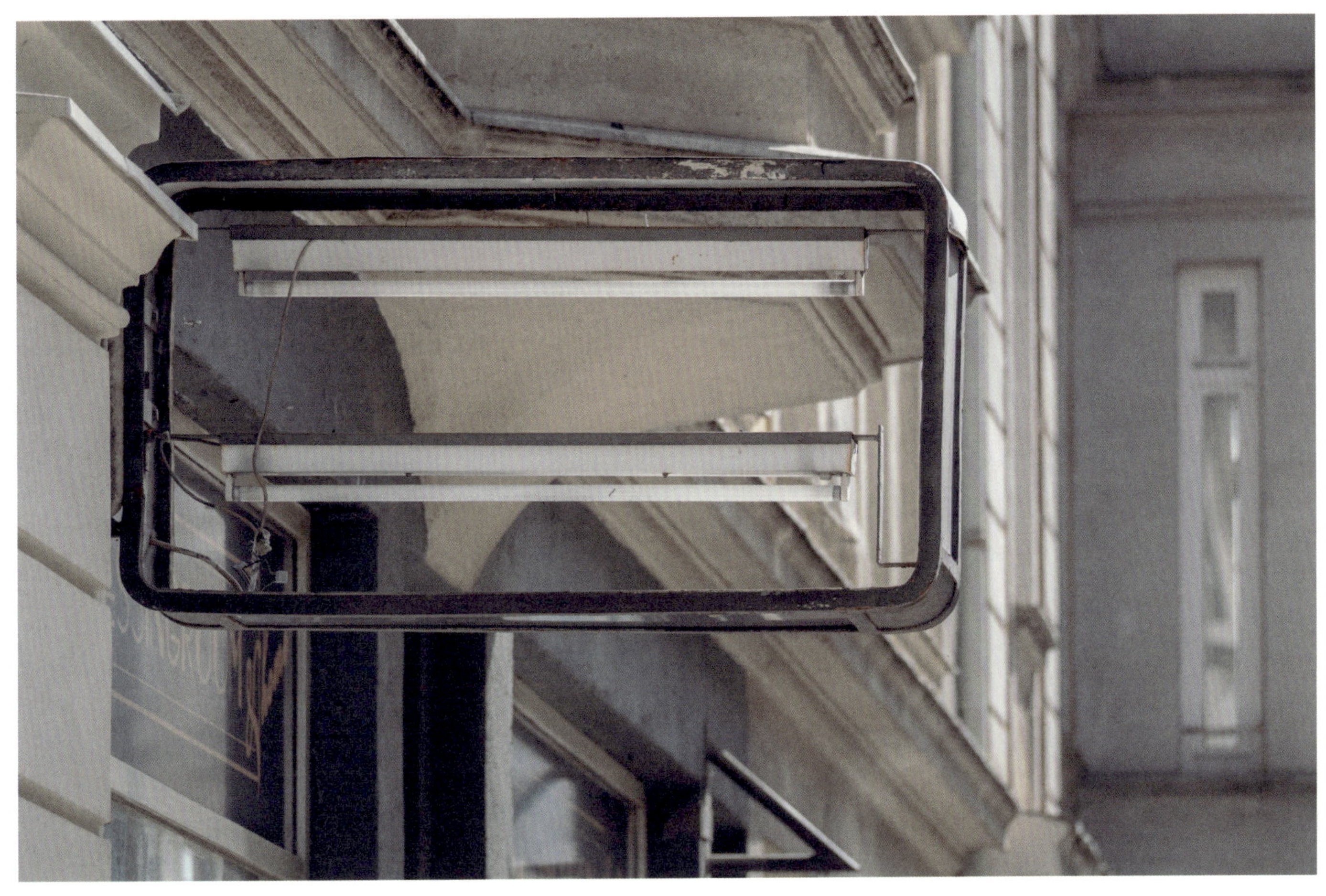

115__Akademie-Buchhandlung
Türkenstraße 58

1950er-Jahre
Die „Akademie-Buchhandlung" verkaufte keine Bücher. Sie war eine Scheinfirma des deutschen Geheimdienstes (Org). Die örtliche Nähe der Firma zur Kunstakademie und die damalige Ferne der Kunstakademie zur Theorie machten die Bezeichnung „Akademie-Buchhandlung" zu einem schwer entschlüsselbaren Code.

115__Akademie Buchhandlung
Türkenstraße 58

1950s
The Academy Bookstore did not sell books. It was a bogus company of the German Intelligence Service (Org). The company's close physical proximity to the art academy and the art academy's remoteness at the time from theory ensured that the code name "Akademie Buchhandlung" was difficult to crack.

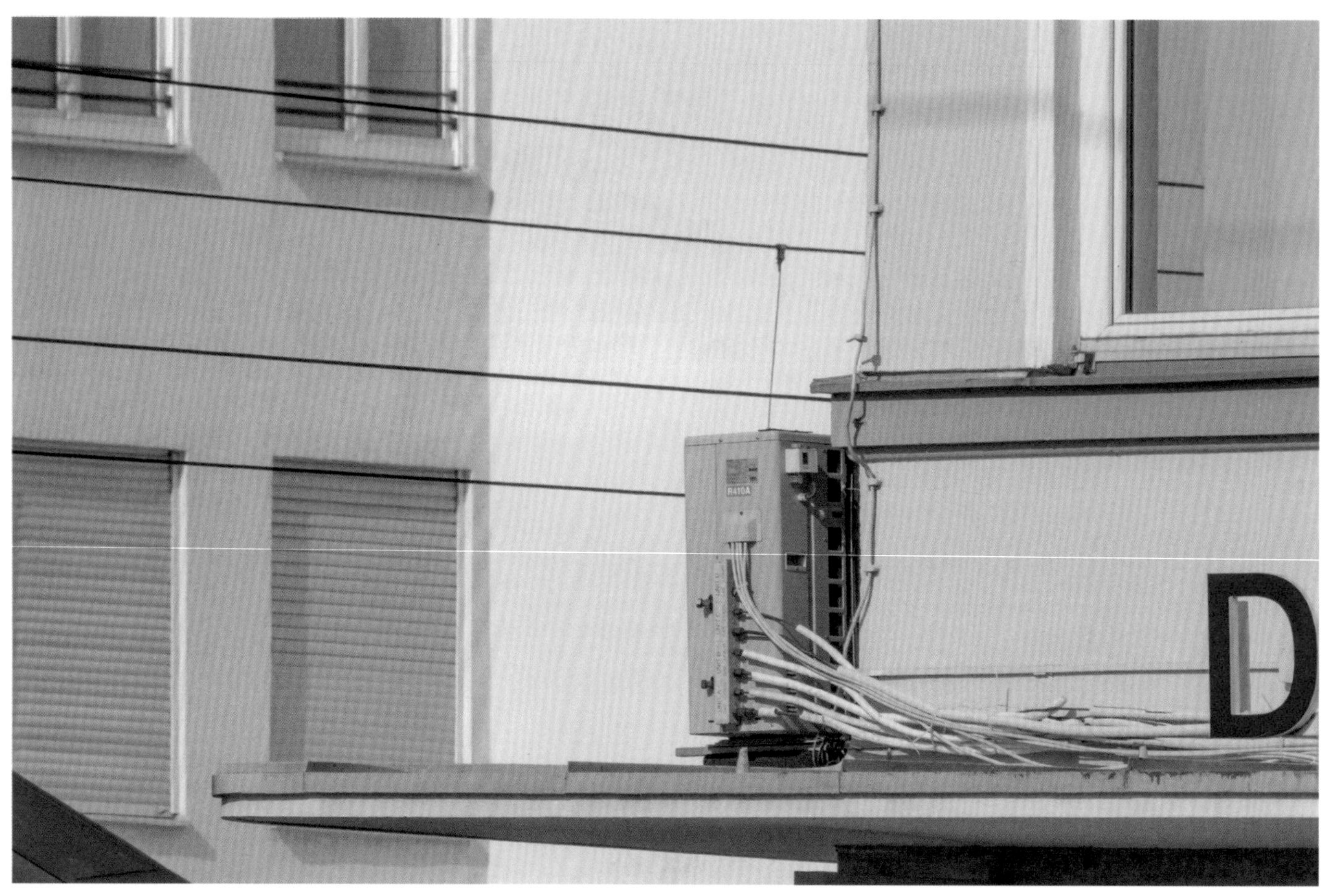

80__Öffentlichkeitsarbeit
Nymphenburger Straße 160

Vermutlich 1960er-Jahre bis 1972
Zur Beeinflussung der öffentlichen Wahrnehmung baute der BND Sonderverbindungen zu Journalist*innen auf. Eine Liste aus den 1970er-Jahren registriert 230 Medienkontakte, um die sich 35 Angestellte des Referats „Presseführung“ kümmerten. 1972 löste der BND das geheime Referat auf, um eine offizielle Pressestelle einzurichten.

80__Public Relations
Nymphenburger Straße 160

Presumably 1960s to 1972
To influence public perception, the BND established special relationships to journalists. A list from the 1970s registers 230 media contacts, who were taken care of by 35 employees of the department of press management. In 1972, the BND dissolved the secret department to set up an official press office.

16__Marketing
Eininger Straße 4

2010
In einer Befragung des Bundesnachrichtendienstes sagte ein Asylbewerber, der Irak baue Biowaffen. Seine Angaben waren falsch, aber geheimdienstlich relevant. Der BND gab sie an die USA weiter, die damit 2003 den Angriff auf den Irak begründeten. Der Asylsuchende erhielt den Codenamen „Curveball“ und arbeitete bei der Werbeagentur Thiele und Friedrichs Marketing GbR, einer Tarnfirma des BND.

16__Marketing
Eininger Straße 4

2010
During a BND interrogation, an asylum seeker said that Iraq was building biological weapons. His statements were false but relevant in terms of intelligence. The BND passed the information along to the US, which used it in 2003 as grounds for attacking Iraq. The asylum seeker was given the codename “Curveball” and worked at the ad agency Thiele und Friedrichs Marketing GbR, a front company of the BND.

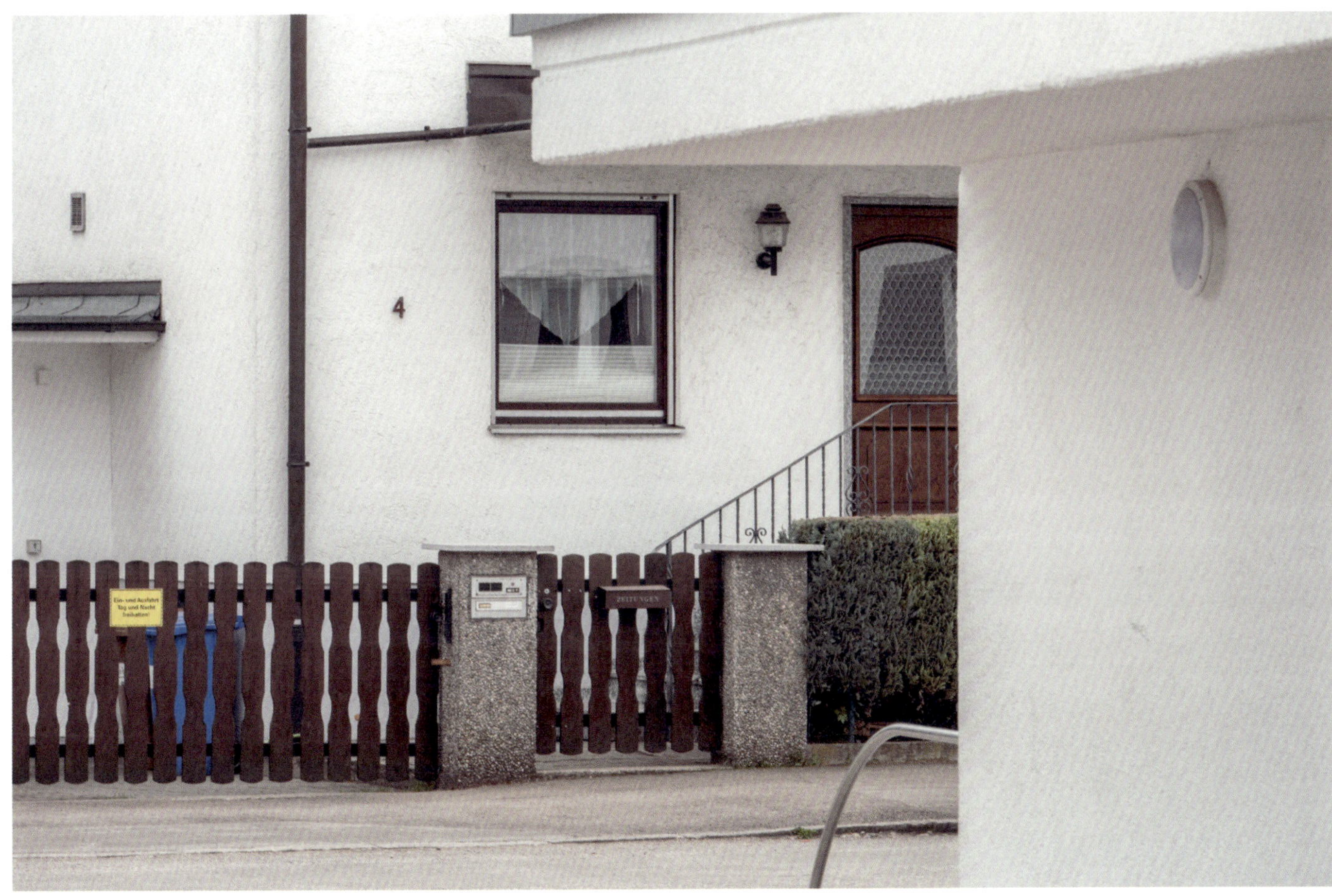

20__Schauspiel
Elsenheimerstraße 21

1971 bis 1981
Heidrun Hofer arbeitete in der Zentralstelle für Verkehrsgeographie der Bundeswehr. Bei einem Dienstaufenthalt in Paris verliebte sie sich in Hans Puschke. Er stellte sich der rechtsradikalen BND-Sekretärin als Mitarbeiter der Altnazi-Organisation „Überlebensträger" vor. Sie verriet ihm BND-Geheimnisse über NATO-Operationen. „Hans Puschke" war ein russischer Romeo-Agent und die Altnazi-Organisation „Überlebensträger" mit Sitz in Südamerika eine Erfindung des sowjetischen Geheimdienstes KGB. Heidrun Hofer lernte auch den Überlebensträger-Vorstand „Baron von Hohenstein" kennen. Der KGB-Agent Jurij Drosdow, der ihn verkörperte, hatte dafür Schauspielunterricht am Max Reinhardt Seminar genommen.

20__Theatrical Performance
Elsenheimerstraße 21

1971 to 1981
Heidrun Hofer worked at the Central Office for Transport Geography of the German Armed Forces (Zentralstelle für Verkehrsgeographie der Bundeswehr). During a period of service in Paris, she fell in love with Hans Puschke. He introduced himself to the radical right-wing BND secretary as a member of the die-hard Nazi organization "Überlebensträger." She disclosed BND secrets to him about NATO operations. "Hans Puschke" was a Russian "Romeo" agent and the die-hard Nazi organization "Überlebensträger," with its main office in South America, was an invention of the KGB. Heidrun Hofer also made the acquaintance of the Überlebensträger chairman "Baron von Hohenstein." The KGB agent Yuri Drosdov, who portrayed him, had taken acting lessons for the role at the Max Reinhardt Seminar.

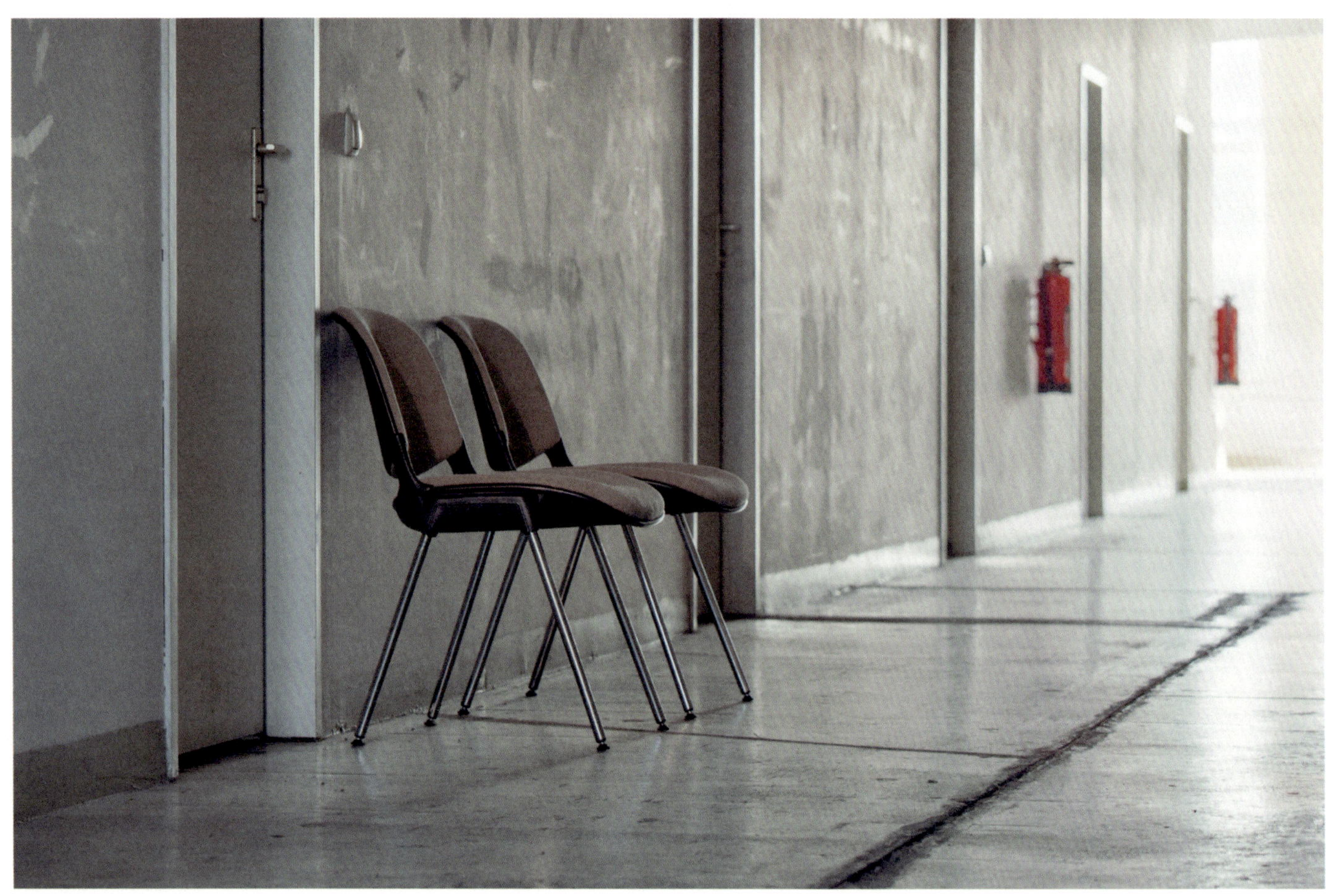

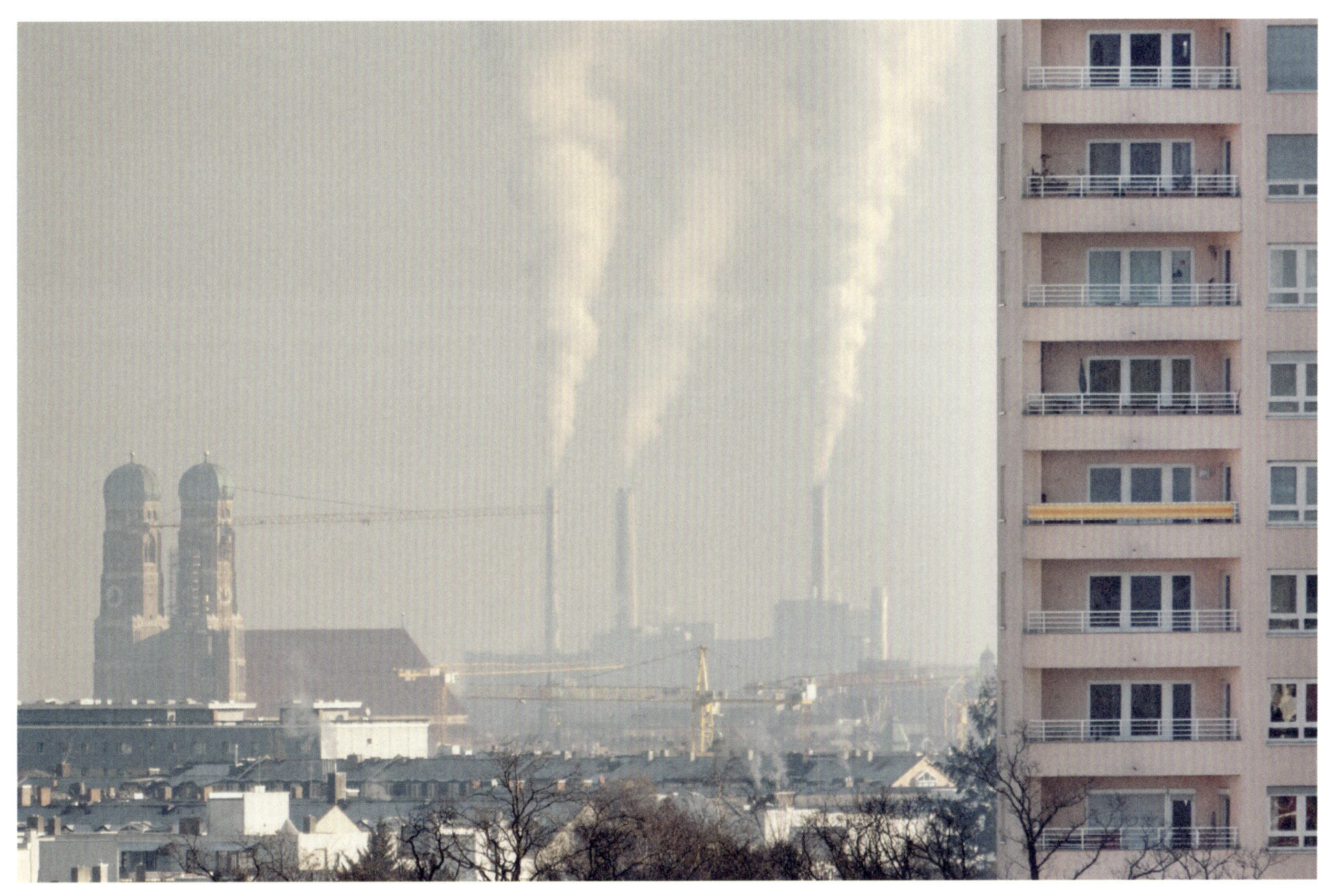

25__Secret Service Landmark
Frauenplatz 12

Seit vor dem Mauerfall (1989)
Das Observationskommando QB30 des BND betreibt zwei getarnte Funkkreise mit den Decknamen „Saturn“ und „Merkur“. Die Funkleitzellen sind im Nordturm der Münchner Frauenkirche untergebracht. Eine offizielle Anfrage von Public Art Munich beantwortete die Pressestelle des Erzbischöflichen Ordinariats am 2. März 2018: „Zu einer Einrichtung namens QB30 des BND ist uns nichts bekannt.“

25__Secret Service Landmark
Frauenplatz 12

Since before the fall of the Berlin Wall (1989)
The surveillance command QB30 of the BND operates two disguised radio stations with the cover names Saturn and Mercury. The radio relay stations are housed in the north bell tower of Munich's Frauenkirche. An official request for information by Public Art Munich was answered by the press office of the archiepiscopal chancery on March 2, 2018 as follows: “Nothing about an entity named QB30 of the BND is known to us.”

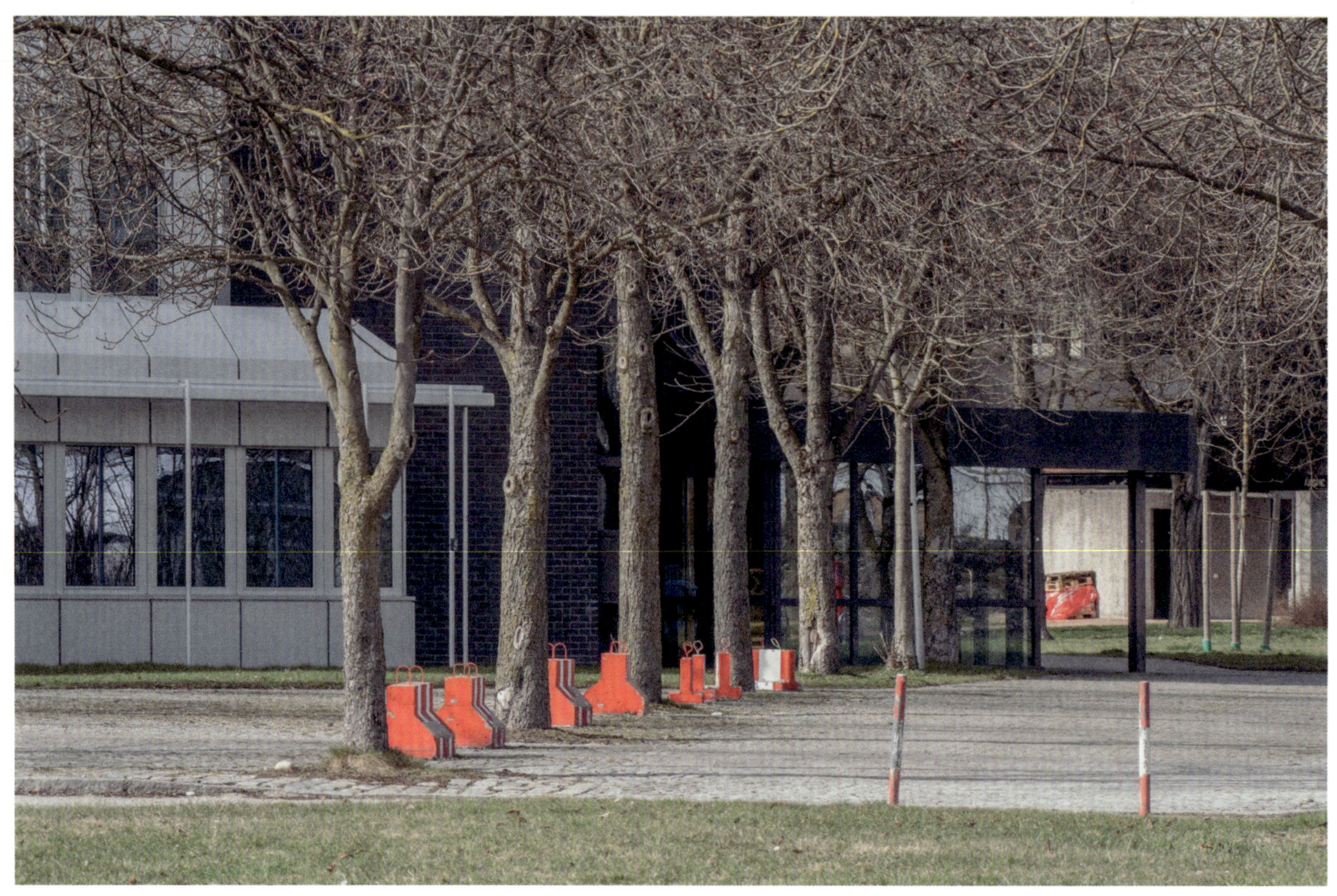

11__Saturn und Merkur
Dachauer Straße 128 (zuvor Hedwig-Dransfeld-Allee 6)

Seit 1996
Das Observationskommando QB30 des BND operiert unter dem Tarnnamen „Technische Revisionsstelle der Bundesverkehrsverwaltung“ und überwachte bisher Diplomat*innen, Agent*innen und Journalist*innen. Im selben Komplex befinden sich auch Einrichtungen des Militärischen Abschirmdienstes (MAD).

11__Saturn and Mercury
Dachauer Straße 128 (previously Hedwig-Dransfeld-Allee 6)

Since 1996
The surveillance command QB30 of the BND operates under the cover name “Technical Audit Office of the Federal Transport Administration” (Technische Revisionsstelle der Bundesverkehrsverwaltung) and has thus far conducted surveillance on diplomats, agents, and journalists. Facilities of the Military Counterintelligence Service (Militärischer Abschirmdienst: MAD) are located in the same complex.

48__Optik

Elsenheimerstraße 33 (vor 2012 in der Isartalstraße 39–43)

1950er-Jahre

Die Südamerika-Abteilung der Optischen Werke Rodenstock galt laut CIA als geheimdienstliche Sonderverbindung der Organisation Gehlen. In den 1920er-Jahren stellte das Unternehmen Kameraobjektive her, für das NS-Regime auch Zielfernrohre für Panzer. Die Geheimdienste anderer Staaten benennt der BND intern mit Blumennamen. Der Löwenzahn ist in dieser „Fleurop-Liste" noch nicht verzeichnet.

48__Optics

Elsenheimerstraße 33 (before 2012 at Isartalstraße 39–43)

1950s

According to the CIA, the South America department of the Rodenstock Optical Works was an informant of the Gehlen Organization. In the 1920s, the company manufactured camera lenses and also telescopic sights for tanks for the Nazi regime. The BND uses the names of flowers to refer internally to the intelligence agencies of other countries. The dandelion is not included in this "Fleurop List."

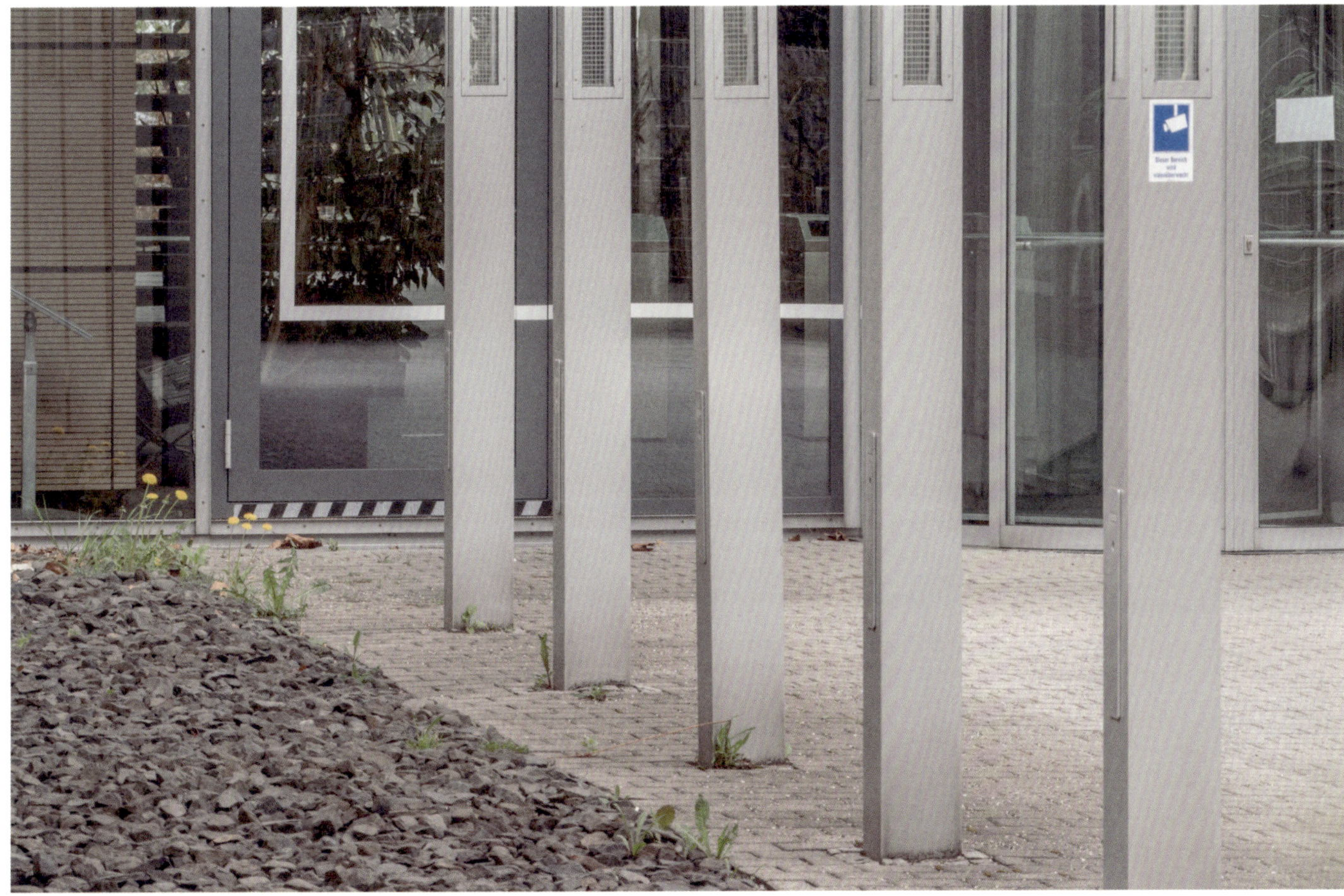

Im geheimdienstlichen Funkverkehr werden Signale oft temporär stark begrenzt gesendet (zum Beispiel einmal pro Woche für zwei Sekunden), um nicht erwünschten Empfänger*innen den Informationszugang zu erschweren.

In secret service radio communications, signals are often transmitted for a very limited period of time (for example once a week for two seconds) in order to make it difficult for unwanted recipients to access information.

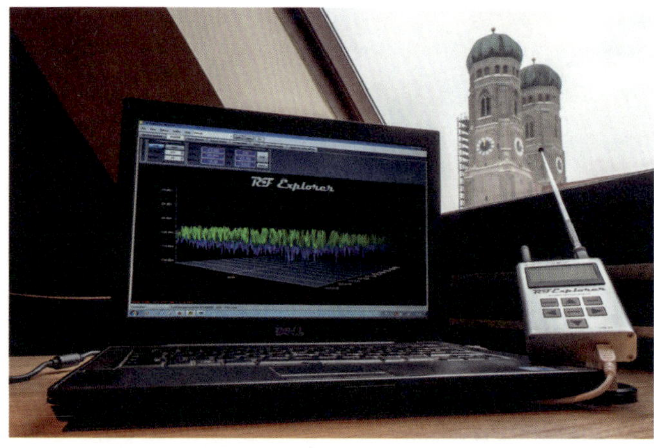

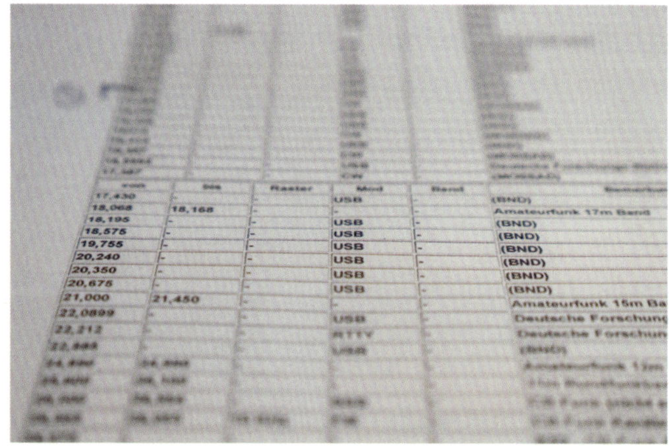

Frequenzanalyse, München, 2018
Frequency analysis, Munich, 2018

In dieser Publikation genannte und abgebildete / Illustrated and named in this publication:

Ausstellungen / Exhibitions

2020 *Rencontres Internationales Paris / Berlin, Underdox – Dokument & Experiment*, Goethe-Institut, Paris, kuratiert von / curated by Dunja Bialas, Bernd Brehmer, Matthias von Tesmar und / and Katharina Scriba

2018 *Public Art Munich*, in Kollaboration mit / in collaboration with *X Shared Spaces,* Münchner Kammerspiele
Public Art Munich, kuratiert von / curated by Joanna Warsza
X Shared Spaces, Münchner Kammerspiele, Konzept / Concept: Matthias Lilienthal, Christoph Gurk, kuratiert von / curated by Christoph Gurk, Helena Eckert und / and Martin Valdés-Stauber

2017 *After the Fact. Propaganda im 21. Jahrhundert / Propaganda in the 21st Century*, Städtische Galerie im Lenbachhaus und Kunstbau München / Munich, kuratiert von / curated by Stephanie Weber
No Secrets! – Bilder der Überwachung, Stadtmuseum München, Sammlung Fotografie / Munich City Museum, Photography Collection, kuratiert von / curated by Rudolf Scheutle

2016 *Favoriten III*, Städtische Galerie im Lenbachhaus und Kunstbau München / Munich, kuratiert von / curated by Eva Huttenlauch und / and Stephanie Weber

2015 *DUAL-USE*, Einzelausstellung / solo exhibition, Perspektiven Kunstpreis / Perspectives Art Award, Platform München / Munich, kuratiert von / curated by Radmila Krstajić

Arbeiten / Works

2019 *Bereinigung I–II*, szenischer Text / *Decontamination I–II*, scenic text
Beschränkung I–II, szenischer Text / *Limitation I–II*, scenic text
From Camp to Campus, HD video, 10 min.
Die Befragung / The Interrogation, HD video, 7 min.

2018 *Die Befragung*, szenischer Text, Theaterperformance (situativer Loop)
The Interrogation, scenic text, theatre production (situational loop)
*Secret Guide, Grundkurs Geheimdienst, Basiswissen für Agent*innen, Lektion 3_Die Befragung* und *Lektion 4_Die Außenstellen*, Faltplan, 59 x 95 cm, Maßstab 1:25000
Secret Guide, Intelligence 101, Basics for Agents, Lesson 3_The Interrogation, Lesson 4_The Outposts, folding map, 59 x 95 cm, scale 1:25,000
Secret Sites, Fotoreihe, Text-Bild-Konstellation / photo series, text-image constellation

2017 *Battle Management Drawings I–V,* 5-Kanal-Installation mit wechselnden Text-Bild-Konstellationen / 5-channel installation with alternating text-image constellations
Ortsanalyse I–II, öffentliche Raumuntersuchung / *Site Analysis I–II*, public space exploration

2016 *DUAL-USE I–V*, 5-Kanal-Installation / 5-channel installation, Sammlung / Collection of the Städtische Galerie im Lenbachhaus und Kunstbau München / Munich
DUAL-USE I: Global Cocktail, HD video loop, 4 min.
DUAL-USE II: Biosprengstoff / Environmentally Friendly Explosives, HD video loop, 1 min.
DUAL-USE III: Kampfmodel / Combat Model, HD video loop, 3 min.
DUAL-USE IV: Or do we have the same?, HD video loop, 11 min.
DUAL-USE V: Weltverzweiflungsmaschine / World Desperation Machine, program code (ChucK), – ∞

Lecture Performances

2019 *Battle Management Language. Sprachlose Mythen militärischer Strukturen II*
Speechless Myths of Military Structures II
Vortrag im Haus der Wissenschaft Bremen / Lecture at the House of Science, Bremen, Robotik und KI / Robotics and AI, Cyberspace-Forum

2017 *From Camp to Campus,* videografischer Vortrag zu den *Ortsanalysen I und II*
Videographic lecture on the *Site Analyses I and II*, Georg-Knorr-Saal, Städtische Galerie im Lenbachhaus und Kunstbau München / Munich
Battle Management Language. Sprachlose Mythen militärischer Strukturen I
Speechless Myths of Military Structures I
Vortrag beim Jahreskongress der Informationsstelle Militarisierung e. V., Tübingen
Lecture at the annual congress of the Informationsstelle Militarisierung e. V., Tübingen

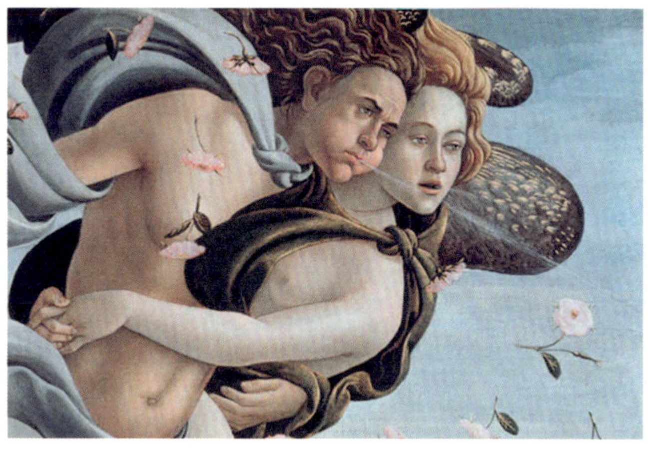

From Camp to Campus, Stills, 2019, siehe Seite 42
From Camp to Campus, stills, 2019, see page 42

From Camp to Campus, Stills, 2019, siehe Seite 42
From Camp to Campus, stills, 2019, see page 42

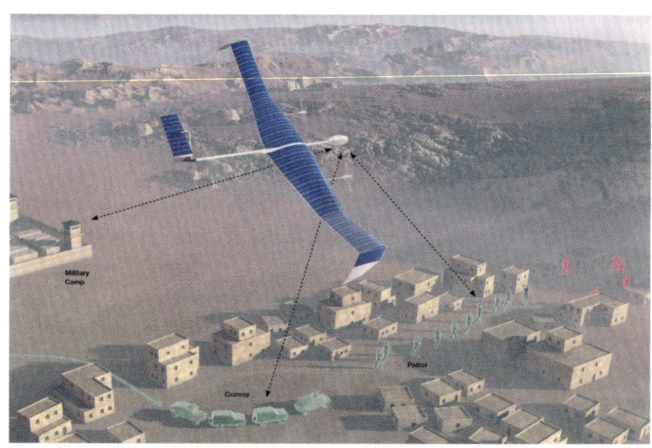

From Camp to Campus, Erzählstimme, 2019
Ein Forschungsinhalt am Ludwig Bölkow Campus ist *Zephyr.* Die Drohne ist nach dem griechischen Gott Zephyros benannt, der Westwind erzeugt. Ihr Hersteller Airbus illustriert, wie Soldat*innen über die Drohne mit dem Militärlager kommunizieren. Wenn sie auf Widerstand stoßen, fordern sie Verstärkung an. Berglandschaft und Architektur machen deutlich, dass die Kampfzone außerhalb der westlichen Welt liegt. Die Feind*innen am Bildrand sind rot abgebildet, die Soldat*innen und ihr Konvoi sind grün dargestellt. Die Laufrichtung führt von links nach rechts.

From Camp to Campus, voice-over, 2019
One research subject at the Ludwig Bölkow Campus is *Zephyr.* The drone is named after Zephyrus, the Greek god of the west wind. Its manufacturer, Airbus, illustrates how soldiers communicate with the military camp via the drone. Whenever they encounter resistance, they call for reinforcements. The mountainous landscape and the architecture make it clear that the combat zone lies outside the Western world. The foes at the edge of the frame are depicted in red, the soldiers and their convoy in green. The direction of movement is from left to right.

Franz Wanner (geb. 1975 in Bad Tölz) arbeitet seit 2000 unter dem Pseudonym Franz Wanner. Seine zuletzt realisierten Arbeiten waren 2020 im Goethe-Institut Paris im Rahmen des Festivals *Rencontres Internationales Paris / Berlin* und 2018 in Russland im Museum of Moscow zur Ausstellung *18 +/- Voluntary Self-Control* zu sehen. Die vorliegende Publikation entstand 2019 während der index Freiraum Artist Residency in Zürich.
Franz Wanner (born in Bad Tölz, Germany, in 1975) has worked under the pseudonym Franz Wanner since 2000. His most recent works were shown at the Goethe-Institut Paris as part of the festival *Rencontres Internationales Paris / Berlin* in 2020, and in Russia at the Museum of Moscow in the exhibition *18 +/- Voluntary Self-Control* in 2018. The present publication was created during the index Freiraum Artist Residency in Zurich, Switzerland, in 2019.

Stephanie Weber ist seit 2014 Kuratorin für Gegenwartskunst an der Städtischen Galerie im Lenbachhaus und Kunstbau München, wo sie Ausstellungen zum Werk von Senga Nengudi (2019) und Lea Lublin (2015) kuratierte und die korrespondierenden monografischen Publikationen herausgab. 2017 organisierte sie die thematische Ausstellung *After The Fact. Propaganda im 21. Jahrhundert.* Von 2010 bis 2014 arbeitete sie in der Abteilung für Medienkunst und Performance am Museum of Modern Art in New York.
Stephanie Weber Curator for Contemporary Art at the Städtische Galerie im Lenbachhaus und Kunstbau München in Munich since 2014, where she has curated exhibitions on the work of Senga Nengudi (2019) and Lea Lublin (2015) and edited the accompanying monographic publications. In 2017, she organized the thematic exhibition *After The Fact. Propaganda in the 21st Century.* From 2010 to 2014, she worked in the Department of Media and Performance Art at the Museum of Modern Art (MoMA) in New York.

Maria Muhle ist Professorin für Philosophie und Ästhetische Theorie an der Akademie der Bildenden Künste München und Mitbegründerin des August Verlags Berlin. Ihre Forschungsschwerpunkte sind Politische Ästhetik, Medien der Geschichte und Biopolitik.
Maria Muhle is Professor of Philosophy and Aesthetic Theory at the Academy of Fine Arts in Munich and cofounder of the August Verlag, Berlin. Her main areas of research are political aesthetics, historical media, and biopolitics.

Gefördert von / Supported by

STIFTUNG KUNSTFONDS

LfA FÖRDERBANK BAYERN

KUNST club 13

Im Verborgenen Gutes tun!

Impressum / Colophon

Herausgeberin / Editor
Stephanie Weber

Konzeption / Concept
Franz Wanner

Gestaltung / Design
Doris Maximiliane Würgert

Texte / Texts
Stephanie Weber, Maria Muhle, Franz Wanner

Übersetzung / Translation
Cynthia Hall, Jane Michael, Warren Niesłuchowski

Lektorat / Copy Editing
Ursula Fethke (Deutsch), Danko Szabó (English)

Abbildungsnachweis / Image Credits
Amelie Gerhard, S. / p. 41
Florian Peljak, S. / p. 53 (unten / bottom)
Christian Schmieder, S. / pp. 45, 47, 53 (oben / top), 57
Sandra Singh, S. / p. 87
Øystein Sørbye (Hg. / ed.), Originalzeichnung / Original drawing in: *Natzweilerfange Nummer 20266 Hans Grinde og andre fangeberetninger fra Ottobrunn*, Natzweilergruppen 2006, Norwegen / Norway, S. / p. 43
Franz Wanner, S. / pp. 6–10, 18–20, 29, 32–39, 42, 48–51, 62–63, 67, 73–75, 80–82, 91–106
Herburg Weiland (Design, Flyer *After the Fact*), S. / pp. 58–59

Lithografie / Image Editing
Kilian Blees

Produktion / Production Management
DISTANZ Verlag

Gesamtherstellung / Printing and Binding
optimal media GmbH, Röbel/Müritz

Vertrieb / Distribution
edel Germany GmbH
www.edel.com
international-books@edel.com

ISBN 978-3-95476-318-4
Printed in Germany

Erschienen im / Published by
DISTANZ Verlag
www.distanz.de

Dank an / Thanks to
Monika Bayer-Wermuth, Babylonia Constantinides, Gürsoy Doğtaş, Beate Engl und / and, Justin Lieberman

Die auf dem Cover verzeichneten und nummerierten Orte sind dem *Secret Guide* entnommen. Der unter diesem Titel herausgegebene Faltplan (59 x 95 cm) erschien zur Theaterperformance *Die Befragung* (Franz Wanner, 2018) an den Münchner Kammerspielen. Die Adressen, Tarnbezeichnungen, Funktionen und Datierungen der geheimdienstlichen Außenstellen (München, 1946 bis 2018) sind dort und in der folgenden Legende aufgeführt. Die mit * ausgewiesenen Orte liegen außerhalb der hier auf dem Cover abgebildeten Karte.

The numbered sites indicated on the cover have been taken from the *Secret Guide*. The folding map (59 x 95 cm) issued by the Münchner Kammerspiele under this title was published for the theatrical performance *The Interrogation* (Franz Wanner, 2018). The addresses, code names, functions, and dates of the secret service outposts (Munich, 1946 to 2018) are listed there and in the following legend. The locations marked with a * lie beyond the map as shown on the cover.

1__ Ainmillerstr. 22, **Kontax, Walter Taxmann – Consulting GmbH** (1980er-Jahre), als Meinungsforschungsinstitut getarnte Scheinfirma des Bundesnachrichtendienstes (BND) für Hausbefragungen mit Filiale in Kiel
Bogus Bundesnachrichtendienst (BND) company (1980s) disguised as an opinion research institute for household surveys, with branch office in Kiel

2__ Augustenstr. 46 IV, **Süddeutsche Warenvertriebs GmbH**, Scheinfirma der Organisation Gehlen (Org) für Finanzen und spezielle Beschaffungen
Bogus Org company for finances and special procurements

3__ Augustenstr. 78, **Siegert & Co. GmbH**, Scheinfirma der Org und des BND, die den ehemaligen stellvertretenden Gestapo-Chef Wilhelm Krichbaum beschäftigte
Bogus Org and BND company that employed former deputy Gestapo chief Wilhelm Krichbaum

4__ Bauerstr. 28, **Teppich- und Textilindustrie – TETEX** und **Europa Textil**, Scheinfirmen als Unterkunft und zur Führung von Sonderverbindungen (Filiale Leopoldstr. 26)
Bogus companies as lodging and for directing informants (branch office Leopoldstr. 26)

5__ Bayerstr. 8, **Rechnungsprüfungsstelle**, Außenstelle des BND
Outpost of the BND

6__ Bayerstr. 57 III, **Sudetendeutscher Verlag**, Scheinfirma der Org
Bogus Org company

7__ Biedersteiner Str. 41, **Betreuungsgesellschaft für private Vermögensanlagen**, konspirative Beobachtung von ausländischen Diplomat*innen und Agent*innen, Journalist*innen und unter Feindverdacht stehenden Angehörigen des eigenen Dienstes
Conspiratorial surveillance of foreign diplomats and agents, journalists, and members of one's own agency suspected of being enemies

8__ Böcklinstr. 55, **Südtechnik (Schmidt & Co.)**, Tarnfirma der Org für das Stay-Behind-Programm: Agenten und Truppen sollten sich im Fall eines Angriffs durch den Ostblock „überrollen" lassen, um dann im besetzten Gebiet Sabotageakte auszuführen
Org front company for the Stay Behind Program: In the event of attack by the Eastern Bloc, agents and troops were to allow themselves to be "rolled over" in order to conduct acts of sabotage in the occupied territory

9__ Brienner Str. 47, **Gesellschaft für Wehrkunde**, Tarnorganisation der Org zur Stärkung des „Wehrwillens" der BRD
Front organization of the Org for strengthening the Federal Republic of Germany's "will to fight"

10*__ Cincinnatistr. 63a, **Studienstelle für Auslandsfragen** (später Diefenbachstr. 30), BND-Dienststelle zur Auswertung
BND office for analysis (later Diefenbachstr. 30)

11__ Dachauer Str. 128, **Technische Revisionsstelle der Bundesverkehrsverwaltung** (S. / p. 104)

12*__ Diefenbachstr. 30, **Studienstelle für Auslandsfragen**, BND-Dienststelle zur Auswertung
BND office for analysis

13__ Dienerstr. 17, Ausbildungsräume der Org (Eingang Altenhofstr. 17)
Training rooms of the Org (entrance on Altenhofstr. 17)

14__ Donnersbergerstr. 7, **Dr. Starke & Co.**, Scheinfirma der Org für Personal- und Finanzverwaltung
Bogus Org company for personnel and financial administration

15__ Düsseldorfer Str., Kontaktbüro des BND-Referats „Presseführung" (siehe Nymphenburger Str. 160)
Contact office of the BND department of press management (see Nymphenburger Str. 160)

16__ Eininger Str. 4, **Thiele und Friedrichs Marketing GbR** (S. / p. 101)

17__ Elisabethstr. 18–20, **Schwäbische Industrieberatungs GmbH**, Treffpunkt der Org mit Partnerdiensten
Meeting place of the Org with partner agencies

18__ Elisabethstr. 33, **Filiale 121**, Wohnsitz von Org-Mitarbeiter*innen der operativen Beschaffung
Place of residence of Org members of operative procurements

19__ Elisabethstr. 35, **Schwäbischer Bilderdienst GmbH**, Tochterfirma der gleichnamigen Bauberatungsfirma der Org in Stuttgart; in den 1970er-Jahren BND-Außenstelle zur politischen, wirtschaftlichen und technischen Observation der DDR; diese BND-Dienstelle wurde wiederum durch die Stasi observiert
Subsidiary of the Org construction consulting company in Stuttgart with the same name; in the 1970s, BND outpost for the political, economic, and technological surveillance of the DDR; this BND office was, in turn, under surveillance by the Stasi

20__ Elsenheimerstr. 21, **Zentralstelle für Verkehrsgeographie der Bundeswehr**, BND-Außenstelle für den Krisen- und Verteidigungsfall, der militärischen Komponente des Stay-Behind-Programms (S. 102)
BND outpost in case of crises and defense situations, the military component of the Stay Behind Program (p. 102)

21*__ Emil-Geis-Str. 50, **Süddeutsche Industrieberatungsgesellschaft**, Scheinfirma der Org für Auswertung, Spionageabwehr und für die Sichtungsgruppe Marine
Bogus Org company for analysis, counterespionage, and for the information-gathering group Marine

22__ Ettalstr. 3, operative Dienststelle der Org
Operative office of the Org

23__ Feilitzschstr. 2a, **Südbayerische Industrieverwertungsgesellschaft**, Sitz der Beschaffungsdienststelle des Bayern-Büros der Org (zuvor Montsalvatstr. 7)
Main procurement office of the Bavaria office of the Org (previously Montsalvatstr. 7)

24*__ Frankfurter Ring 227, **Bayerisches Leichtmetallwerk** (früher Freimannerstr. 227), Dienststelle für Sonderverbindungen der Org
Office for Org informants (previously Freimannerstr. 227)

25__ Frauenplatz 12, Funkanlagen des Observationskommandos QB30 (S. 103)
Radio stations of the surveillance command QB30 (p. 103)

26__ Fraunhoferstr. 39, **Firma Ernst Lautenbacher**, operative Einrichtung der Org
Operative facility of the Org

27__ Friedrich-Herschel-Straße 12, **Terramar**, Ableger der Hamburger Rüstungsfirma im Besitz des Org-Mitarbeiters Franz-Peter Studermayer
Offshoot of the Hamburg armaments company owned by Org member Franz-Peter Studermayer

28*__ Gabriel-Max-Str., BND-Konferenzzentrum; in den 1980er- und 1990er-Jahren fanden hier Treffen mit dem dänischen Geheimdienst statt
BND conference center; in the 1980s and 1990s, meetings with the Danish Intelligence Service took place here

29__ Gaiglstr. 10 II, **Spezialarchiv für Wirtschaft und Technik**, Scheinfirma der Org, später des BND für die allgemeine Verwaltung
Bogus company of the Org, later of the BND for general administration

30__ Geyerstr. 9 I, **Lichtbildverlag**, Scheinfirma der Org für die taktische und strategische Aufklärung der UdSSR und Polens; der in Polen als Kriegsverbrecher gesuchte ehemalige Stabsoffizier der Wehrmacht Dr. Heinrich Anton Kurts (Deckname Kelling) verrichtete von hier aus operative Arbeit gegen Polen
Bogus Org company for tactical and strategic reconnaissance of the USSR and Poland; the former Wehrmacht staff officer Dr. Heinrich Anton Kurts (cover name Kelling), sought in Poland as war criminal, carried out operations against Poland from this site

31__ Goethestr., Nachwuchstreffpunkt der Org / des BND (siehe Leopoldstr. 62)
Meeting place for Org / BND recruits (see Leopoldstr. 62)

32*__ Goldbergstr. 6, **Industrial Research Unit** (später **SINDUVER**), Scheinfirmen der Org
Industrial Research Unit (later SINDUVER), bogus Org company

33__ Graf-Lehndorff-Str. 49, Safe House und Treffpunkt der Org für das Stay-Behind-Wesen (siehe Böcklinstr. 55)
Org safehouse and meeting place for the Stay Behind Program (see Böcklinstr. 55)

34__ Grillparzerstr. 46 I, **Auskunftei Dun Europa** (Dun & Bradstreet), operative Scheinfirma der Org mit Filiale in Frankfurt
Operative bogus Org company with branch office in Frankfurt

35*__ Grünwalderstr. 26, **Firma Horst Weisch**, Scheinfirma der Org
Bogus company of the Org

36*__ Grünwalderstr. 61, **Wehrbereichsverwaltung VI** (ab 1997 Rauchstr. 16), Verbindungsreferat des BND zur Landesregierung in Bayern
BND liaison department to the Bavarian State Government (from 1997: Rauchstr. 16)

37__ Habsburgerplatz 1/1, seit 1962 **Verein zur Erforschung sozialpolitischer Verhältnisse**, 1966 in **Deutsche Arbeitsgruppe für West-Ost-Beziehungen e.V.** umbenannt, Außenstelle des deutsch-niederländischen Geheimdienstprojekts INTERDOC zur psychologischen Kriegsführung gegen den Ostblock, an dem sich weitere NATO-Staaten beteiligten
Since 1962: Verein zur Erforschung sozialpolitischer Verhältnisse; 1966: renamed Deutsche Arbeitsgruppe für West-Ost-Beziehungen e.V, outpost of the German-Dutch intelligence project INTERDOC for psychological warfare against the Eastern Bloc, in which other NATO states also participated

38__ Habsburgerstr. 10, **LABORA Außenhandelsagentur Lauterbacher & Co.**, auf Nordafrika und Nah-/Mittelost ausgerichtete Tarnfirma der Org, später des BND, deren Inhaber seit 1959/60 der ehemalige SS-Obergruppenführer Hartmann Lauterbacher war
Front company of the Org, and later of the BND, directed at North Africa and the Near and Middle East, occupied from 1959/60 by the former SS-Obergruppenführer Hartmann Lauterbacher

39__ Hackenstr. 3, **Akademischer Gemeinschaftsverlag**, Scheinfirma der Org zur Spionage in Österreich, Ungarn, der CSSR und Jugoslawien mit Muttergesellschaft in Salzburg
Bogus Org company for espionage in Austria, Hungary, Czechoslovakia, and Yugoslavia with parent company in Salzburg

40__ Hedwig-Dransfeld-Allee 6, **Technische Revisionsstelle der Bundesverkehrsverwaltung**, Observationskommando QB30 (siehe Dachauer Str. 128)
Surveillance command QB30 (see Dachauer Str. 128)

41*__ Heidemannstr. 50, Bayern-Kaserne, **Amt für Militärkunde**, personalführende Dienststelle für alle beim BND beschäftigten Bundeswehrsoldaten mit Filiale in Berlin
Human resources office for all Bundeswehr soldiers active in the BND, with branch office in Berlin

42__ Helene-Weber-Allee 23, **Bundesvermögensverwaltung, Abteilung Sondervermögen – Außenstelle München** (S./pp. 94–95)

43__ Herzog-Wilhelm-Str. 3, **Süddeutsche Industrieberatungsgesellschaft**, Scheinfirma der Org für Auswertung, Spionageabwehr und für die Sichtungsgruppe Marine
Bogus Org company for analysis, counterespionage and for the information-gathering group Marine

44__ Heßstr. 53, **Untervertretung 71**, Büro und Wohnungen der Org zur operativen Beschaffung
Office and apartments of the Org for operative procurement

45__ Hohenstaufenstr. 1, **Pension Descano** (frühere Agent*innenschule), Ausbildungsstätte der Org
Pension Descano (formerly Agentenschule), Org training site

46__ Isabellastr. 7, **Süddeutsche Industrieberatungen**, Scheinfirma der Org zur operativen Beschaffung
Bogus Org company for operative procurement

47__ Isabellastr. 30, **H. Bohn**, Tarnfirma für Kraftfahrzeuge der Org
Front company for Org automobiles

48__ Isartalstr. 39–43, **Optische Werke Rodenstock**, seit 2012 Elsenheimerstr. 33 (S. 105)
From 2012: Elsenheimerstr. 33 (p. 105)

49__ Ismaninger Str. 98, **Südlabor GmbH**, Scheinfirma des BND, Fälscherwerkstatt (später Dienerstr. und Traubinger Str. 67), verfügte in den 1980er-Jahren über eine Papierproduktion und eine der größten Stempelsammlungen der Welt; später war hier auch eine gegen die DDR gerichtete Aufklärungsstation, die erst im Februar 1991 aufgelöst wurde
Bogus company of the BND, forgery workshop (later Dienerstr. and Traubinger Str. 67), in the 1980s, it owned a paper-manufacturing facility and one of the world's largest collections of rubber stamps; later, a reconnaissance station directed against the DDR was also located here and was not dismantled until February 1991

50__ Kardinal-Faulhaber-Str. 15, **Kohlenhandlung Raab und Karcher GmbH**, Tarnfirma der Org
Org front company

51__ Karl-Theodor-Str. 55, geheime BND-Dienststelle des Stay-Behind-Wesens (siehe Böcklinstr. 55) zur militärischen Aufklärung der DDR; die BND-Dienststelle wurde durch die Stasi observiert
Secret BND office of the Stay Behind Program (see Böcklinstr. 55) for military reconnaissance of the DDR; the BND office was surveilled by the Stasi

52__ Karlsplatz 7a, **Bundesstelle für Fernmeldestatistik** (zuvor Weinstr. 6), ab 1970 fernmelde-elektronische Aufklärungsstelle des BND
Bundesstelle für Fernmeldestatistik (previously Weinstr. 6), from 1970: signal-electronic reconnaissance site of the BND

53__ Karlsplatz 11–12, **Firma Erich Eger & Co.**, Scheinfirma der Org
Bogus Org company

54__ Karlsplatz 11, **Sudetendeutsche Landsmannschaft Bayern e. V.**, Scheinfirma der Org mit dem ehemaligen SS-Hauptsturmführer Dr. Herbert Böhrsch als Kontaktmann
Bogus Org company with former SS-Hauptsturmführer Dr. Herbert Böhrsch as contact man

55__ Karlsplatz 19, **Gloria Filmverleih GmbH** (S. / p. 96)

56__ Kaufingerstr. 33/3, **Carlheinz Schultz Pelzmoden**, Scheinfirma, Büro eines Spionageabwehrleiters der Org (Filiale Sporerstr. 4)
Bogus company, office of an Org counterespionage director (branch office Sporerstr. 4)

57*__ Knorrstr. 139c, gegenwärtiger Sitz des **Landesamts für Verfassungsschutz**
Current location of the State Office for the Protection of the Constitution

58__ Königinstr. 17, Sitz des **Landesamts für Verfassungsschutz** von 1949 bis 1959 (Filiale Neuhauser Str. 51)
Location of the State Office for the Protection of the Constitution from 1949 to 1959 (branch office Neuhauser Str. 51)

59__ Lampadiusstr. 12 II, **Gesellschaft für Politik**, Scheinfirma der Org, u. a. für Spionageeinsätze in Österreich
Bogus Org company for, among other things, espionage operations in Austria

60__ Landshuter Allee, BND-Außenstelle zur politischen, wirtschaftlichen und technischen Aufklärung der DDR
Landshuter Allee, BND outpost for political, economic, and technological reconnaissance of the DDR

61__ Landwehrstr. 35, **Südtechnik**, Scheinfirma zur Ausbildung von Mitarbeiter*innen der Org und des BND (S. 91)
Bogus company for training Org and BND employees (p. 91)

62__ Lenbachplatz, **Amt für Fernmeldestatistik**, in den 1980er-Jahren Außenstelle der Technischen Aufklärung
In the 1980s, outpost for technical reconnaissance

63__ Leopoldstr. 26, **Teppich- und Textilindustrie – TETEX** und **Europa Textil** (siehe Bauerstr. 28)
Teppich- und Textilindustrie – TETEX and Europa Textil (see Bauerstr. 28)

64__ Leopoldstr. 62, Nachwuchszentrum (BND-intern als „Babyclub“ bezeichnet), 1950er- bis 1970er-Jahre, Söhne und Töchter von Geheimdienst-Angestellten trafen sich über dem Café Rialto, um in den Beruf ihrer Eltern eingeführt zu werden. Sie erhielten Ferienjobs in der BND-Zentrale und die Aussicht auf eine Finanzierung ihres Studiums
Recruits center (referred to within the BND as “Babyclub”); from the 1950s to 1970s, the sons and daughters of intelligence service agents met above the Café Rialto, to be introduced to their parents' profession. They were given vacation jobs in the BND central office and offered the prospect of having their studies financed

65__ Lessingstr. 14, **Bundesvermögensverwaltung, Abteilung Sondervermögen – Außenstelle München**, Dienststelle für Arbeits- und Gehaltsbescheinigungen für BND-Mitarbeiter*innen
Office for work and salary attestations for BND employees

66__ Ludwigstr. 9, **Süddeutsche Boden-Kredit-Bank**, Tarnfirma der Org mit Büro des leitenden Org-Mitarbeiters Dietz von dem Knesebeck
Org front company with office of senior Org employee Dietz von dem Knesebeck

67__ Maffeistr. 6, **Arztpraxis Dr. med. Karl Ihm**, ehemaliger SS-Hauptsturmführer, seit 1953 Mitarbeiter der Org
Medical office of Dr. med. Karl Ihm, former SS-Hauptsturmführer, from 1953: member of the Org

68__ Malsenstr. 66, Dienststelle der Org zur psychologischen Kriegsführung und politischen Berichterstattung, zu deren Leitung der ehemalige Generalmajor der Wehrmacht Friedrich Foertsch zählte
Org office for psychological warfare and political reporting, whose directors included the former Wehrmacht major general Friedrich Foertsch

69__ Maria-Theresia-Str. 16, **Hauptstelle für Befragungswesen** (S. 97)
Main Office of Interrogation (p. 97)

70__ Maria-Theresia-Str. 16a, **Ausbildungsstab für Verwendung in integrierten Stäben – Dokumentation**, geheime Dienststelle des BND (1990er-Jahre)
Secret office of the BND (1990s)

71__ Marsstr. 4, ehemaliger Standort der **Garner-Stiftung**, Scheinfirma des BND, finanziert angeworbene Studierende und hilft verhafteten BND-Angestellten; 1959 gegründet, befindet sich gegenwärtig in der Helene-Weber-Allee 23
Former location of the Garner-Stiftung, bogus BND company, finances recruited students and helps apprehended BND employees; founded in 1959, presently located in the Helene-Weber-Allee 23

72__ Maximilianstr. 3 II, **Simon & Co.**, Scheinfirma der Org zur operativen Beschaffung
Bogus Org company for operative procurement

73__ Maximilianstr. 43, **ANORGANA GmbH**, Tarnfirma der Org zur konspirativen Zusammenzuführung nachrichtendienstlicher Informationen, Güter und Personen
Org front company for the conspiratorial consolidation of agency information, goods, and persons

74__ Montsalvatstr. 7, **Südbayerische Industrieverwertungsgesellschaft** (siehe Feilitzschstr. 2a)
Südbayerische Industrieverwertungsgesellschaft (see Feilitzschstr. 2a)

75__ Montenstr. 7, Begegnungsort für Treffen mit Partnerdiensten
Rendezvous point for meetings with partner agencies

76__ Mottlstr. 6, **Süddeutsche Industrieverwertungsgesellschaft**, Scheinfirma der Org für Leitungspersonal der Liegenschaftsverwaltung und für die Auswertung
Bogus company for management of Org properties and for analysis

77__ Neuhauser Str. 51, Filiale des **Landesamts für Verfassungsschutz** (siehe Königinstr. 17)
Branch of the State Office for the Protection of the Constitution (see Königinstr. 17)

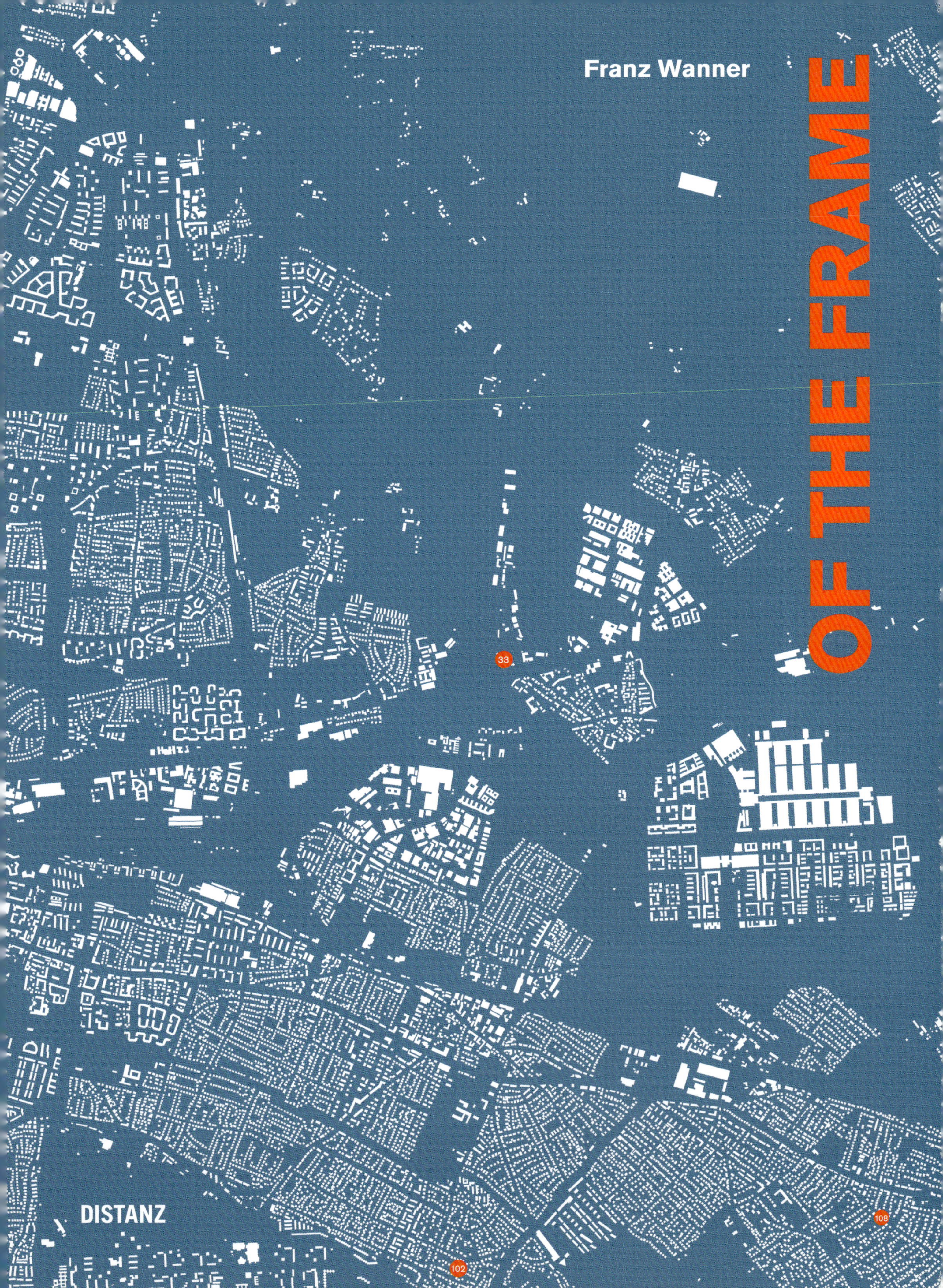
Franz Wanner
OF THE FRAME
33
DISTANZ
108
102

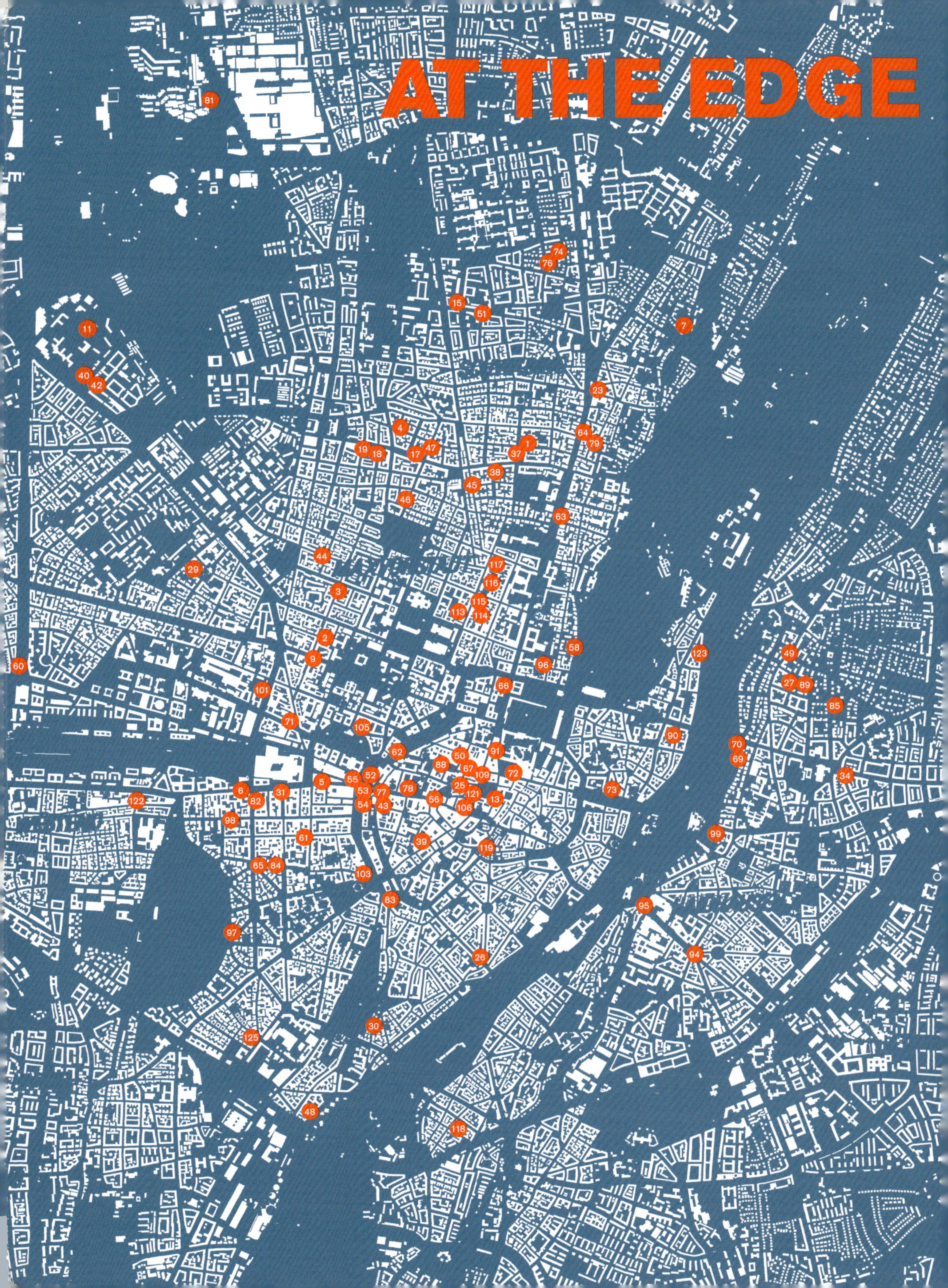
AT THE EDGE

78__ Neuhauser Str. 8 und 10, seit 1959 Sitz des **Landesamts für Verfassungsschutz** (heute Knorrstr. 139c)
From 1959: location of the State Office for the Protection of the Constitution (currently Knorrstr. 139c)

79__ Nikolaistr. 1, **Sinduva (Süddeutsche Industrievertretung) GmbH** (zuvor Schönfeldstr. 11), Scheinfirma der Org
Bogus Org company (previously Schönfeldstr. 11)

80__ Nymphenburger Str. 160, BND-Referat „Presseführung“ mit Kontaktbüro in der Düsseldorferstr. (S. 100)
BND department of press management with contact office on Düsseldorferstr. (p. 100)

81__ Olympiazentrum, Filiale der Münchner Führungsaußenstelle in Laim, deren übergeordnete Generalvertretung G in Frankfurt lag; eine weitere Filiale befand sich am Viktualienmarkt
Office of the Munich management outpost in Laim, whose superordinate Chief Administration G was in Frankfurt; an additional branch office was at the Viktualienmarkt

82__ Paul-Heyse-Str., **Forschungsinstitut für zwischenstaatliche Wirtschaftsfragen GmbH**, Scheininstitut der Org zur Gegenspionage und Spionageabwehr, in der der ehemalige SS-Obergruppenführer Hartmann Lauterbacher tätig war
Bogus Org company for counterespionage and counter-intelligence, in which former SS-Obergruppenführer Hartmann Lauterbacher was active

83__ Pestalozzistr. 2–4, Internat der ehemals auf Schloss Weidenkam bei Münsing gelegenen Org-Ausbildungsstätte, die von einem früheren Wehrmachtsgeneral (Deckname Kerner) geleitet wurde und deren Lehrpersonal zum großen Teil aus früheren Nationalsozialisten, wie dem SS-Standartenführer Rudolf Roeder, bestand
Residential school of the Org training site formerly located at Schloss Weidenkam near Münsing, directed by a former Wehrmacht general (cover name Kerner) and whose teaching personnel was composed largely of former Nazis, such as SS-Standartenführer Rudolf Roeder

84__ Pettenkoferstr. 21, **Firma Donauhandel**, Scheinfirma der Org zur Überwachung von Geschäftsbeziehungen deutscher Unternehmen mit dem Osten
Bogus Org company for surveillance of business relations of German companies with the East

85__ Possart-Platz 3 (heißt heute / today named Shakespeare-Platz), 1948 bis 1962 US-Marinenachrichtendienst **Office of Naval Intelligence (ONI)** zur politischen und wirtschaftlichen Aufklärung sowie für Flüchtlingsbefragungen; enge Zusammenarbeit mit der Marineauswertung der Org und des BND; bis Ende 2010 Verbindungsstelle der Defense Intelligence Agency (DIA) der US-Streitkräfte
1948 to 1962: US ONI (Office of Naval Intelligence) for political and economic reconnaissance and interrogation of refugees; close collaboration with the Org and BND Marine analysis; until the end of 2010: liaison site to the Defense Intelligence Agency (DIA) of the US Armed Forces

86*__ Pössenbacherstr. 21, **Studienstelle für Auslandsfragen** mit ca. 50 Angestellten, bis 1971 Außenstelle des deutsch-niederländischen Geheimdienstprojekts INTERDOC zur psychologischen Kriegsführung gegen den Ostblock, an dem sich weitere NATO-Staaten beteiligten; hier wurden Propagandatexte verfasst, die als scheinbar neutrale Werke im Ilmgau-Verlag Pfaffenhofen erschienen
Studienstelle für Auslandsfragen with ca. 50 employees, until 1971: outpost of the German-Dutch intelligence agency project INTERDOC for psychological warfare against the Eastern Bloc, in which other NATO states also participated; propaganda texts were written here and later published by Ilmgau-Verlag Pfaffenhofen as apparently neutral works

87__ Postillonstraße 4, Außenstelle des **Friedrich-Wilhelm-Heinz-Dienstes** (siehe Rosenheimer Platz 59)
Outpost of the Friedrich-Wilhelm-Heinz-Dienstes (see Rosenheimer Platz 59)

88__ Promenadeplatz, **Spezialarchiv für Wirtschaft und Technik** (später Reulandstr. 6), Scheinfirma der Org, später des BND, für die allgemeine Verwaltung
Bogus ORG company, later of the BND, for general administration (later Reulandstr. 6)

89__ Rauchstr. 16, **Wehrbereichsverwaltung VI** (bis 1997 Grünwalderstr. 61), Verbindungsreferat des BND zur Landesregierung in Bayern
BND liaison department to the Bavarian State Government, (until 1997 Grünwalderstr. 61)

90__ Reitmorstr. 27 (Parterre links), Appartement für operative Org-Agent*innen
Apartment for operating Org agents (ground floor, left)

91__ Residenzstr. 25, **Technisch-wissenschaftliches Büro des Spezialarchivs für Wirtschaft und Technik**, Scheinfirma für das Stay-Behind-Programm (siehe Böcklinstr. 55), Konferenz- und Ausbildungszentrum
Bogus company for the Stay Behind Program (see Böcklinstr. 55), conference and training center

92__ Reulandstr. 6, **Spezialarchiv für Wirtschaft und Technik** (siehe Promenadeplatz)
See Promenadeplatz

93__ Reulandstr. 41, Treffort und Büro der allgemeinen Verwaltung der Org und später des BND
Meeting point and office for general administration of the Org and later the BND

94__ Rosenheimer Platz 59, **Außenstelle des Friedrich-Wilhelm-Heinz-Dienstes** (als Untermieter der Löwen–brauerei); der FWH-Dienst war ein deutscher Geheimdienst, der von 1950 bis 1956 neben der Org existierte, sich auf die Spionage auf dem Balkan und im Nahen Osten fokussierte und das Stay-Behind-Wesen im Alpenraum plante
Outpost of the Friedrich-Wilhelm-Heinz (FWH) Agency (as subleaser of the Löwenbrauerei); the FWH agency was a German intelligence agency that existed from 1950 to 1956 alongside the Org, focused on espionage in the Balkans and the Near East and planned the Stay Behind Program in the Alpine regions

95__ Rosenheimer Str., **Industriekontor München GmbH**, Scheinfirma der Org zur operativen Beschaffung
Bogus Org company for operative procurement

96__ Schönfeldstr. 11, **Sinduva (Süddeutsche Industrie-vertretung) GmbH** (siehe Nikolaistr. 1)
See Nikolaistr. 1

97__ Schubertstr. 12, **Technische Revisionsstelle der Bundesverkehrsverwaltung** (bis 1996), Außenstelle der Sicherheitsabteilung für Observationen
Outpost of the Security Department for Surveillance (until 1996)

98__ Schwanthaler Str. 81, **Bayern-Büro**, „Beschaffungsstelle Balkan“ der Org
Org's “Balkans Procurements Point”

99__ Sckellstr. 4, **Habis Hotel & Cafe**, Safe House der Org-Dienststelle 5
Safe house of Org Office 5

100__ Seefelderstr. 8, **OTAUI** (zuvor **Technische Handelsgesellschaft**, Funkgegenstelle für die Kommunikation mit

Westberlin), Scheinfirma der Org für Beschaffung sowie Praxis des Org-Arztes Dr. Hans Dietrich Schneemilch, später Treffort für Sonderverbindungen
OTAUI (previously Technische Handelsgesellschaft, remote receiving station for communication with West Berlin), bogus Org company for procurement and office of Org doctor Dr. Hans Dietrich Schneemilch, later a meeting point for informants

101__ Seidlstr. 11 III, **Gesellschaft für Auslandskunde**, Mitarbeiter*innen und Sonderverbindungen der Org

102__ Semmeringstr., **Süddeutsche Industrieberatungsgesellschaft SIBEG**, ab 1955 größte Scheinfirma der Org für die Auswertung
From 1955: largest bogus ORG company for analysis

103__ Sendlinger-Tor-Platz 8, Tarnfirma zum Transfer von Operativgeldern zwischen der Schweiz, Österreich, der CSSR und Italien
Front company for the transfer of operative funds between Switzerland, Austria, Czechoslovakia and Italy

104*__ Sonnenweg 24, Nebenstelle der Bundesvermögensverwaltung, Abteilung Sondervermögen – Außenstelle München (100 bis 200 Mitarbeiter*innen), Dienststelle für Arbeits- und Gehaltsbescheinigungen für BND-Mitarbeiter*innen sowie Referate für Wirtschaft, Technik und Medizin mit Zeichen- und Karthografenbüro, Lichtpaus- und Fotoanstalt, Druckerei und Zentrallaboratorium
Sonnenweg 24, Munich branch of the Federal Property Management Division, Special Assets Department (100 to 200 employees) for work and salary attestations for BND employees and department for Economy, Technology, and Medicine, with a drafting and cartography office, blueprint and photography shop, printer and central laboratory

105__ Sophienstr. 6, **Amt für Schadensabwicklung**, Scheinfirma des BND
Bogus BND company

106__ Sporerstr. 4, **Carlheinz Schultz Pelzmoden** (siehe Kaufingerstr. 33/3)
See Kaufingerstr. 33/3

107__ Stöberlstr. 2, **Firma Schultz & Co.**, geheime Dienststelle der Org für das Stay-Behind-Wesen (siehe Böcklinstr. 55)
Secret Org office for the Stay Behind Program (see Böcklinstr. 55)

108__ Tangastr. 22, Bund der Unfähigen (S. 98)
Coalition of the Unable (p. 98)

109__ Theatinerstr. 7, **Kühne und Nagel**, laut der Central Intelligence Agency (CIA) vermutlich eine Tarnfirma der Org und des BND
According to the CIA, probably a front company of the Org and the BND

110__ Tizianstr. 90, Leitung des Strategischen Dienstes der Org
Directorate of the Org Strategic Service

111*__ Traubinger Str. 67, **Südlabor GmbH**, Scheinfirma des BND, Fälscherwerkstatt (siehe Ismaninger Str. 98)
Bogus company, forgery workshop (see Ismaninger Str. 98)

112*__ Tölzerstr. 3, **Atlashandel GmbH**, Grünwald, Scheinfirma der Org (mit Ablegern in Gütersloh und Cuxhaven) zur Überwachung von Geschäftsbeziehungen deutscher Unternehmen mit dem Osten
Bogus Org company (with branches in Gütersloh and Cuxhaven) for surveillance of business relations between German companies and the East

113__ Türkenstr. 29, Filiale von **Simon & Co.**, Scheinfirma für Finanzverwaltung, Leitungspersonal und Kommunikation, in der der ehemalige SS-Sturmbannführer Emil Augsburg tätig war, der bis 1968 beim BND arbeitete
Branch of Simon & Co., bogus company for financial administration, managerial staff, and communication in which former SS-Sturmbannführer Emil Augsburg (who worked for the BND until 1968) was active

114__ Türkenstr. 50, **Simon & Co.**, Scheinfirma für Finanzverwaltung, Leitungspersonal und Kommunikation; laut CIA fanden hier Treffen der Org mit dem norwegischen Geheimdienst statt
Bogus company for financial administration, managerial staff, and communication; according to the CIA, meetings between the Org and the Norwegian intelligence agency took place here

115__ Türkenstr. 58, **Akademie-Buchhandlung GmbH**, Versandbuchhandlung (S. 99)
Academy Bookstore, mail order bookstore (p. 99)

116__ Türkenstr. 74, **Schmöger & Co.**, Scheinfirma der Org, später des BND für die Untervertretung 5000
Bogus Org (later BND) company for Untervertretung 5000

117__ Türkenstr. 90, **Simon & Co.** (Filiale), Scheinfirma für Finanzverwaltung, Leitungspersonal und Kommunikation
Simon & Co. (branch), bogus company for financial administration, managerial staff, and communication

118__ Untere Weidenstr. 21, **Süddeutsche Warenvertriebs GmbH**, Scheinfirma der Org, Büro und Lagerräume
Bogus Org company, office, and storage space

119__ Viktualienmarkt, Filiale der Münchner Führungsaußenstelle (siehe Olympiazentrum)
Viktualienmarkt, branch of the Munich management outpost (see Olympiazentrum)

120__ Walhallastr. 7, **Hans Richter & Co.**, bis 1953 Kryptostelle der Org und Führungsstelle für Sonderverbindungen in die Wirtschaft sowie Leitung des Strategischen Dienstes
Until 1953: concealed Org site and directorate for informants in the economy as well as administration of the strategic office

121__ Weinstr. 6, **Bundesstelle für Fernmeldestatistik** (siehe Karlsplatz 7a)
See Karlsplatz 7a

122__ Westendstr. 30, **Süddeutsche Warenvertriebs GmbH** (siehe Augustenstr. 46 IV)
See Augustenstr. 46 IV

123__ Wiedenmayerstr. 39, **Süd-Film-Vertriebs GmbH**, Tarnfirma der Org, Vorläufer der Gloria Filmverleih GmbH am Karlsplatz 19
Org front company, predecessor of the film distributor Gloria Filmverleih GmbH at Karlsplatz 19

124__ Würzburger Str. 6, **Überregionale Aufklärung Wirtschaft, Technik und Wissenschaft**, in den 1980er-Jahren operative Außenstelle des BND
In the 1980s, operative BND outpost

125__ Zenettistr. 23, **Barth & Söhnlein**, Scheinfirma der Org für psychologische Kriegsführung
Bogus Org company for psychological warfare

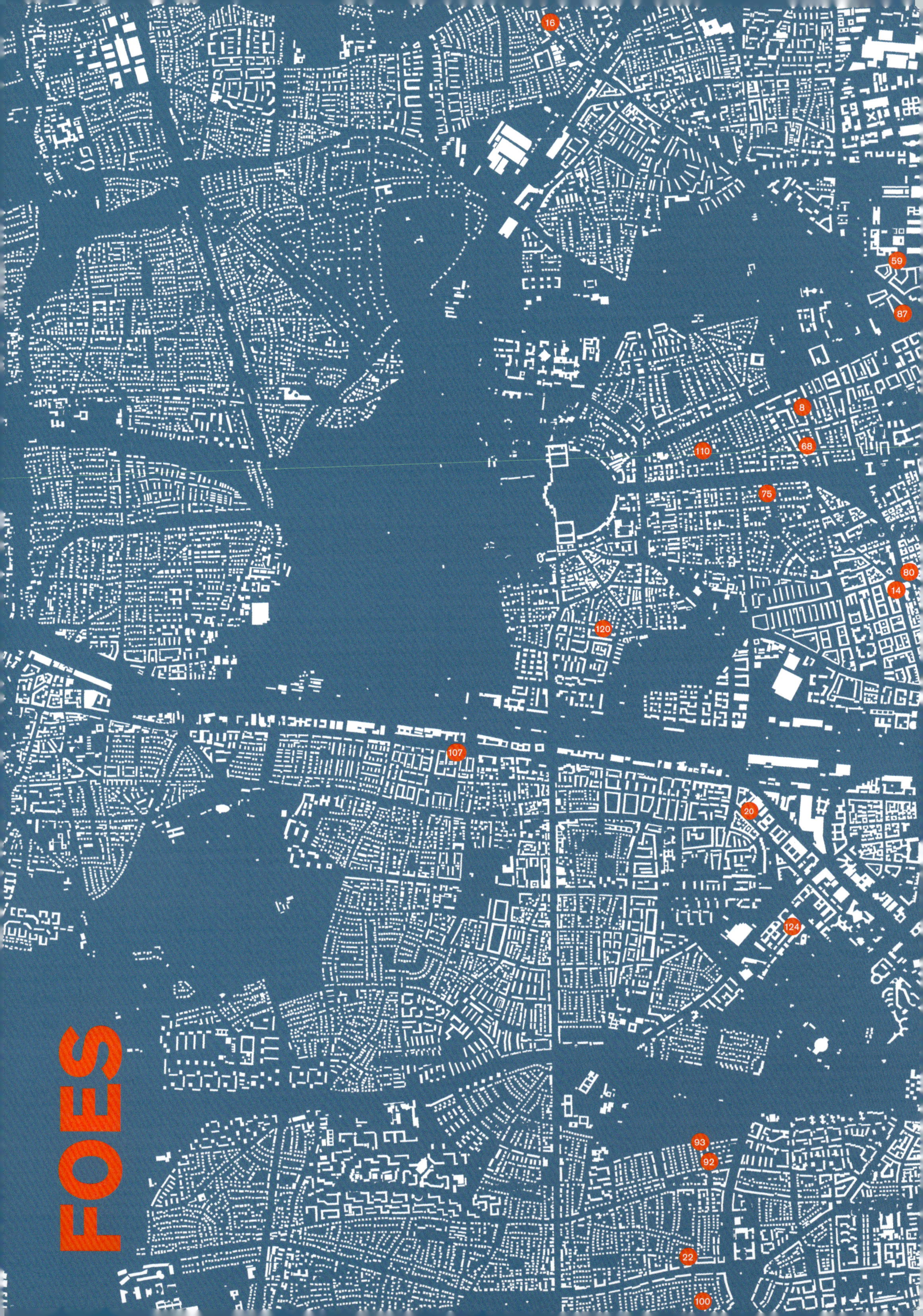
FOES
16
59
87
8
68
110
75
80
14
120
107
20
124
93
92
22
100